W9-DBE-925

A FRIENDSHIP

A FRIENDSHIP

*The Letters of Dan Rowan
and John D. MacDonald
1967–1974*

 Alfred A. Knopf   New York   1986

THIS IS A BORZOI BOOK
PUBLISHED BY ALFRED A. KNOPF, INC.

Copyright © 1986 by John D. MacDonald Publishing, Inc., and Dan Rowan Enterprises.
All rights reserved under International and Pan-American Copyright Conventions.
Published in the United States by Alfred A. Knopf, Inc., New York,
and simultaneously in Canada by Random House of Canada Limited, Toronto.
Distributed by Random House, Inc., New York.

Grateful acknowledgment is made to News America Syndicate for permission to reprint
an excerpt from "The Only Good Debates Are Between Friends" by Sydney J. Harris.
© by and permission of News America Syndicate.

Library of Congress Cataloging-in-Publication Data
Rowan, Dan.
A friendship:
the letters of Dan Rowan and John D. McDonald, 1967–1974.
1. Rowan, Dan—Correspondence.
2. MacDonald, John D. (John Dann), [date]—Correspondence.
3. Rowan and Martin's Laugh-In (Television program)
4. Comedians—United States—Correspondence.
5. Novelists, American—20th century—Correspondence.
I. MacDonald, John D. (John Dann), [date].
II. Title.
PN2287.R77A4   1986   791.45′028′0924 [B]   86-45305
ISBN 0-394-55269-5

Manufactured in the United States of America
First Edition

Adriana Rowan disagrees with certain of Dan Rowan's
statements about her in this book.

An enemy can partly ruin a man, but it takes a good-natured injudicious friend to complete the thing and make it perfect.

MARK TWAIN

Do not remove a fly from your friend's forehead with a hatchet.

CHINESE PROVERB

A man cannot speak to his son but as a father, to his wife but as a husband, to his enemy but upon terms; whereas a friend may speak as the case requires and not as it sorteth with the person.

FRANCIS BACON

INTRODUCTION

by John D. MacDonald

This is a strange preoccupation for a novelist and an entertainer, to collect and publish their letters written to each other years ago. We have worked together on the task. I was the pack rat, tucking away Dan's letters and my carbons in one of my files.

The motive is not exhibitionism. We value our privacy. One motive was to reveal to the reading public the inner workings of a highly rated, long-running television show—how it was born and just how it died. I have always been curious about everything which goes on behind the scenes in various occupations and professions. Also it reveals the novelist's attitudes toward the disciplines of his own work. I think that the letters illuminate both these areas of effort with more truth and reality than if we had each sat down to write about what our lives were like from 1967 to 1974.

The other motive was to explore through our letters the strange and sudden collapse of a valued friendship. We can expect empathy, because this has happened at least once in everyone's life. It leaves one dreary and with a sense of emotional impoverishment.

Perhaps it was not quite as sudden as the letters would imply. I remember that when the four of us flew down to Port-au-Prince, Haiti, for several days during one of the last of Dan's spring vacations from taping the show, strain had begun to evidence itself in small and almost intangible ways. What had been placid discussion had begun to be a kind of argumentation. Of course environment may have had something to do with it. Port-au-Prince, as a garden spot, ranks right up there with Djakarta, Calcutta, New Orleans and Shanghai.

There was a lot of editing. There had to be. Without editing the book would have been twice as long and would have contained areas of a dullness which would have felled the reader faster than Valium. We deleted such subjects as literary rights and finding a good agent and how one might keep the Florida bays from being filled by the developers. But there were no changes at all made to make either of us sound cleverer or more poetic or less tasteless. We were tempted, but abstained.

Now friendship has been restored. Dan took the initiative. I am glad he did. It is not the same as it once was. We are each a little bit wary, I think—perhaps because we are more than a little bit older. But we share a lot. It was a hell of a time, and it was good to be there when it was happening.

INTRODUCTION

by Dan Rowan

A mutual friend mentioned in the letters, architect Tim Seibert, approached John and me separately to inquire if we would like to have lunch together. It had been almost 10 years since we had talked face to face. I was happy to accept because the loss of our friendship had left a void which none other had filled and there had been many times over those years in which I needed, or badly wanted, to talk to John.

Almost the first words from John were to the effect that he had saved our letters, some of which comprise this book, and that he felt there was a book in them. Here it is.

Motivation? Here was a man, who should know, suggesting that I could receive some money for something that I had written years ago. It surprised me that John D. thought anyone would find our letters of sufficient interest to pay money to read them, but I sure as hell was willing to find out.

Typically, generously, John D. also suggested a fifty-fifty split on any proceeds from the sale. It isn't fair to him, since he is the one who saved the letters, did most of the work collating, typing, copying, used his agent to sell the book and his publisher to publish it. For one of the first times in my life, I feel I'm on a pass. It feels great!

The friendship. In his introduction John said it was sudden and strange in its collapse but not, possibly, as sudden as the letters suggest. It was sudden, for me. I did not see it coming. John D. and I are such different men it is strange, retrospectively, that we had such a deep friendship at all. I commit totally and trust absolutely. He is much slower at that than I. He is smarter and more perceptive than I, and was undoubtedly watching me more closely than I him, but as a life-long observer of the human condition, John D. would naturally do so.

Introduction

It is possible, some would say probable, that the success of Rowan and Martin's TV show, Laugh-In, changed me, my attitudes and behavior. It would be sort of weird if it didn't. But John D.'s success with his books other than those in the already successful McGee series, the increased critical acclaim and almost automatic inclusion of his name on best-seller lists upon publication of each new book, all this had its effect on him. Success begets confidence. And other qualities less attractive.

John D. in his introduction brought up the editing which was done. Neither of us ever had any idea when we were writing these letters that others would read them someday. My partner, Dick Martin, is one of the funniest men I ever met, and one of the nicest. He knows I feel that way and the fact I never said anything about that in letters to my friend John D. will have no effect on him, but I make this statement here for the information of others.

I don't know about you, but in a busy, varied and much-traveled life I have not made so many solid and worthwhile friendships that I can afford to lose one. I am happy that we are friends again, John D. and I. It's not like before. But neither are we. I miss the time we lost. I hold dear the time we had. I look forward to what's to come.

Thank you, John.

Manasota Key
January 1986

A FRIENDSHIP

1967

From Mrs. Erskine Caldwell

May 26, 1967

Dear Dorothy and John,

Last week Erskine and I were at Lake Tahoe and we spent some time with Dan Rowan and his lovely Australian wife, Adriana. He is one half of the Rowan and Martin comedy team.

They have read all your books and the last time they were in Miami they tried to locate you . . . they want very much to meet you and, also, Dan thinks a marvelous TV serial could be woven around Travis McGee and I sort of gathered that he identified with the character because among other things he loves boats, and some day they would like to retire to Florida, West Coast.

Dan was a pilot in World War II and was a scriptwriter in Hollywood before he teamed up with Martin. I think that both of you would enjoy meeting them and if you wanted to let them know how to get in touch with you their address is: Mr. and Mrs. Dan Rowan, 9353 Nightingale Drive, Los Angeles, California 90069.

We have decided we have been in California long enough and are talking about the next place to live. To me there is only one place, Sarasota, but I have an awful lot of relatives in and out of there who might make it too crowded for my isolationist husband. Do you know any other spot in Florida that is comparable? If so we would certainly appreciate knowing your ideas!

3

I hope that you will get to know the Rowans and that we, too, will see you again in Sarasota one of these days.

Best,
Virginia

From John MacDonald to Virginia Caldwell

May 29, 1967

Dear Virginia,

Thanks for being a go-between. I think they are very, very good and any friend of McGee is a friend of mine. Copy of my letter to him is enclosed. I'm sure he'll understand how I feel about the serial television thing.

We had a month in Naples. We *like* Naples. More than we thought we would. There are some pretty ridiculous people around there, but I guess they're everywhere anyway. It would, I suspect, suit that noted recluse to whom you are wed.

We are going to move within the year . . . 25 miles further south. Down to an empty chunk of Manasota Key which we have owned for a long time. If that is far enough away from Sarasota for you, take a look at it.

Our love . . .

John

MacDonald to Rowan

May 29, 1967

Dear Dan Rowan,

A very nice note from that very nice Virginia arrived today with the happy information that you and your Adriana can be numbered among My People. Tis only fair, as Dorothy and I joined Your People some time ago. [We'd seen Rowan and Martin as summer replacements on the Dean Martin Show in 1966.]

Next time you are in the area, please send a letter or wire to this address ahead of time, and we will get out the good jelly glasses, and ride around in my very very small boat. (21' T-Craft w/2 OMC 120's)

The enclosed release of two weeks ago explains what *could* happen to ol' Trav. [The release concerned a motion picture to be made from "Darker Than Amber" by an independent called Major Pictures.] Their option is ended on Jan 1st, but I suspect they now have their deal with a major lined up. I put so many restrictive clauses in the option agreement they've had problems peddling the merchandise. One item is that the serial television rights are completely escrowed, sequestered or whatever you call it. The McGee books are to keep me in boats and baubles during my declining years, and I have said to those who would have him on the TV screen that it isn't very likely right now that any huge swarm of people would run to their favorite newsstand and snap up new novels featuring Ben Casey. Or Sgt Bilko.

The people I had the most trouble explaining this to were a sort of matched set of about four fellows from Goodson-Todman. They jollied me up at the Oak Room at the Plaza, phones on the table amid the raw meat etc. Seems some overconfident type on the coast had conned them into thinking he had the lock on the television rights, and so they had gone ahead with script and contracts with sponsors and network folk and all that, and had, bless my heart, signed one Chuck Connors. All this was two years ago, and after the long talk with me, they gave Connors a broken saber and had him march out of the fort without his buttons. They kept saying "How much?" and I kept saying I wasn't going to talk price because he wasn't for sale, not to G-T, not to anybody. They had those pained little half smiles, half frowns, and they were wearing those giant cuff links that must be full of helium or they couldn't get a hand up to their mouth to take a tranquilizer. You know, I feel like a pretty standard true-blue middle-aged American boy until I get with those types and then somehow I begin to feel like some very stupid broad must feel in a hotel bar lounge when three or four salesmen are trying to talk her into coming up to the suite, honey.

Later it was Mr. G or Mr. T, I forget which, told my agent, Max Wilkinson, that it was extraordinarily difficult to find the right approach to a writer who doesn't believe in television. He was wrong. I believe in it. One percent of it is very very good. And one percent of all writing, painting, sculpture, dance, acting, comedy, circus, basket-weaving etc is also good. And 99 percent of everything is and always has been schlock. I just don't want Trav to undergo that simplistifying (new word!) change which the series tube requires, nor do I want the angle of approach wrenched this way and that when the ratings don't move and everybody starts to get frightened, and they start trying this and trying that.

Incidentally, this is a long letter because I am waiting for a phone call and can't work anyway.

I am intrigued to learn you were a scriptwriter. How come I never heard that anywhere? Maybe I heard it and thought it was a fragment of a routine. Anyway, those now trying to steer McGee through choppy waters have weeded their prospective writer list down to the following: Sidney Carroll, Hal Feinberg, Eric Ruran, Bill Goldman, the Carringtons, Paul Dehn, Carraway and Ruran, Waterhouse and Hall, and Bill Fairchild. Now it is the question of availability and, I suppose, how well they like and react to T. McGee. I liked very much the touches Goldman had in Harper. But all good people, impressive credits, and on a budget of 2.5 they should be able to get the best, and because you give me the consistent impression of being tasteful (and now that I know something of your reading habits, I am *positive*), how about telling me secretly who you'd take dead aim at out of that list, knowing McGee as you do?

Once again, make a notation about those jelly glasses, and write sometime when you're waiting for a phone call.

Cordially,

John D.

Rowan to MacDonald

June 6, 1967

Listen!

I haven't had a thrill like this . . . hell, there hasn't been another to compare. Now I can understand, faintly, some of the mail I have had in which fans have explained this is their first fan letter, they are not easily swayed, they are hard to please, etc. Somehow it's important to the idolater that the idolized realize the importance and value of the esteem.

In February R & M played a date at a joint in Fort L. and the first day there, Adriana and I (I turned her onto MacDonald and it's a valuable and closely held in common affair we three have . . . you are the only writer she can read on a plane . . . and since she is the President of the White Knuckle Flyers Club, that's no mean accolade) went to Bahia Mar and looked for the Busted Flush. We prowled the entire marina and came up with a McDonald, a MacDonough, and one drunk who steered me to a bust-out crap game when I asked for the B.F.; but no J. D. Mac.

A few years ago, playing the Copa, my partner and I were interviewed on a now defunct radio show which emanated from Sardi's. Erskine was also on the show and we became acquainted. From time to time we would be in the same city and, well, never became pals, but were pleased to meet again. When Erskine sent a note backstage, I had Virginia and him up for drinks and chat. Again, as had been my custom, I mentioned you as my favorite writer (In such a way, I hope, that I didn't seem churlish to Erskine) and for the first time, DAMN! They know you. Virginia gave me your address and you were going to get a letter . . . not this one . . . when I got home.

John, there were many reasons for my wanting to write you, not the least of which was to simply say thanks for the books. Split infinitives aside, the most recent Travis McGee left me feeling a little funny. For some reason, near the end of the tale you sounded a little down, discouraged, sort of, "hell, I've tilted at this windmill long enough and nobody is listening," style. I wanted to write you and say, "Hey, pal, stop that! I'M out here and all ears. I hear you and you're doing real good." Then while this unborn letter was gestating, I read "The Last One Left" (Congratulations on the United Artists Sale) and that negated the reason for the letter.

Oh, you have some wonderful people for us to meet in this one! I was thinking of "Please Write for Details" and the one, Title escapes me, in which a gang of motorists are held up on the road and get involved in each other's lives. [It was "The Damned."] So few fellas can get folks together and make them work as you do. Enough of that, I am sure you don't need a critique from me.

About Trav. I have wanted to play him since the first book. And for all the wrong reasons. An actor is supposed to seek a challenge, or see some hidden nuance that only he could deliver. I simply wanted to be like him, to have all those qualities and by association be admired. And, of course, I am as wrong as Connors. He is a typical Hollywood choice, you see. They only see the exterior and Trav is a big guy and Connors is a big guy, so there you are.

So anyway . . . this is the next morning, and from the way I was beginning to ramble, a good thing. You see we closed at the Sahara Tahoe Monday night, stayed up to catch a 6:40 A.M. flight home and stayed up through the day. I opened my mail, saw your letter and sat down and started an answer. So with a cup of coffee and your letter in front of me, let's finish and hope you're waiting for a phone call and can find time to finish this getting longer letter.

Point Crisp Road. I don't remember Sarasota well enough to know where that is. During several periods of the Big War I was stationed down there. Flew out of Sarasota for a time and spent a good deal of time at Pinellas in St. Pete. In those days my interests were broads, booze and fighter airplanes . . . not necessarily in that order . . . and boats weren't in the picture. After a hitch in New Guinea in P-40's, 39's and 38's, I came back to Pinellas for almost a year. So I know your country well enough to envy you. But not from the water. Today it would be from the water. I am so hung up on sailing there's little time for anything else, my golf clubs are gathering dust, and my old golfing buddies are being replaced with saltier types. Pretty good types, the boat folks.

I too, liked Harper. Don't know Goldman, but the screenplay was tight and good, but who directed? It was fine, and it's hard to know sometimes where credit duly lies. It's been such a long time, John, since my Paramount days, and I'm very concerned about answering current questions on screen writers apart from the comedy field. Beware of teams. That is, if they present a team and credits, make sure that this is the team that wrote it together and you're not getting the breast-beating half of a now broken team and that the guy who ground it out quietly away from the writer's conferences is writing with someone else, or is solo. You probably know all this, but I would dislike to see Trav slicked and primped beyond all recognition. And keep all the control you can, pal. Out here they can make a wanton of St. Joan . . . and damn near did.

TV. Not for Trav. Not now. Maybe in a special or two a year from now with big budget and tight control, and foreign rights etc. A la Universal's features for TV. But I can't for the life of me think why you should. Aside from boats and baubles . . . good things, my friend . . . they—TV—must by their nature corrupt good work. That one percent you mentioned gets produced despite TV people, not because of them. The success of Travis McGee is an honest success, and your own integrity and purpose must never be aborted to fit the smaller minds and limited imaginations that run this industry.

Should you ever make a series of Trav, however, you may be wrong in thinking it would damage your box office at the book stalls. Hasn't the Matt Helm series Dean [Martin] is doing helped [Donald] Hamilton? For God's sake don't think I'm making a qualitative comparison here, only a commercial one. Exposure, unless it's terrible, can only help, has been my experience. (What kind of sentence is that? Do I have to write well to be a fan? Excuse: I'm beginning to rush because the phone is jumping and I'm running late today.)

My partner and I are preparing a TV special for NBC. They have come up with ¼ million for some more schlock, and that's what they'll get. It's their store, pal, and that's what they want. We aren't handicapped with your integrity and high standards. It's now grab the money and run. Get me some of that residual money and let me sail over and visit the MacDonalds and cruise the islands, and live the quiet, strong worthwhile life on the sea. How about that Chichester? [Circumnavigation of globe—alone!] And 65! There's still time, maybe, for us older types to do something.

At this length a letter is becoming an imposition. Just never did know when to go home from a good party. If I were more articulate I could thank you properly for the letter. It was a great thing for you to do. When do we hear from Travis again? And what about When? Coppolino? does that one come out? You know, I expect that Bailey has his own TV show now? I think Ev Dirksen is singing the title song. And although I haven't read "Bisco" (Is that the title?) of Caldwell's, I will look it up and do so. Used to be fond of Nevil Shute. You? Hesitate to say the ones I like, because one day a fan said, "You're my favorite, you and Homer and Jethro." Ouch!

I consider the jelly glasses an invite and accept. Will let you know when, maybe next winter if we play Miami we can stop on the way. With great respect and, again, many thanks.

Dan

MacDonald to Rowan

June 12, 1967

Dear Dan,

A good letter to get. I don't mind long ones. I write long ones, but at erratic intervals. Faithless correspondent.

Point Crisp Road was devised by a robber baron now dead name of Tom Crisp, who bought a mangrove spit of land sticking out into Little Sarasota Bay about ¾ of the way down Siesta Key, and built tract houses on it, after he filled it, and sold the one at the end to me after we got tired of living in Mexico, Texas, New York and renting and so on. On the nineteen aught eight maps, it was called "Mosquito Use." A Use was something you could take title to by homesteading. We did not get here early enough.

Should you go anywhere near Bahia Mar, through a very fortunate coincidence there was a big shake-up less than a year ago in ownership and management, and a friend of mine who used to be a PR guy with Lifelines Marine Public Relations in Fort Lauderdale became manager. Irv Deibert, a very solid and good man, who intends to put a small "reserved" plaque on F-18 or has done so already.

You are so right about the last McGee. It was from being pooped from "The Last One Left," and being pressured by Fawcett (which is the last time I'll ever let a book out of my hands before I am sure it is right. I had made that resolution before, but it went and happened again.)

Thank you for the word on the scripting people, and the avoidance of the team effort. Do not credit me with knowing these things. I know nothing about the organized hallucinations of H'Wood.

I made the decision to avoid the responsibility of any artistic control of anything in any other medium, figuring that perhaps I could achieve the same result by dealing only with people I think might be tasty, and then sticking them severely enough so that they have to go to top talent to get their bait back. For example, the next option that will be picked up (according to their man, Gordon Carroll) is Jack Lemmon's on "The Girl, the Gold Watch & Everything." A few years ago Mr. Peck turned "The Executioners" into Cape Fear with Mitchum, Peck, P. Bergen, Barry Chase etc, and it was a dreary moving, I mean unmoving picture. Mr. Jaffe of UA has indicated that Mr. Mankiewicz will direct The Last One Left, which would seem to put that one on the safe side.

I keep thinking this way: Artistic control on any continuing basis would mean accepting the responsibility, and doing some work, and making decisions, and I would rather channel all such effort into whatever book or books are on the fire at the time. And I cannot for the life of me adjust to sitting down and talking to people about what should be done about this and that. It gives me an itch I can't reach.

Shute, yes. Charles Williams, yes. Peter De Vries, yes. Cheever, yes. Bourjaily and J. Hersey, yes. Michener, Robbins, Wallace, Drury, Uris and friends—no no no no no.

To show you what a strange kind of special discipline I am into on this 1000 page ms on the Coppolino bit, I have selected some pages and run them off on my handy home Xerox for you. It is a departure. And a struggle. But I think I now have it nailed to the point where I can do a fascinating book without violating objectivity.

The next McGee, "Pale Gray for Guilt," will be out, they tell me, in October.

In the jelly glasses I shall make you all a drink known hereabouts as a McGee. Fill glass ⅔rds full of cracked ice. Slosh in an unmeasured amount of very pale dry sherry—domestic or imported. Hold ice in with spread fingers and immediately throw away the sherry. Fill with Plymouth gin, pinch a little citrus oil thereon, lean back, drink, and feel the lips go pleasantly numb, and the old war lies start flowing.

Best regards,

John D.

Rowan to MacDonald

July 8, 1967

Hi!

Well, I'm back. (You are? I didn't know you'd been gone.)

Sure, I've been gone. We've been to New York and to Las Vegas. There's a couple of swell spots, Harvey. Ought to take the little woman out there to the desert for a visit. God! I hate Las Vegas. Wouldn't you know? My partner loves it. We played the Sands on a fast pick-up date because Jack Entratter got some dates fouled up, and we did well enough that my agent called yesterday with the happy news (he gets 10% and can stay here except for opening night) that we have been booked for three or four weeks a year for the next three years. So in exchange for a measure of financial security I have to work that drag until at least 1970.

You must not like Las Vegas either, if your attitudes are truly reflected in your books. I read a couple of yours that told it like it is there. But maybe that isn't truly the way you feel. I remember my disillusionment when a guy I know well who has no need for lying told me that Hemingway was not only a bad shot but a coward. Speaking specifically of Africa-style hunting. And Lord knows to read him one would have to believe he'd be first choice for a hunting companion. Wonder if he was the same with the big fish. Hope not. In your quick list you didn't mention Hemingway but my guess would have you digging his short stories and lamenting his attempts to lengthen them into novels. Shalt thou blow the bridge, John? And will Brett marry the bullfighter or wait till our hero gets his cojones fixed? But he had it many times, and I guess it was the times he didn't that bugged him to the point of a shotgun against the palate. I want to be great too, but come on!

And Cheever! Well, he's fine. Have you read the fairly recent Thornton Wilder? Strange and fairly compelling. "The Eighth Day." You mention a certain novelist. We met him through some mutual friends and he's a great con man. Also very rich and very bright and shall we make a list of commercial people with his name at the top? Wow! Speak to him of writing and he has some kind of strange ideas. Writes an entire 15 million word best-seller in 4 days. Says he never rewrites, never edits, just sits down and it all pours out. All over the page. Isn't that grand? A real freaky little guy, John. If you get the chance to meet him, cancel anything else to do so, because he is as fascinating as a Siamese twin making it with a hump-back. Is that repelling and odd? Well, you get the picture.

I am being interrupted, but shall return—

And I did. The interruption was from the producer and R & M's partner in the special we are preparing to film and tape the next two weeks at NBC. This project is the first real shot the team has had in the majors. We have done many guest shots on most of the three networks' shows, and hosted for Dean's summer show last year, but this time at the plate we need a home run. We are calling it Rowan & Martin's Laugh-In, and there is no format, and no story line. The idea simply put is to try anything wild and different which seems to hold a spark of humor, and remain fairly honest. Damn, it's hard to do anything different in this medium. NBC is putting up the bread, and Timex has bought the hour. We will be on September 9 at 9, just preceding the Miss America Pageant, so the time spot is good due to the Pageant being a big rating show every year, and that is supposed to help the rating on lead-in and following shows.

Today, Sunday, my call was for 10 A.M. for a writer's meeting, then to the studio at 1 P.M. for a full cast read-through of the first script, then independent rehearsals for the rest of the day. Back home again at 7, and the schedule will pick up from there. Usually 8 A.M. calls lasting until 10 or 11 P.M. Of course we are over budget, and of course the direction we started has been changed several times, and many things we wanted to do can't be done for one silly reason or another. The first script is longer than Anthony Adverse, and heavier than the "Random House Dictionary." Anthony Adverse! So there is trimming and cutting to do and when you deal with actors and start cutting their lines you will witness diplomacy that shames anything at the U.N. Would much prefer right now to be sitting down to a McGee and let everything go numb and pleasant. And if that action were taking place on the afterdeck of Aisling, well—it don't get better than that, pal.

Ah, yes. Aisling. Being a Celt you know that's Gaelic, and pronounced

ASH-ling, and is that essence of beauty, of dreams of all things good and fine, and literally in this case—Dreamboat. She's a 35 foot ketch, Bill Garden design and where I most want to be, but surely I have told you all about her? Perkins diesel auxiliary—seldom used because we sail in our family, sir—and sleeps six if they are friendly enough. Slip D-6 at Villa del Mar, Marina del Rey, where dock boxes rent for $4.00 a month and $2.00 a foot per month for the slip. There is, incidentally, a Tolleycraft office at the end of our dock, and they are selling boats there faster than the Smiling Irishman sells used Fords. I was a little disappointed, frankly, to find you are a power boat fella (Oh feet of clay!), but in your waters probably a good idea. Don't know what the sailing is like on that side of the State, but it is surely great on the Lauderdale side. Here, there's Catalina and maybe the Channel Islands and rarely down to Mexico.

One paragraph of your letters really grabbed me. I'm not rating the paragraphs, but this one hit home. It was the one regarding your feelings about artistic control on MacDonald properties sold to the movies. Man, you are so right! And for such good reasons. But I shouldn't be surprised at this reluctance to divert your creative energies. Another thing that impresses me is your evident discipline. Of course the fact of your prolific and steady output at a high quality level demands a man spend his hours economically and well, but people who regulate their time, spend certain portions on work, on diet, exercise, play, reading and get everything done, are probably the same ones who don't spill water from the ice cube tray on the way to the freezer and take paper clips from dry-cleaned clothing without ripping the cloth. I admire you, friend.

But so many of the people I know want to be with the production staff, want to perform, direct, write, orchestrate, choreograph, light the sets, etc. And a steady concentration on a basic talent would reap them so many more dividends in quality and results.

The Coppolino sample was provocative. My own interest is not on the accused, nor sadly enough on the victim, but legal procedure and technique is fascinating, and Bailey should be tremendously interesting to watch. I can't wait for the book.

I enjoy this correspondence more than anything in its nature in years, but have a monologue to write, several sketches to fix and some blackouts to dream up, so will have to get cracking.

As ever,
Dan

A FRIENDSHIP

MacDonald to Rowan

July 12, 1967

Dear Dan,

Look, my attitudes except when I am laying the con on somebody in a small aside here and there, or doing the interior monologue thing with a fairly finky sort, are pretty straight in line with what the books say. And Las Vegas really and completely spooks me. I guess it is maybe because money is, everywhere else, a sort of second-hand symbol of survival, and there it is so immediate and ever-present it becomes survival itself, and survival in a certain mode. I do not like the way it ruptures a lot of person to person membranes because maybe, in other places, no strain was placed on them to that degree. I do not like to be looked at by some chicklet with that warm personal speculative look which means she is wondering if she can pull the handle and my forehead will light up "Jackpot" and she can pull the certified check out from between my aging fangs.

Also, they keep the insides of their damned snake pits so cold I can't hardly stand it.

I think the guy who told you Hemingway was a bad shot and a coward, with no need to lie, is full of some special kind of bullshit. Maybe he is full of the kind which lets him know he chokes when the shot is really important, and lets him remember he ran when he shouldn't have, so the cheap little satisfaction is in badmouthing a far better man down to his own level. No, that spectacularly romantic and myth-addicted old man was pure guts, foolish guts, and until his eyes started to go, was a superb wingshot and better than average with a rifle. Maybe your informer meant Ruark?

The famous novelist analogy has had me trying to ring changes on it, but I must leave it in its present form, adding only the variation of two hump-backs helping each other make out with one Siamese twin.

Look, I am well-organized for the work bit, but it ends right there. It's the only time I regulate. Regards all else, I am mostly pure slob. Inanimate objects detest me, and bash hell out of me every chance they get.

When you get out from under everything, write again sometime.

Best

John

PS: The way I enjoy sailboats is like that ancient joke of the dentist who meets a recent patient and sees the guy all bent over and hobbling on crutches and asks what happened, and the man said he rented a boat to go fishing and his wife fell out and couldn't swim and he dived after her in such a hurry he caught himself in the groin on an oarlock. "But for a minute or two there, Doc, these new false teeth didn't bother me a bit."

Rowan to MacDonald

August 9, 1967

Listen, my talented friend,

I am damned sorry for the reference to E. Hemingway, it was a stupid thing to repeat, and you are right for being indignant at this useless hearsay slander, and I sure as hell don't want you sore at me. If for no other reason than you're the only guy I know with inter-changeable heads on his IBM. Since writing that letter to you and receiving your answer I have spent, among other days, 10 days at my annual retreat in the redwood forests of Northern California and met several men there who knew E.H., and two of them who have shot with him. One, an unforgettable character type, named Ken Knick-erbocker, repeats your estimate of his wing-shooting ability and further states he was a very gutsy fella indeed and quoted me verse and chapter. All this not by way of corroboration mind you, but simply to let you know that I do indeed feel chastened, will try to avoid making that sort of error again, AND SO—

John, I feel a little as I imagine you may feel after wrapping up a good book. I really think we have a good hour TV show, one that most people will be able to watch and smile and laugh out loud a couple of places. Man that feels so good! I have just come from seeing a rough cut, and qualifying my objectivity of course, which looks awfully funny in most places. We all worked damn hard, but that doesn't ever make a good pudding necessarily. This one is *different*. Now we are all hoping that it's different good. Not in any mold, in nobody's bag but ours, not a message in a carload, and pretty close to the target we had. If you're near a set that night, NBC 9 P.M. Eastern Sept 9, please look and advise.

Now it's about time to start the Rowan and Martin rat race again. This Sunday night we work in Vegas at the Sands for Dean Martin while he flies in to tape his TV show, back home Monday for some legal meetings (we are in process of changing all our legal and business help in the hope our business affairs can get cleared up without costing us every bean we've been working ours off for), then the rest of the week in packing and crating (we're leasing our house in town and moving to the Marina to be nearer the boat) then off again the following Sunday, Monday, Tuesday in Vegas, again for Dean, home to NBC Wednesday to tape a Bob Hope TV Special, then to Reno to open Thursday for three weeks in a joint there called the Nugget. Our own special will air in the time we're in Reno, but our producer says he will keep us on top of critical action from here.

Have you spent much time in Reno? It doesn't bug me as Vegas does. Firstly because we can get away from the casino and show business action. A friend has a wonderfully comfortable ranch there and is a fine and relaxed host. I can play golf, there's a good skeet and trap range not far away, we may get a shot at a few chukkers, he has a couple of good saddle horses, so it all adds up to a not bad sort of job arrangement. The job itself is a bit of a drag and not too many laughs and Dick and I usually end up at each other's throat, but that's the name of the game, pal.

Oh, I know what I wanted to tell you, old salt! Last weekend we took our first family cruise in the Aisling, bound for Santa Catalina. Adriana finally consented to an overnight trip (I think I told you that sailing is her next favorite thing to do, the first being to catch an anvil in her teeth with a bad sunburn under her girdle) and my son, who is an eager and able albeit new sailor, and his date, a healthy blonde Nordic type who is a sailing instructor at the local sailing school and knows the local waters etc. At this point I should tell you that my experience previously of Catalina was limited to a flying boat trip many years ago to Avalon, landing at dusk, drunk, spending the evening with an equally drunk pneumatic red-haired over-sexed playmate and flying home the next day neither sad nor wise. Insofar as visual recognition goes I could have been on Capri. Hell, maybe we were. Get the picture? I don't know Catalina at sight from a loaf of moldy bread.

We shoved off at 0800 in ¼ mile visibility, no wind, motoring. Having just installed a knot indicator, and a recently swung compass, I dragged out my charts of these waters, a few navigational aids, and a very rusty memory of how to use these items. Twenty minutes after leaving the breakwater we were in fog, the only people on the water apparently. I laid a course logging every quarter hour speed and compass heading. It's the first time I have ever motored with Aisling except for entering and leaving the slip. Knot indicator showed a steady four knots at 1800 rpm on my trusty Perkins diesel, and, it being thirty nautical miles from Santa Monica to West End point of Catalina, I figured it would take me about 7 and a half hours to fetch my landfall. After 5 hours of putting through the still windless foggy waters, I saw a landmass and called Pitter (the blonde Nordic etc) topside. "What's that?" I queried. "What's the time?" she riposted. "1400" I parried. "We still making four knots?" she inquired. "So indicated," says I. "Well, it can only be Palos Verdes, in which case we are not making four but nearer three knots," she informed.

Thereupon I laid out new course, set my jaw and my hand more firmly on the wheel, laconically refusing a beer (which is hard to drink anyway with your jaw on the wheel) and kept paddling. Don't you know we sailed another five and a half hours, at which time through a rapidly settling darkness and a hole in the cloud bank I saw some land several miles to the east of where I anticipated. By the time we got there, darkness had indeed fallen, and Pitter couldn't identify any land marks, there were no lights where there should have been, and feeling faintly alarmed (you notice the understatement?) I posted Tom in the bow, Pitter on the fathometer, Adriana in the head, and with old Dad at the helm we proceeded dead slow toward land. "Dad, I can't see anything, but I hear breakers!" called Tom. "Oh, hell," said Dad as he wrenched the wheel around. "I can't read this thing," said Pitter. "Can I help?" offered Adriana, not too hopefully. We tried again, this time steering around a large dark rock, unlit. Now there are no lights anywhere, it's pitch dark, and no sign of other boat life. I head to sea. I ask Pitter if she has a clue as to where we are. "It has to be the Isthmus." A part of Catalina, I presumed. "Can we find a mooring buoy, do you think?" "Oh, sure!" she oh sured. Back into the dark harbor the intrepid skipper went.

Well, there weren't any buoys, there weren't any boats. We finally got an anchor down, stood anchor watch all night, slept fitfully, awoke at dawn to discover we arrived in the pitch black night at high tide, over shallow reefs, between two impossible rocks between which I couldn't have gone in daylight at an island called San Clemente. Not only is it off limits to civilians, being a rocket and test-fire range for the Navy, but it is also the last stop between here and Hawaii. Of course what happened is the knot indicator showing four knots was in error by two, what we thought was Palos Verdes was actually West End Point, we had been at Catalina at 2 in the afternoon and sailed on. Some great weekend. Some great persuader I'll have to be to get Adriana out with me again. Out of deference to my pride and my old Army Air Force navigational training I insisted on instrument sailing back and did that all right, but of course the reputation was already established. This sort of news travels, of course.

As I walk down D dock now, all the cheery neighbors insist upon asking my help in charting their Mexico trip, or they want to know if the fishing is really better "down Clemente way," that they have always wanted to go to San Clemente and are proud to know someone who has. My God how embarrassing!

Hope I haven't kept you up. It's almost 1 A.M. and this has been a fun visit for me. I don't have a MacDonald to read, but I am reading the Diaries and Letters of Harold Nicolson. What a priggish, bigoted, but strangely interesting man he was. The local papers are full of the murders of two little girls, sexually molested. First of these particularly sad jobs we've had in these parts for a while. They will likely find some poor demented old aberrant, terrified of life and people, then befriended by the kids, strangled and assaulted them and doesn't truly know why or maybe even if. All this had crowded Reagan off the front page. He's developing a full head of steam out here. I don't know which is more frightening, the thought that this guy could be President, or the thought of insane old men roaming the streets with a manic erection. Well. Hell of a note to say so long on, but so long anyway. Hope all goes well with McGee et Cie.

As ever,

Dan

MacDonald to Rowan

August 15, 1967

Dear Dan,

Goodness gracious, dear heart, I did not intend a runover of spleen onto thee! Only onto the clown who was laying the knock upon the Old One.

Ruark, also as dead as one can be, put the gratuitous knock upon Hemingway shortly after the old man died, and so I dropped a little note to Robert—of whom I was not let us say totally fond—saying that perhaps in all his African experience he might have noticed that when a large animal drops dead, all the smaller ones who've been hiding in the bushes come scuttling out to feed on him.

I shall make a point of being near that dangerous radiation which is emitted by the oscillator on color sets on Sept 9th to see the Team, and mayhaps to marvel that you did what you wanted to do IN SPITE OF all the efforts to warp it into other directions.

Do you possibly realize how your description of the rat race appalled me? Everyone to his own bag. I could not possibly exist like that. I need huge chunks of total alone-ness, and when they are in rare supply I get as mean as a pit viper. Had I to endure that kind of thing for weeks, I would sting myself to death like a scorpion.

I enjoyed your cruise vicariously. I now tout you onto a Columbian 310. They are a marvel, and the D cell power makes them ideal for the wing-rag set.

Do not envy you the legal-business change. I changed my dice as of January 1st, '66. I entered into an Agency Contract with the Trust Department of my bank. They collect all the money, pay all the bills, shunt some into the personal checking account when necessary. I don't have an attorney on a retainer basis. As things come up, I go to the guys who seem to be sharp in whatever area is involved—publishing, motion pictures, television.

I WAS NOT LAYING THE UGLY UPON YOU. OKAY?

Best,

John

MacDonald to Rowan

September 10, 1967

Dear Dan,

It was indeed delicious! [The Rowan and Martin Laugh-In Special aired the previous evening.] Pay no attention to the turgid-heads who will mumble that it went too fast for them. Tell them to tape the reruns on their little Sonys.

Extraordinarily dear to me was the Jap on the elevator bit, the BE FRIENDLY on the biceps, the slow motion big ball bit, the lovely knock at that horrid little broad and her repulsive puppets, the great camera work on the little doll things, and, bless you one and all, that solitary clapping by one person at the final fade. (I enjoyed having you raid the treasure trove of upstairs-downstairs too. There are some pro musica antiqua bits in their old series that never got the exposure they deserve, as well as one fabulous lecture on pot—I think it was in number 2.)

Thank you for a damned good hour, and for not patronizing the troops.

Best,

John

Rowan to MacDonald

September 17, 1967

John,

It's not that I don't appreciate your very kind note, and it has nothing to do with the fact that I just got it today because I owe you one for the great letter with the joke I stole and have become famous with, it's that we no sooner closed in Reno than we were made to go right to Las Vegas—again—and fill in for Sinatra at the Sands. Mr. Entratter now has a show booked starting tonight, and it would appear that we can expect a home stand of about two weeks.

Ah! Two weeks with nothing to do but write, rehearse, and tape a Hollywood Palace this week, plus a game show interview on ABC on something called Keep Talking, plus write and prepare a special we are doing with Perry Como on NBC. That effing boat of mine could have sunk for all I know. Now about that special.

Your note was so perceptive, you picked the nuggets, except for my own favorite, the musical comedy news. That idea has really haunted me for a couple of years. I thought we would do it one time on the Andy Williams Show, but the network balked at the last minute. I almost always get the news from TV, and galling as it becomes, always watch national, international and even local, and the local guys are usually the worst offenders. They, most of them, read the news in almost the same unknowing way J—— used to conduct interviews. Maybe still does, last I heard of him he was in Chicago and I am sure he must be broadcasting someplace even now. "And tell me, Miss Suzy Stareyes, how long have you been an actress?" "Oh, ever since I was released from prison on those narcotic charges." "That's nice, and are you married?" "My husband just died horribly of cancer." "Isn't that sweet? And what are you etc. etc. etc." So illustrative and typical, this sort of guy, of the general world at large. They just don't listen, care, hear.

And the news talkers on TV who report disaster as cheerfully as ball scores continue making their unique contributions to this idiot culture. (Remember I have just returned from a month in Nevada) MY GOD, I get the feeling every now and then that I will fly through the top of my head. In a terrible way I become so misanthropic in Nevada, and it seems to take increasingly longer to simmer back down and not slap waiters in the face; not ram my car into hesitant senile ladies in traffic; not bust Adriana in the nose for making me wait 15 minutes outside a ladies' john at the airport while all the time she was waiting for me at another appointed place; not run screaming from the phone "NO NO LEAVE ME ALONE FOR CHRIST'S SWEET SAKE" to the phonies and their party invites—now when things are rolling a little bit and not before, when I was wriggling.

I weep to exchange places with that gifted fella in Florida who mostly holds his own counsel, works when the fluids are flowing, fishes, rides his boat, sips his McGees, loves his wife and fellow man, and turns out good meaningful stuff. Or is it that way? Don't deny it. Somehow I must know that someone has things taped better than I and these other treadmill trodders out here.

The Laugh-In did well with most critics, and did very well in some places where it counts. However, while Dick and I were away, our producer-partner copped the credits, "forgot" to give us writer credit on the crawl and in the ads, and succeeded in giving the industry the impression that it was his concept, his formula, and that we came in, were handed the book and performed as we were told. DAMN. Everything that Dick and I have always wanted to do on a free hour of our own. As you know from my letters, this is really the first time we could make a full statement of comedy of our own. We hired, we conceived, we insisted that what went on the air went on the air. And now there is nothing to do about it. His production firm has reaped full rewards already, and, as I say, there's nothing we can do now nor say that wouldn't sound like sour grapes.

Some consoling thought that we can maybe do it again, and he couldn't do it once. But I feel like a guy who has stood at the crap table for a week losing, finally hocking his last bauble, rolls eleven and the man next to him picks up the money.

Listen, idol-of-mine, a pause just occurred and upon my return to the Olivetti, I reread this and discover that not only am I rambling, but am unloading in a most unseemly way upon a guy who neither needs it nor deserves it, so will rack it up until in better fettle. I do appreciate your watching the show, glad you liked it, and thank you for the review-letter. John, I am weary. It's to the Chivas and water, dinner and bed. The only J.D.MacD I could find on the road was "April

Evil" which I reread, enjoyed. I can always seem to find somebody
I know in your books. Unfortunately they were the bad guys in this
one.

If interested, can give you the inside-casino story on the Sinatra
fracas. Sorry to have dumped this one on you, pal.

as ever,

Dan

MacDonald to Rowan

Sept 22, 1967

Dear Dan,

Well, yes, it is pretty good. There is this guy in Florida etc, etc—
But there is one thing that kind of baffles and scalds me about it, and
irks my lady Dorothy too.

My doing pretty good is a kind of test of fire for old friends, especially
those in the same trade. And by God, it is funny and unexpected how
many of them drop off. They have to invent some reason for so doing,
I guess. Like I have gotten the big-head, or I don't have time for old
buddies, or I am taking myself seriously or something. Every little word,
gesture, sign of irritability, tendency to dispute etc that would have
passed unnoticed a long time ago now gets a big white light directed
upon it, and becomes SIGNIFICANT, for chrissake. So in social intercourse, even with old friends (not the rare and special and good and
lasting ones who know I am the same tiresome fink I always was, with
a good moment here and there) I feel like I have to walk through the
conversation in stocking feet on tiptoe. I have to be a gentle Jesus and
wear the benign smile and evidence such a tremendous interest in
all their doings that I feel like some kind of hypocritical Dale Carnegie.
So it just is more restful not to see them, and then that compounds
the goddamn thing.

Then there is another distressing thing which is kind of a horse's
ass change in my outward deportment. For a long time I could not
figure out what the hell was going on. For me, of course, it is in far
smaller dimension than you with your face hanging out there in mid-
air like a constant fireworks display. But finally I nailed it down. It
is laziness. People get a certain conviction somehow that you are X.
Now you know goddamn well that you are actually Y. So for a long
time when you meet strangers and they try to turn you into X, your
hackles rise and you hardnose them into comprehending that you are

Y, that you are you, by God. But it takes emotional and nervous effort, and with some of them you never get through, because they cherish the image of you as X, ridiculous though that image may seem to you. So, to save hassling, you begin to settle for being XY. And finally it saves strain, wear and tear to say the hell with it, so in public I will be that jackass X of the preconception. I think that it is realization that people who are in the public eye in any way shape or form must hang onto desperately—the awareness that their profession has demanded of them a controlled schizophrenia, because you and I know the ones who haven't been able to check the process and have become X all the way through, and lost the Y identity entirely—and it was the Y part of them that was responsible in the beginning for their ever getting a chance to be X. So when the image and the guy merge and the guy disappears publicly and privately, it has to be downhill from then on because the motor is gone.

Please read that over. I just did, and I think I understand it, even. Anyway, it is the one thing that makes a burr under the saddle.

Want to fix the producer-partner deliciously? You could use the same kind of approach as in the bit where you are teaching Dick to play The Game. Only you are the writer-comedian explaining what kind of show you want to do, and he is the producer who keeps darting off in bad directions and you keep hauling him back and saying, "Did you ever produce anything before? You're sure?" He keeps repeating the concept as you lay it out and in the end when you get to the story boards and credits, Dick goggles at you blankly and says, "Buddy, I just worked out the whole format for you off the top of the head, right? What do you want a writing credit for? You on some kind of intellectual bag?"

Don't enough people in the Industry catch you to enjoy the in-joke and wouldn't it make a reasonably entertaining routine for the layman?

Evermore,

John

Rowan to MacDonald

October 11, 1967

Well, John, here we are in sunny Las Vegas—

and you know how happy I am about that. But, let's be fair, with this sudden flush of success that R&M are having, I am getting that old shit-heel feeling (surely you know that old Broadway wheeze) and enjoy lapping up the cream of those absolutely inconsequential but delicious things that happen for "stars."

Christ, it's nice to have all those doors, upon which we've been knocking these 15 years, swing inward. We are doing big business for the hotel (to my surprise, pal), Jack Entratter is a hero with Howard Hughes, our new boss since we are now working for the Hughes Tool Co. along with half the rest of Nevada, and on Adriana's and my visits to the other spas on the strip, the other hoods turned hosts, stumble over themselves to pick up our checks. How sweet it it! as the Great One says.

There's other news from here, but I have exhausted my three typing fingers. I have, sorry to say since I had sworn off, been shooting craps and got badly hooked. After sitting around sick for a couple of days, have gone to get my markers back with a discipline that has been working, and I have paid them down to a couple of thousand now and feel as if I should leave it at that, but will take a couple of more runs before I leave.

Which brings me to closing and to say that we moved into the new apartment just before we came here. Adriana and I have a nice, though fairly small, apartment with an extra bedroom into which we would delightedly install you if you were in the West for any reason, and probably could give you a car to get about in and that measure of seclusion you indicate a liking for. Know you don't dig sailing, but have friends with power boats. Not any empty invite, my friend, would love to have you. And if we were away and you didn't use the apartment, well shame!

As ever

Dan

PS: Where the hell is the new T. McGee—Been watching the stands—Didn't you say October?

Rowan to MacDonald

December 23, 1967

Well, Happy Holidays, Ho-Ho-Ho and hello there, John.

Unless the letter I wrote several months ago went astray this one is being written without one from you to answer, so you'll just have to let me pick the subject for tonight. In the happy, and I hope not deluded hope that you are interested in the situation with me out here, here's the news. Time to call 'em as we see 'em.

NBC has ordered 13 shows, starting January 22, modeled on the Laugh-In special. I think anyone is out of their tree to think that sort of show can be done every week, but when this industry waves the carrot, all us donkeys trot. When the order came Dick and I were almost at the parting of the ways with the production people who did the special with us. You remember the beef? It went on from there.

Recap: NBC indicated to Dick and me that they would like us to do an hour special, they would put up $250,000, we would give them an hour of comedy-variety, anything that we wanted to do, they had a sponsor—Timex Watches—and they had a time slot for the show. George Schlatter, a bright, hustling type we have known for years, called us for a lunch date to discuss his producing the show. We were talking to producers and went to talk to him. We three sat and talked away most of an afternoon at the Beverly Hills Polo Lounge and came away with a handshake agreement to do a show together.

George had a lot of clever ideas, new ideas and new slants, and that's what we wanted to do. Something different. The ideas he had we never used on the show, but we liked his enthusiasm and his wildness. After several other meetings in which we grew even more convinced we had the right guy, the agents and lawyers forged ahead to a standstill. Schlatter wanted to own half the deal. I felt it should be equal, i.e. one third each Dick and I and one third George. No. That deal they say couldn't be made. He would own half, we would own half. I was talked into accepting this. He wanted to start hiring people and we three agreed all the way on most of the people we used. Some people we knew he didn't and some he did we didn't, but we got a staff and crew and cast.

At this point we were asked by our lawyers (subsequently discharged and replaced by Ed Hookstratten) to sign a letter of agreement. This was to be the working paper until details of the contracts could be settled. Now the letter of agreement was signed between Romart (Dick and me) and George Schlatter Productions, a joint venture. The letter stated that we would produce an hour special for such and such and that NBC would have an option by specified date to buy the show as either a weekly series or a series of specials. At that time we were all agreed that a series of specials was the only way the network could go because of the composition of the show.

Somewhere in here a joint venture agreement was sent to our former lawyers for us to sign. They advised us that it was unacceptable and would have to be worked on, and we also about that time, for other reasons, changed lawyers. The special was done, was well received, gained some fine critical praise and pleased NBC.

Now the network is considering the show for a fall start. It seems generally agreed that there will be no spot for it in the mid-winter schedule. The lawyers, our new one (we call him The Hook) and theirs. The agreement they want us to sign is piratical. But I didn't like the deal long before I saw the agreement. For instance: The weekly series to have a budget of $140,000. Agency commission (Their agents and ours split, getting 5% each) is off the top figured at 10% of the package price. $14,000 a week. S-F and Romart each agreed to take $10,000 a week. This adds up to the ridiculous fact that my agent is getting $7,000 a week on a show that I am getting 5. Forget that neither agent, theirs nor ours, had one goddamn thing to do with selling this deal. Nor will they have anything to do with keeping it on the air. They will help us book the show and that is about it.

I stood up and declared to all parties that I would never sign such a deal. That I would continue working saloons the rest of my life if necessary before paying a damned agent more money on my own show that I was making. Time rolled on. Agents and lawyers continued to negotiate.

In the midst of this hassle, NBC called and said they were exercising their option and wanted the show to go on in January. Now, remember, there's *nothing* signed between Romart and S-F. There's only this letter of agreement signed last summer, and Friendly isn't even on that paper. Well S-F called to tell us that the series was on, isn't that great, etc. I said bullshit, you got no show. I won't work. I was still beefing about the agents. Through all this my partner is silent. He says he doesn't care what the agents make, and the show is going to make us stars and we'll get rich making personals. (DEAR JOHN: I didn't know this was going to take so long, but it's the first time I have written it down and it's just spilling over. For Christ's Sake, please excuse me.)

Well, now, a whole gang of pressure was brought to bear on me. My partner, finally, my agent, S-F, and the Hook said, "Dan, you're right. I agree with you. But it looks like if you want to make this series, you'll have to make this deal." Adriana finally said I was becoming manic about it and for God's sake either sign it or don't, but stop brooding about it. We were working every night at this period at the Cocoanut Grove, and George and Ed are down there talking every night. Finally, when I saw that Dick was getting very uptight, I said Okay, what the hell, let's do it. Wheels started turning and people were being hired.

THEN, for the first time, I read the agreement they wanted me to sign, and now the agent's commission was forgotten. This agreement says that S-F owns the concept, format, theme and title of the show. S-F owns all materials done on the show. S-F has the right to do the Laugh-In anytime, anyplace, without our consent and without our participation. In fact the only 50/50 agreement in the paper is when it comes to liability. If the show goes over budget, Romart agrees to pay half the overage.

I got a copy to Dick, which after reading he threw to the floor and said he would *never* sign. And that's where it still is. In the meantime production continues apace. We have already shot some stuff. S-F has moved into large grand offices, beautifully furnished and equipped, charged it to show budget, have a staff of people, all paid by the show. NBC is apparently unaware this is all going on, and that they are starting a series in a few weeks with some people they don't have under contract. If the show is a hit, it seems to me we should have them by the short hairs.

So this being the Christmas weekend, I worked most of today on script changes, and intend to slack off and sail, watch the Rams do it to the Packers, get boozed, and then back in the saddle which galls on Tuesday. I had almost written you a letter shortly after we closed in Vegas saying Adriana and I were going to stop in Sarasota for that drink this winter. We had a date booked in Miami at the new hotel, Hilton something or other or Plaza, anyway that date is now cancelled as was the Waldorf and the rest.

I hope that my not hearing from you is not a reflection of your poor health or anything of that sort. Don't think I'm pressing for answers, I'm not. You are always busier than anyone I know and correspondence sometimes is just not convenient. You know, looking back through this year just ending, I really think that meeting you through the mails as we've done is one of the bright spots of the year.

Instead of sending you a card, Adriana and I wish you and your Lady every possible good thing for the next year, and much happiness.

Sorry to have written all this, in a way, because it looks like I'm using you. Maybe I am. You strike me as being smarter than most folks I know, certainly smarter than I, and I guess I wanted someone like you to say, yeah, Dan, you're right. You been screwed but etc. etc. It's the etc. etc. I'm interested in.

Again, Merry, Merry and Happy New Year and much, much respect.

As ever,

Dan

MacDonald to Rowan

December 27, 1967

Dear Dan,

A bore is somebody—you ask him how he is, he tells you. Right? So you asked me how I am.

Look, right in the midst of rounding the clubhouse turn on the great big long son of a bitch of a Coppolino book, now delivered to Doubleday 793 pages, 240,000 words, Sept publication at $7.95 titled "No Deadly Drug," massive promotion etc etc, I got pains in my left hind leg. Finally couldn't sleep. Got sent to orthopedic guy. Did exercises. In Oct I suddenly got "drop foot." Nerve damage. Foot seminumb, wouldn't work, dragged toe, etc etc. So they argue. Neurologist says disc, Orthopod says no disc. Got tired of confusion. Went up to Columbia Presbyterian where both the neurosurgeon and orthopedic surgeon said disc or discs, and possibly fusion required. Made date to go into Columbia Presbyterian on December 20th. But I had the feeling *everybody* was wrong. I think the body has a kind of way of sensing its own problems. So I decided to go in down here for a myelogram, which is the bit about taking out 10 cc's of spinal fluid and replacing it with a sophisticated fraction of peanut oil and iodine, and putting me on a tilt table and watching the progress of the slow oil and dye, while Xrays being taken. Figured on local man doing a simple disc removal if required. So after it was over (last Friday) and I was trundled back to the room, the anaesthesiologist came in and told me to expect a sore throat because they were going to shove a breathing tube into me on account of administering a muscle relaxant that would immobilize the lungs too, then in came the neurosurgeon, Ben Sullivan, to sigh and say he was not going to operate, that the spine area where, in theory, the sciatic nerve was being pinched, was wide open, wider than normal, nothing in the way, plenty of room for the nerve. Diagnosis: I already had, and recovered from, a form of toxic neuritis given me by a virus-carrying mosquito of the same species that has been giving people encephalitis in the Tampa and St. Pete area for the last seven years. Ben had five cases remotely similar to mine in the last three months. So I am now left with the same kind of left foot one would expect from a mild case of polio. I now take therapy. They are deciding whether a brace will aid recovery or impede it. I walk okay, but use all wrong muscles because the ones I used to use are kaput, and so the foot in the morning when I clamber from the sack feels like somebody has been tapping it with a sledge. In six months I will know how much function I will regain, and it can be all, or none, or anything in between. Got home from the hospital Christmas eve after 48 hours of staying flat in bed to avoid the spinal headache you otherwise get from a myelogram. I felt so curiously let down after being prepared for the knife I asked Ben if there was any other little thing he might like to do, but he couldn't think of a thing. When I think of the places where the viral neuritis could have settled—optic nerve, brain, arm and hand—it is very nice to realize that if I had to make a list of the things I could get along pretty well without, ol' Left Foot would have been pretty high on the list.

Hope you're not sorry you asked.

Now then, a couple of weeks ago I saw a thing in TV Guide saying that Rowan and Martin were going to do Laugh-In as a series. My immediate reaction was to take the possible variations of this grotesque plan:

1. Somebody got the facts wrong.
2. It is a situation type comedy borrowing the title from the Special. (a lousy idea)
3. R&M have finally flipped out.

Last night I used my handy insomniac period to dwell upon your problem as outlined in the letter.

The final conclusion is that even were they to lay truly massive quantities of bread upon you, it could not help but be a form of professional suicide. You people and your work and your special ablility are not geared to the old cookie cutter, and the inevitable outcome would be a total expenditure of energy which results inevitably in a veritable dog of a show which would gut you for good and all in the marts of the audio-visual trade.

The option on series usage was a goof on your part (a goof because it assumed intelligence on the part of the network people) but I suspect that a letter agreement made with a production organization which in truth no longer exists would not be finally binding upon you. You had a deal with George Schlatter Productions. George Schlatter Productions no longer exists. A different mushroom has sprung up, named Schlatter-Friendly Enterprises. You have no agreement in writing with that corporate entity. I do not believe that the piece of paper can be transferred as an asset from the original corporation to that one because the piece of paper called for the performance of certain personal services by Schlatter under a certain organizational situation which no longer exists. An agreement on personal services cannot be transferred except with the written consent of all parties seeking to benefit from those services. So I think that piece of paper is stone dead and along with it the option on series presentation of Laugh-In.

Analogy: Were my agent to take in a new partner and form a new agency, he could not consider my agency contract an instrument which could be transferred to the new setup as a corporate asset unless he had my written permission to do so.

USE YOUR LEVERAGE! Goddamn it man, as an ex scriptwriter, you know the power of the grievance committee—and that is but a small part of the credits you should have in this venture!

I suggest you focus on one thing. TRYING TO DO LAUGH-IN AS A SERIES WOULD BE A CLASSIC DISASTER. So don't do it. Tell Schlatter and Friendly to go urinate up a twisted rope.

But the negative bit is not entirely constructive. I would, were I you, make a deal with NBC which would be ass-breaking to fulfill, but would give you your maximum leverage, without spoiling your material, the kind you do best. You have to get another pipeline to NBC, which you should be able to arrange because you have CLOUT and LEVERAGE. The substance of your discussion with NBC should be: (a.) Your option is not valid. You can try to enforce it by legal means, but we'll fight it and you'll have no show. (b.) We are willing to enter into an agreement to provide you with six specials, two weeks apart minimum, or at whatever interval will best fit scheduling. (c.) Under our new agreements the shows will be co-produced by Romart and X, with proper protection on materials, title, format etc residing in Romart. (d.) Because we could not sustain, nor could anyone, the pace achieved in Laugh-In, and because the whole bit of Love-In, Live-In etc is becoming a dated argot, we wish to title each special separately, based on the preponderance of the material we use in each one, with the true identifying signature being Rowan and Martin. We have thought of using a Bobbsey Twins type title each time, like Rowan and Martin Go to the Beach, Rowan and Martin Go to Washington, etc. In these specials Rowan and Martin will get other credits where due—i.e. for direction, writing, etc and will get that portion of the budget allotted for those purposes, with full residual percentages.

I do not think you can fight that 10% off the top of the agency arrangement. It is too standard in the field. Forget it, and settle for fattening your end of it, your end of the budget monies in line with what services you will perform to make your show work.

I believe that a co-producer satisfactory to NBC should receive a third of the deal on an ownership basis, but on a practical basis you could certainly part with half ownership of the show itself because there is absolutely no money in owning a piece of a show for the first two or three years anyway, no matter how well it goes over. Use ownership pieces of the show itself as trading material to fatten your return under the budget and thus on the residual monies.

Now then, I do not know how competent the Hook might be, nor how loyal to your interests. But when a fellow is sick, nobody can object if he does a little doctor-shopping.

Above all, Dan, please do *not* fall for that typical Bull Shit which attempts to rationalize a bad deal by saying that it doesn't matter, that you will make a mint later just because of having had the series show. Look, how big a deal could F. Lee Bailey swing in the Industry right now? Who needs him for anything? That kind of series overexposure could ruin you for good if it should happen to work (which is dubious) and tie the big can to you if it doesn't—which you and I know is highly probable. Your stuff does not fit the weekly concept, and praise God, it never will.

Best to you and that Adriana girl,

John

1968

January 19, 1968

John, your special delivery letter got to me last night. I'm so damned mad! It was addressed to the Nightingale number and then forwarded to the office and there it sat until yesterday. I have chewed a few rear ends and they say it won't happen again. Plus which, the letter had been opened and I don't know who or if they read it. Anyway, you are so damned right about everything it is painful.

First of all, however, I am damn sorry to hear of your neuritis. Whatever else life hands us there is no substitute for health. Don't you wish you had said that? You know what I mean, though, pal. Deadlines, contracts, people, money, debts, etc. are as nothing. Let's hope that you won't have to get along without "ol' left foot." Damnedest thing about your being home in bed Christmas eve because I came within an eyelash of calling you that night to wish you a Merry Christmas.

We didn't send cards again this year, and I like to call pals or write a letter. You were on my mind a lot over that period. Nothing mystical or psychic. I didn't suspect you were going through that kind of scene, but we had gotten a card from Virginia and Erskine Caldwell to the effect they were in Florida looking for a new billet, and since you and Florida are usually in the same thought, I was wondering what you were doing. I had you placed on the boat or visiting family someplace. Instead you unlucky bastard are going through all that jazz with the doctor types. Whooee! Don't you guys know about spraying the waters with oil or something? Mosquitoes went out some time ago.

After sitting down to write a Christmas letter and then unloading the whole megillah on you, I was going to tear that letter up and just write a happy little note to wish you and all there a happy holiday, but the mail went with the letter in it. Now I feel a good deal like a family pet pooch who has just crapped on the carpet, and comes to the master with tail between legs hopeful that I'll just get whipped and not sent to the pound.

We're doing the goddamned series.

This Monday night is premiere night, and we have three finished and are shooting the fourth this afternoon and evening. I have been spending all day every day on the show, have been writing, editing, directing, rehearsing, and getting no more credit on it than on the special. Why? I have been thinking of all the reasons I could give you, but actually, in order to keep at least a *small* measure of your respect I will be deep real honest—I guess the fact is I am chickenshit. I just couldn't or didn't have the stomach anyway to fight off all the heat and pressure.

The first few will be all right, I believe. It is surprising what you can do when you *have* to. But from the 4th or 5th show on it will begin to show the strain. Others are now being nice enough to say I was right in not wanting to go weekly. But, John, it was this or nothing. We could have had a deal with CBS, but it, too, was a weekly show, and we would have had to start from scratch. If we can get to a position of any strength at all, then it should be possible to make them listen to once a month time. At least it proved that way for Danny Thomas and Hope.

There was a time when I was younger and more daring—and less in debt, that I could have told them to bag their ass, but now I am at the stage of rationalizing what I know are the actions of a standard show biz boob.

Do you *know* just how independent *you* are? In the first place you write alone. You don't have a partner. You are already a success. You know that you can write and you know that you can turn out winners, and if you never write another line, you are established. I don't have any of that going for me.

I have a partner. We are, as a *team*, just beginning to "make it." A step or two that is wrong right here can put us back into saloons for the rest of our careers and since both of us hate them, it would be the end of the act and I really don't have any plans beyond *that* eventuality.

Hell! Adriana just yelled at me that it's time to head for NBC. I'll mail this incomplete letter to let you know that I did get yours. I wish you would address me here at the apartment and then I know I would get the mail. At least when we're in town, which we'll be for a couple of months. Hey, pal, take care for Chrissake! We haven't been fishing yet, or any of that stuff. And I'll write more completely in answer to yours soon as I can.

As ever,

Dan

MacDonald to Rowan

January 23, 1968

Dear Dan,

Well, I am one of these pollyanna types who says well, hell, if he got the letter when he should have, maybe it would have tipped the scales and maybe he would have gone uglying around and bitched himself back into the saloons.

Buddy, I too am chickenshit. On account of that I had a case of the quease about sending you that letter and, in effect, taking the responsibility of gratuitous meddling in the career of somebody else.

Anyway, the shape of things is clear right now. You *have* to make it work thirteen times, and in so doing you have to stay clear of all options and commitments for more of the same suicidal programming.

We did enjoy it last night. I quite failed to dig the hirsute falsetto musician [Tiny Tim's debut], except in Dick's expressions, but there the camera work was ragged, trying to alternate between the two shot and the closeup instead of locking onto a closeup from a side angle which would have kept the "singer" in view.

Naturally you know my favorite thing. "David Susskind loves David Susskind."

As a confirmed meddler, may I suggest some bits of business for the future. All through the show you could keep coming back to a whole series of switches on the supermarket grocery cart thing. Like a ladylike lady who, once she gets her hands on the cart, becomes bestial, grows fangs, goes ramming the cart into any damned thing that moves. And maybe two muscular husky matrons meeting in the narrow aisle with full carts, and going into that same kind of duel as in the dodge 'em amusement park thing, going "Hah!" and "Ho!" like the judo bag. Camera could come back from time to time to show each in a more extreme case of disrepair until finally they end up with pieces of the handles, standing among the wreckage, doing that saber fight bit, clang, clang. There should be other shoppers and store clerks paying not the slightest bit of attention to them.

Another thing which I have not seen done and which has nice wistful overtones is the host (Dick?) taking a party to a restaurant where he is well known, where the food is superb, the service incomparable etc etc. But on arrival he finds that the restaurant has changed hands, and the personnel, food, service etc have all become chain-store type, but he tries to cover.

Do you want any additional crap like this, designed only to stir the imagination? If so, whistle.

NBC has ten thousand miles of pro football clips. What about a sequence of nice dreamy slow motion shots of people getting brutally and disastrously clobbered, with some Sugarplum Fairy music, and unctuous voice over, telling how football builds character, conditions the body, builds happy healthy young Americans, a contact sport in the beautiful out-of-doors, which could end up with one of those long slow mud-slides on repeat.

My foot seems to be responding to tender loving care. But I keep knocking it into things, and sometimes, to get even, it wilts at the ankle and knocks me into things. Apparently the objective measure of improvement is whether I can walk on my heels, the feet uptilted. Left Foot seems to be making a better effort to accomplish same, but cannot yet manage it.

The Ping-Pong return of the white egg was good. And I am tantalized by some subliminal glimpse of some pink hairy monster where I blinked at the wrong moment and didn't get to read what kind of a sign he had.

A guy down here invented the goddamnedest eeriest looking costume about ten years ago for an artists' ball. Maybe you could use somehow. He built an oversized female picture-hat that concealed his whole head and sort of rested on his shoulders. The big brim was uptilted in back, and on his bare back he had an artist paint a very realistic gigantic female face, the eyes on his shoulderblades. He had wads of blonde greasy locks hanging out from under the hat. So in effect his hips were the shoulders for the female, and he wore a kind of semi-off the shoulder, scoop neck gown that turned the cheeks of his behind into a décolletage. Two stuffed stubby little arms less than a foot long hung from the "shoulders." The gown came to floor length, and he had built some kind of fantastic backward shoes, so that the pointed toes came out from under the hem of the gown as he walked backward, slowly, seeing where he had been by means of holes in the hat tilted down over his face. Honest to God, it made such a hideous stumpy little woman with an *enormous* face, that it became a series of that kind of double take that jumps back and forth from fantasy to reality, and it gave one calm lass in our group a genuine case of hysterics. Squire Sessler, the man in the costume, kept his own arms out of sight, folded across his belly.

Hang tough,

John

Rowan to MacDonald

January 24, 1968

Hey, John, what a nice fella you are.

You haven't enough to do, right? You have to send me material for my shticky show. And I don't think you should ever feel constrained to apologize for giving asked-for advice to a friend who needs it. Matter of fact, that sort of "meddling" is what can sometimes keep a man's anchor hooked into reality.

I remember shortly after Marilyn Monroe killed herself, many of our group out here were wondering why, and several people who knew her far better than I did said she was lonely, and really felt out of it and not liked. Steve Allen told me that he and his wife had intended to call her for dinner because Jayne knew she was feeling down and bluesy, but they just didn't want to meddle. Steve is a dreamer, but said that maybe if they *had* called, *had* spent some time with her just then and *had* meddled, maybe she would have gone a different route.

A poor analogy except that when a man I respect as much as I do you, takes the time to have an interest in and good intentions for me, it is a bit more than heart-warming, it is complimentary and worthwhile. So meddle. Anytime.

About staying clear of options and commitments. The only paper we have signed, as I say, is one of intent to produce and co-star in a special—which we did—and (NBC) were to have the right to ask for either a series of specials or a series based on that special. Now they may ask us for a fall renewal, and if they do we would be committed to give them a show next season. I don't know what that show would be, but they would expect something like this one.

Let me tell you what has happened. We are, in terms of this silly phantom place, a pretty good-sized hit. The N.Y. Times was a love-letter, the L.A. papers the same, the show is sold in Canada and they called it a "secret weapon to clobber all competition." The overnight in New York (Christ, they've got me doing it!) gave us 58% more market than Gunsmoke and 27% more than Lucy and both those shows are in the top ten and have steadily murdered NBC Monday nights forever. ABC show with Chuck Connors—Cowboy in Africa—is being watched apparently by Mr. Connors and family, and he must be single. The final rating result isn't in yet and the vast unwashed have yet to be heard from, but already the network is getting critical mail and wires and calls.

They say we are naughty, and are pushing pot, and are degenerate and deviates. I must say I have never pushed pot, whatever that is, in my life.

I haven't touched on the material ideas. Incidentally if you see a cartoon, hear a joke, remember one, send it along. The supermarket idea is a dandy, and will be worked on. I see it as a series of panels, running through one and maybe two shows.

The restaurant thing is beautiful and finds me relating to it, since it just happened to me, but is expensive and a little complicated to do right now. It is filed. The football idea proves we are sympatico; I've been trying to get just that idea in the works and haven't had the time yet to go through the footage, and check clearances. But there will be a time when we are saluting sport or some such and that section will be useful.

The pink hairy monster is Morgul the friendly Drelb, and if you ask me what *that* is supposed to be, I'm afraid I'll have to belt you.

The picture hat and the body credits you describe so well, simply point out—old recluse—that you get out about as often as Willy Sutton. There have been several dozen chorus numbers using that get-up for a number of years. Sure you wouldn't like to be my guest in Vegas next time we go? I could bring you up to date on all that sort of stuff. But the first time you see it, it *is* weirdly funny. Besides the specific ideas, when we step on our joint in your opinion I would appreciate a nod and the back of your hand. Some things get past me by majority vote, but I'm afraid I can't cop out on most of it. You know, I'm working my ass off and having a ball. Right now, for instance, it's 20 past 2 in the ayem, I have a section of the news to rewrite and lines to learn and have a 10 o'clock call. But I had to sit down and thank you for your very kind help and assistance and let you know that you knock me out.

Oh! And, pal, I'm *delighted* to hear the good report on "ol' left foot." Incidently, I didn't know what bad shape I was in until I tried to walk on my heels with my toes up. Think some of those mosquitoes migrated to California?

I really have to stop visiting and get to work. Thanks again, John. Talk to you soon.

As ever,
Dan

MacDonald to Rowan

January 30, 1968

Dear Dan,

For CHRISSAKE, man, do NOT spend any of your energy trying to answer anything from me while you are rolling the monstrous rock up the mountain once a week. It will make me feel too guilty to even try to comment.

Okay—last night—Numero Dos—an epic which must now seem to you like something out of the misty past.

Lovelies were:

Remember Perle Mesta
Beware of Dog
Lower the Age of Puberty
The Pill Stops Inflation
Tinker Bell is a Fairy

Does the name MacDonald ring a bell? Hmmm. MacBell? Donald Bell? BellDonald? Shit no, chief. It went over my head.

Last night was fine. Held up. But my cold and skeptical eye detected a small conceptual flaw I think.

Try this for size. Number One was a smash. And every pattern was random. It went without pre-familiarity. At the end of last night I found myself thinking: "Hmmm. ALWAYS the Ping-Pong? ALWAYS the elevator? ALWAYS the windows in the psychedelic wooden wall? ALWAYS the cocktail party?"

Always means, of course, 13 time, so does it mean eleven more switches on the same series of visuals and same settings for jokes?

No, I said. They are brighter than that. They will not trap themselves into a situation where each week the original shock of newness is ever more diluted, no matter how wild the ringing of the changes. So abruptly the Ping-Pong table will go, maybe next time when cutie in a horrid frenzy of frustration takes an ax to it, and then there will be another continuity to last three weeks, four, two, or happen once and be gone forever. Otherwise there is lost the "What are they going to do next?" flavor, and it changes to, "Next comes the girl in the body paint with sayings written on her, Mama."

You know the bit in the TV jingle: Nothing exceeds like excess. And so we can reasonably expect a lot of imitations. So what hath R&M that others do not. (1.) They have an "easiness" with each other, a tolerance that has in it a flavor of warmth, so that as a duo it is a very effective tool for reacting and interacting to outside stimuli, in contrast to that tangible ego-tension between most duos which gives one the uneasy feeling they are trying to feed upon each other. (2.) They have the practice in pace to handle the fast shift without stepping on the bits of business. (3.) They have the intelligence to operate on two simultaneous levels, one of which is sort of a put-on of the other.

Now *anybody* can go buy the services of the outrageous off-beat minds floating around insofar as comic invention is concerned, and come up as you all have with a contemporary amalgam of Hellzapoppin, Upstairs at the Downstairs and hallucinatory drugs. But I do *not* think there is another duo around who can wing it within that kind of frame.

WAIT A MINUTE!!!! I just read what I had written up to now, and the impression is wrong. Look. You can go with the same frame, wring it out right to the final thirteenth time, saving the most outrageous to the last, and the momentum is going to carry you. Ratings have a built-in durabililty based on the idea that a new show becomes bartalk and cocktail-talk, and there is upmanship about seeing it first and telling the others, and so the others see it and the word goes, and you do not have a 39 week monster to sweat.

You are, bless your anxious heart, a New Household Word, and you will soon know it for sure, and you have escaped the saloons forever, and with smart handling the new leverage and clout can be turned into security forever and cartons of small bills stashed in the utility room. Just be very very glad that you got to be mature before the Big One happened, because that is our modern process whereby potential people are turned into permanent infants.

My quibbling is predicated on the belief, from corresponding with you, that you share my belief that one never rides with anything, because that is the way to dull up the world. One tries to improve everything with the tools available: imagination, mischief, irony and the marvelous knowledge that the world is mad.

Back to the other letter. I looked back to see when Squire Sessler came up with that rig, and I find that it was at the Beaux Arts Ball of the Sarasota Art Association in 1956. This circus contingent in our town spreads things far and wide. (I wrote a nonsense political speech for Emmett Kelly to give to the State Legislature a few years ago, and he has now given it at maybe 18,000 luncheons.) Yes, I am a recluse as far as night spots concerned. What I and my lady do is try to find a dark corner in a place where the music is small, and sufficiently Jo Joneslike inventive to guarantee the attention of the trade, and where one does not find cement-heads rapping out the beat with their swizzle sticks.

I do like the De Gaulle bit you quoted.

Stay in there,

John

Rowan to MacDonald

February 7, 1968

2:30 A.M.

I am afraid, John, that I am getting to be the fatuous actor-type who says "Enough about me, what did *you* think of my last picture?"

Your letter was a groove as the kooks on this show of ours would say. Matter of fact, it was so perceptive and pertinent that I had it Xeroxed and gave it to the staff to read. Hope you don't mind, and it's a little stupid to ask at this point, but the next day the letter went to work with me, and first I showed it to George Schlatter, then Dick M. and then I figured from their positive reaction that the writers should see it, so—

The reason I liked it, of course, is that the letter reflected most of my own opinions, and said several things that I had said, but it was better said by you. So far as results go, you won't see much change for a few weeks, of course, because once you start one of these things it's almost impossible to stop it. Plus we are shooting three weeks ahead, plus the format is one we are apparently married to, and plus, always, it's easier to do it the way we are doing it, so that's the way most of the rest will be done.

I'm not going to fight terribly hard, though, for what seems at this time to me a practical reason. The show is kicking hell out of Lucy and Gunsmoke's ratings—we are not beating them, but have moved Lucy, for instance, from 1st and 2nd spot to 19th. This means lots of money to NBC, and may even mean enough to them to overlook the bad mail we are getting from the card and letter writing boobs. Please don't think I feel every bad or against letter is written by bigots and racists—God love those who feel it is truly wrong to speak of the things we do in the way we do—but the letters are marvels. Anyway, there are a lot of them. If NBC likes our position in the ratings well enough, they may insist we do a show next year, and that is when I can insist with more strength on changes.

Some screwy things have happened: In three different towns around this wonderful country, telephone calls from concerned people have sent police cars to TV stations to rescue whoever it was that sent a message on our flashcaster "help help I'm being held prisoner in the news room." The US Public Health Service requested a clip of our Salute to Smoking piece, saying that we did more in five minutes for their cause than they have been able to do in two years. One delightful letter, incidentally written on blue paper bordered with little yellow flowers, said: "Your show is just disgraceful. We can't take our children to the movies anymore, now we can't let them watch TV, pretty soon we will have to start talking to each other."

The show continues essentially the same look. There are a few spots in each of them I am fairly proud of, but I can't really say to you, drop everything Monday nights and watch. Finally, dear friend, thanks again and again for your critical comment. Time may permit to thank you properly. Tut, tut, I know you didn't do it looking for thanks. Now, let's see.

Is the foot better? Or rather is the problem that makes your foot poorly better? It's just not a compatible picture picture of my hero dragging his ass around, so correct that stat.

Hey! Where the hell is McGee? I asked before and didn't get an answer. It would be delightful to be able to curl up and read of Trav again. And I asked at Martindale's about Coppolino, but I guess that one's not out yet. You *are* working? You're *not* devoting all your time trying to correct this meshugah series, are you? Let's get to where it's really at, and whip out something for the folks to sink their teeth into.

We have been working so *damn* hard. Taping days have been Thursdays and Fridays and this week is the end of that schedule. Starting next week we tape on Saturday and Sunday, and that means I am going to take Monday and part of Tuesday off for sailing. I bought myself a very fast very tender day-sailer two weeks ago. It's a Super Satellite, don't know if you have them in your parts. 14 footer, glass boat, tender as a dinghy, sloop-rig and have been clocked at 15 knots. Hiking gear, trapeze and all that jazz. But's a gas to sail. When I have an hour or two, I can run up the sails and get out fast and back. By the time I uncover and rig Aisling the time's gone. I just love it, but am having trouble getting what's-her-name to go with me. She says it's "tippy," what the hell ever that means.

When the show is finished shooting, I hope to take off for ten days or so and am thinking of going to Lauderdale to sail. Are you going to be at home and receptive in the Spring? Maybe we can fly your way for a quick stop on our way there. Don't be afraid, ol' chum, we'll run in and right out and expect nothing but a handshake, but I would like a confrontation. The way your health is going, could we make it soon? That's a bum joke when a guy is hurting—I take it back. But if we can make it, it would be dandy if your lady or your secretary or whoever could get us a place at the Bide-A-Wee for the night. Did I ever tell you I was stationed at Sarasota once for about 20 minutes back during the days of the Big War? I can remember little of it, except a place called, I believe, Lido. On a peninsula, place to dance and drink beer. Probably another town.

But I do remember the circus used to winter there, and it seemed to me that someone once pointed out Al Capone's winter residence. Do I have the right place? Adriana has never seen the west coast of Florida, and it is really a very nice sort of place, or have you discovered that for yourself? I can see I am getting punchy and writing bullshit chitchat, so goodnight John MacDonald, whoever you are.

As ever—

Dan

MacDonald to Rowan

February 8, 1968

Dear Dan,

Okay, Okay, Okay, dammit!!! I should have known better than to belabor the obvious. You all did not do what I thought you were going to do, so all is well.

Now as to last Monday, the things I liked best—(as if you were aiming at an audience composed of several million of me).

The clumsy juggler.
De Gaulle's world wide tour of France.
The duel where they both shot the girl second.
Write to a shut-in. Hoffa.
The knife that was a gun.
The Nelson Eddy–Jeanette (steel butterfly) MacDonald takeoff.
And hail to the stork which brought him.

Off on Sunday for my junket amidst the wholesalers and distributors in Washington, Baltimore, Philadelphia. Then to Vermont to see the grandbaby, back to the Gonk on Monday the 19th, a week of futzing with the publishing trade, and then back here on the 25th or 26th.

Some eager young PR lady at Fawcett wanted to set me up with the TV interview trade, and had the idiot suggestion that in order to set me up with those who had never heard of me, I should write out the questions to be asked and the answers I would make.

Stay in there. Number three show passes number two in quality thus far. And so you are on maybe number ten, which makes it like a damned all-class sailing race, where you can't tell how you placed until the slide rule people figure it out the day after you cross the finish line.

Luck and control,

John

MacDonald to Rowan

March 6, 1968

Dear Dan,

The hustlers and the cuff-linked ones kept me so goddamn busy with their nonsense during my 3 Mondays away that the one time I got to the set in time, the set in the suite in the Gonk was kaput.

So I was back by my dish and my reliable antique color Zenith on Monday the 4th, and by God there you were on schedule and I liked the John Wayne—Dick Martin—Trap Door bit very much. Also Wayne asking, "Is that dirty?" I'm just a kid, but I didn't think so. Maybe I'm a dumb kid. Very nice too was the Lord taketh away but is not an Indian giver, and the necessary shortening of the Lord's Prayer.

Hilarious (and I am not being over-effusive) was the Girls' production number parody of production numbers.

I missed the random signs, bumper stickers and graffiti.

So here are some for your solemn deliberation and discard:

Theater Marquee Graffiti:
    Richard Chamberlain plays Katharine Hepburn
    Revival: Spencer Tracy as Gertrude Stein
    Biblical Epic: Cool Hand Luke, Matthew, Mark & John
    Ernest Borgnine stars as Jackie Kennedy

Miscellany
    Jerry Lewis cuts Hugh Downs' hair.
    Hugh Downs cuts Jerry Lewis' hair.
    Nobody could be named Stokeley Carmichael, or Claude Kirk,
        or Percy Foreman.
    Johnnie Ray has Bawls.

Congratulations on nice words in Time, sir.

I am tentatively scheduled for the Tonight Show on Monday the 11th, which they will let me know about tomorrow. Prolly in the writer's ghetto period beginning at 12:47, ho-hum time.

Keep it waving,

John

Rowan to MacDonald

March 16, 1968

Well, I was never so goddamn mad!

Monday night I set aside so that I could see you interviewed, and then was called to a long distance phone call that kept me away from the set, then outside to see to the mooring lines on Aisling, it started blowing a near gale, and so I didn't see Monday night and thought I missed you.

On Tuesday I asked Paul Keyes, our head writer and my friend, if he had seen the show and he hadn't and asked why and I told him I was trying to see you. Anyway—I had to fly to New York very early Thursday morning and when I got home Wednesday night, the night we have celestial navigation class, it was about 10 and I took a sleep bomb and since I rarely take them—when I do they are near-lethal, and I finished up a couple of things and snuggled down into the sack when the phone rang and it was Paul. He told me that you were on the Tonight Show later.

So I sat through Florence Henderson's fascinating chat, and the rest of what must have been the dullest show John's ever had (Carson, that is) and I say "must have been" only because I haven't seen them all and I was so dopey by then I couldn't be called a competent judge. Anyway I just kept watching the clock, and thought he would *never* call you out. But I saw your seven or eight minutes. Did you get to see it?

I thought you made a very good impression. You must realize I had never heard your voice and was most curious about that, and your looks. Then I heard you tell Johnny about the writer's ghetto, and said, "Good on you, John, give it to 'em." Then when you described the promo tour and that the books were sold before you got there, so why go? and Carson said something to the effect that it *did* really help, didn't it? and proved that he wasn't really listening to you, I just flipped. My God! You better have a sense of humor, pal, or you will never leave your home again. I can't blame you for feeling as if you had participated in a monumental waste of time, and I would have to agree that you were shamefully treated and sluffed off in a way, but I am glad you did the show.

You have sold a helluva lot of books, and have made fans of most of the people who have read them and it was a treat for *this* particular fan to see and hear you, and I am sure that was true for quite a few others. So apart from whatever promo value those things have, they do serve that rather nice purpose.

Thursday night Dick and I entertained at something called the IRTS which is a society of TV and Radio news guys. We were getting an award, all three networks wanted us there and the brass from NBC made a pointed request and politically it was the thing to do. But we found out back there that the show is reordered for the fall season and that contrary to reports published here, we are being given the same time period next year, so that was good news.

In the meantime, we finish taping the 27th, fly to Miami the 28th to work the Hilton Plaza Hotel for 10 days and then take off for a vacation, returning to Miami for a one-nighter the 22nd, then to Vancouver for a week. From there we have time play in Tahoe and Reno and then it will be time to start production on the fall series.

We *still* do not have a deal with our "partners," we *still* are fighting the battle of dough, etc. etc. And something had better break fairly soon, or there's going to be all kinds of hell flying. But I know you must have had enough of that from me.

I am not yet set on where we are going after closing Miami, but I know I want to get an open car and drive down the Keys and show them to Adriana, and maybe the Bahamas for a few days, and just ogle, sail, play a little golf and try to relax. If we drive or sail up your way, I have your phone number and will probably call. As I have said before, I am really not a pest, and can be told that you are busy, away, sick, not feeling social, and I will understand, because that's usually the way *I* feel.

But I am sadly out of shape and would like to lean up a bit and get brown and cleaned out from the inside and I know that won't happen in the usual watering holes for vacationers. Maybe one of the St. Pete benches will do me. I am not going to plan it and am really looking forward to it.

Glad you got to see the black-out I used your name on, sorry you missed those three shows, one of them was kind of funny. This Monday we are pre-empted by a Cosby Special, but the following week is the Sammy Davis show and should be a good one. It was sure as hell funny when we were doing it. Thanks for the graffiti and miscellany. I still have not found the new McGee on the stands here.

As ever,

Dan

MacDonald to Rowan

March 21, 1968

Dear Dan'l,

Thank you for being so kind about the Carson thing. When I saw some weeks ago a quite pleasant type there called Shirley Wood, I suggested she tell Fawcett they couldn't use me, on account of if I told Fawcett I wouldn't do it after they had strained to set it up, the PR people at Fawcett would just lie down on the floor and whimper. But she said she could not think of an excuse that would not also knock off guests (what a stupid use of the word guest) of other publishers, etc. And it wouldn't be so bad, would it, etc etc.

The best was behind the scenes as it usually is, I guess. I went into a little room where they have a color monitor, and in comes Ray Bolger and sits diagonally about 6 feet away, and I have admired him for more years than I will admit, a fine gentleman with one of the most expressive and controlled bodies in the world, and, at 64, in better shape than most outfielders. So I am suddenly faced with the problem of trying to say the exact right thing, and not being corny, etc, and just as I am deciding that probably plain sincerity is the best bag, he peers through the gloom, hops over and shakes my hand and says, "Hey, I hope you've got another book coming out, John." Son of a gun. So I told him I had been trying to think of something real straight-eagle to say.

There was a nice wry guy in there. He wasn't on, or part of the show, and I never figured out who he was. But in murmured voices we made an analysis of a giggly little lady guest while she was interminably on the monitor making nit-talk, tugging at her skirt, and we decided that if one could ever get a chance to see the lady unclothed, one would find it was all clear, clean, smooth, pink plastic exactly like a Barbie Doll, which then led into another analysis of the celebrity figures of America, male and female, who might reasonably have the same distinctive plastic body, and it is amazing how many you can identify.

Another nice thing was to have one of those harried chaps behind the curtain, all festooned with cables and anxieties, tell me he had read just about everything I'd done, and giving me the very clear implication that it was kind of pointless for me to be there to be on the show. Constructive disloyalty, I think.

And the best part of it is that I shall not have to become involved in that kind of chronophagistic bullshit again.

Dan, you sound glad the show was reordered for next season. In one sense of *course* you should be glad, but unless there is an arrangement whereby the second time around is going to make you very very rich forever, you should keep remembering that last Monday a week I could see a pretty wearied guy standing there. Like maybe you should run a clip of the very first special, and then a clip of the last one completed, and compare the two Dans, and then compute what it is worth, and get the money or tell them to shove it.

Funny how in all the variety shows since you people hit so big, they are using your shtick—not as deftly, not as wryly, but using it nevertheless. In the nothing-exceeds-like-excess formula of television, by next season it could be like the second year of that ancient series when J. Arness became almost obscured by everybody else's gunsmoke. Nice you made the point last night on Hope of the theft syndrome.

Look, do you open the 28th at the Hilton Plaza? If it is possible for us to do so, would it be a Good Thing to come over to it?

If my math is right, your vacation will be April 8th thru 21st. I do not want to bug you or impose on you or any shit like that, but if before or after you drive down the Keys, you want an "unwinding" place, if you let me know soon enough, I think I can get you a cottage type thing down on Manasota Key some 20 miles south of us, with great hunks of empty beach, distant and totally disinterested neighbors. I could turn over to you the tiny Aquacat, place the Munequita at your disposal, fix you up at a pretty fair golf club, and leave you the hell alone. But, dammit, if we make no chance at all to crack the bird, the bottle and tell old-fud lies, I shall be a touch forlorn and wistful. Nothing I can't get over though, knowing it will happen eventually. But a thought to insert into your computer.

Take good care,

John

MacDonald to Rowan

March 28, 1968

Dear Dan,

On the map see two ways. If in a hurry take the orange line. To see more of the indigenous flavor, take the purple line.

But at all costs avoid the death-trap route of 41 from Naples to Venice. One of the highest mortality rates in America during the tourist season. All locals have alternate ways to avoid it.

We are back-road folk, ourselves.

Now then, orange or purple, you come over 70 and then 72 and stay on 72 to the intersection of 72 and Route 41. There is a traffic light there, and, on your left, a big shopping center called Gulf Gate. Go straight across 41 and you will be on the Stickney Point Road which, though bitched by new road and bridge construction, takes you out onto Siesta Key. Two miles.

Once on the Key you have to turn right or left or proceed into the Gulf. Turn left on the Midnight Pass road (your only left-hand choice) and go exactly one mile and you will see on your left a green street sign that says Point Crisp Road. Turn left and go out to the last house at the end of Point Crisp and that is us. Then we will guide you down to your hideout, which is right at the tip of the black arrow I have drawn on the map.

Actually, maybe I made it sound *too* primitive. It is not. It is a frame beach house with sand & old books by Harold Bell Wright and a porch and good kitchen, 2 bedrooms, good beds, jalousied windows, grass rugs, etc. John Lord is accustomed to all the creature comforts and has them in abundance, except you can't drink the lousy water, so 5 gallon jugs are delivered.

Listen, I suspect you and I share the same kinds of likes and dislikes, and if I had just gone your route I would relish this place because it is the kind of thing, that, if you spend 10 days there it is like 10 days on another planet, or 10 days back in childhood. You can walk miles down the beach, in any direction, pick up sharks' teeth, catch mackerel surf-casting etc. My friend down there is Bill Ward, a magazine writer. He and his wife Ginny have been there for a long time and we have been friends a long time. He found the place. He lives a mile south of you on Manasota, and they are totally occupied with building a new house a couple of hundred yards north of where you'll be, as they sold their house and have to get out by Apr 15th. Bill will fix you up with a card to the Manasota Beach Club, a shacky little place with good food. Here in Sarasota we have a friend who operates something called Sailing, Inc. and has a 26′ fiberglass sloop which he will lease you and go along and show you the waters. April is a good month for it around here.

As to the routes—if you move right along—the orange line takes 4 + hours, the purple line 5 +, longer if you take that crazy little dotted loop road (State 94).

Listen, I realize that I would be a bit skeptical and wary and bemused were somebody I have never seen to go to so much trouble. But actually the trouble was limited to one (1) phone call and (1) ride down to look at Lord's place, and it had been too long since we had seen the Wards and we wanted to see how their house was coming along anyway.

But agreeable as our correspondence has been, sir, I would not risk it had not Virginia given you two her hearty stamp of approval, and she has a very good built-in radar which can detect idiots at a thousand paces.

So I am not going to move in on you with any con job etc etc. The only possible use I think I can make of you, if it ever came to that, would be someday if there is somebody leery of us and we want to meet them, you can tell them we are not idiots. What would it cost you to lie a little.

Why we couldn't come over is on account of a sudden negotiation-type thing which is intricate and requires me to hang close to the files until it is all sorted out.

Best,
John

PS: I was thinking this morning, while feeding Goose and Travis Duck that you have got your partner locked into the partnership, on account of out in the wide world there are singles like Dean Martin, Tony Martin, Mary Martin, Purple Martin, Extra Dry Martin but how many Rowans are there? And then I realized that he could merely get his name changed to Rowan Anne Martin. Wing it well over there on Boob Beach.

Rowan to MacDonald

April 1, 1968
The Hilton Plaza

Boob Beach, indeed, Pal.

It has been eight years since we have played Miami Beach and I had forgotten—mercifully—what it's like. The same audiences who roar in New York or Vegas merely smile down here.

We have a girl on the bill here, Donna Jean Young, who is truly a funny girl, but low-key put-on kind of funny, and I guess you have to be Henny Youngman to kill them here. She is having a disastrous time of it. We fare somewhat better, but that's *only* because they go with the money.

However, I am confident that the hotel's check will be good & that's where it is for us right now.

Got your map and instructions and am currently thinking of going the inland route because it looks a little weird and should be less traveled. Plus Adriana has never seen country like that. The Australian Outback is barren and bone dry and the Big Cypress Swamp should impress her.

We are not going to rush out of here, but sleep until we wake, load up and saunter west. If it starts getting late, we'll haul in someplace snug and proceed next day. In any event we won't come pounding on your door at midnight or such.

Please, sir, don't misunderstand my gratitude for all this. I never suspected any motives on your part. Far from that, as a matter of fact. It's a rare thing for people to get at *all* involved with other people or their needs, and for a pen pal to be as gracious as you and your Dorothy have been is a very nice thing.

I am mostly concerned—and this is a personal hang-up—about my ability or opportunity to reciprocate.

If there's any drastic change in plan, I will call. Meantime, we'll be seeing you guys in about a week's time and I must confess it is an exciting and eagerly anticipated prospect.

As ever,
Dan

MacDonald to Rowan

April 21, 1968

MUSTACHE AND ALL or MOANASOTA BLUES

While the "friendlies" were skinning Dan Row-an
Our Hero stood still as a stow-an
Stood valiantly there
As they peeled hide and hair
With never a whimper nor mow-an.

They cured his pelt with great care
Then with exquisite tailoring flair
And neat little stitches
The sly sons of bitches
Prepared it for Schlatter to wear.

Presented to Himself by telephone on this 21st Day of April 1968 by his fair weather friend:

John D.

Rowan to MacDonald

May 14, 1968
Sahara Tahoe

Dear Hearts, you have been on my mind daily, and I am sorry to be so long in telling you so.

Vancouver was a standout date! We planned it only as a break-in date for the show, but it turned into a real exciting and most successful outing indeed. We did two shows a night and not only were all of our shows sold out, but there were almost 1500 people turned away. The ones who got to see the show were enthusiastic to a silly degree, and every one of our company scored very large. We were there for six days and then opened here at the Lake.

Although we are not in the season for Tahoe yet, we are doing big business here as well. I charted a 27 foot Endeavor, sloop—rigged, Schock-built, keel-boat that belongs to the Dad of the girl whose boat I rented last year. It proved a lot of fun for about ten days and then we blew the mainsail a few days ago. It has been snowing here for the past three days, which takes care of the possibilities of golf, etc. So, unhappily, the evenings have been spent by this particular idiot at the crap tables.

I don't remember whether or not this subject of gambling was covered in any of our seminars, but if it was not—I am one of those pitiable people who gambles compulsively, almost invariably a loser, and gets *no* real fun from it, and, matter of fact, hates the whole establishment simply because there is gambling allowed here. Stupid? Yes. Neurotic? Yes, again. Someone told me once, or I read it somewhere, that it is masochistic. That is equally as much help as someone telling me to stop. In any case, over the past few evenings I have lost the sum equivalent to a very plush guest house on Manasota Key. Ain't that dandy?

Discussions regarding the TV situation continue apace. We are being given a slightly higher stipend; NBC so far has not figured a way to give us any keeping money; the Hook is involved with tax experts at the time trying to figure ways and means.

The redoubtable Schlatter-Friendly duo arrive here tomorrow with the stated intent of settling matters relevant to cast and crew. One of our stalwarts, Digby Wolfe, is not going to be with us next season and that's a loss. He was by way of being assistant head writer, and although he isn't as strong as Paul Keyes, he was very creative and especially good with political humor.

Neither of us remember when you said that you and Dorothy would be leaving Sarasota. Dick and I have a one-nighter in Tampa on our way to the Westbury Music Fair date in June. The date in Tampa is June 7, and we have an extra day in there. We are staying at the Hawaiian Motel. If you're still around and feel so inclined, let us know and we will rent a car and drive over for dinner and a chat. We then go to Long Island.

We close here the 18th, do the Emmy Award show the 19th as presenters and are nominated in 7 categories; then to San Francisco for one night, the 21st; then the 22nd we fly to Honolulu for three working days, the 23, 24 and 25th, and then home for a week of readjustment and work on the concert tour that starts in Westbury.

In line with something you said about the amount of work I am doing, you will be satisfied to hear that I have been turning dates down the past couple of weeks. They have been booking our off days from taping. The plan was, you see, that we would tape 5 days and then tour the two days off. Good plan? No.

Adriana had her birthday, the 5th, and is now an aching 26. MIGOD! Were *we* ever 26? I threw her a party that night and she had a fine time, she says. That gang that is working with us are fine folk. All happy and all fun. Henry Gibson—our kind of guy—became a parent the third time the other night and got bombed, and was the funniest and most dignified drunken performer I ever saw. Denies that he had more than a couple, though they *were* on an empty stomach.

Let's see, what else? Actually, old chum, I am terribly distracted because of the craps loss; it is a worm twisting my innards. I must make a big big effort to try and write those thousands off, and forget it. And not go near it again, etc. etc. ad nauseam. Christ do I miss Manasota! And John and Dorothy. Well.

Maybe we shall meet again in June?

As ever,

Dan

PS: If you and Dorothy would like to see R&M at work—let me know & you can do so in Tampa. This, you understand, is a courtesy attempt and is not meant to be persuasive.

MacDonald to Rowan

May 18, 1968

Dear People, whom we miss, and why aren't you back here where you belong?

God willing, we want to be in Tampa and see you on the 7th. We shall leave it up to you to wedge us somewhere into the eager throng, and we shall arrange our own overnight pad up there.

"Oh to be in Tampa now that June is here!"

Delighted that Vancouver was so great. It is one of those places in the world that I have absolutely *no* image of. I just see hills, evergreens, rain and the very orderly structuring of a Canadian downtown.

I never heard so lousy and idiotic an idea as that dismal bit of taping five days and touring two. That is called accelerated depreciation of asset values, and you end up having to have your ankles taped between every race. In the end they dye you roan and sell you to a Mexican.

As I could not make any comment on the crap table bag which so obviously troubled you, I worked it into a conversation I had with Meyer to see if he had any of his pretentious elliptical sermons to give thereon. I report the gist of his rambling oral essay as best as I can remember it.

"If that is how it is with your friend, then that is how it is. You say he is of a high order of intelligence and perception. So he can work his way out of the delusionary progression of self-analysis which talks about weakness, will power, compulsion and all that shit. Sooner or later he will suddenly realize that what he is actually after is the *remorse itself*. Otherwise why should people with such an instinctive shrewdness about the odds, and perfect knowledge of the house percentages, bet contrary to their own expertise? To achieve an aching remorse in a perfectly acceptable way—a remorse as sizable as one might get from hitting a friend in the face, betraying a dear wife, burning down a treasured home place. So why is remorse and regret a thing somebody wants to achieve? Because it is an immediate and tangible and explicit proof of one's own unworthiness. Masochism? Bullshit! The submerged part of the self, absolutely certain that it has somehow erected a 'good guy' facade, and in a painful honesty wanting to tear down that structure and say 'See? Here I am!' finds a way to demonstrate its perpetual and insecure existence by corrupting the security achieved by the 'good guy.' The inner creature insists on advertising, once enough pressure has been built up—generally by outward success. What it is, is a man standing at a gaming table and reaching into his gut and taking out bits of viscera and playing a game called 'I love me, I love me not.' And it has to come out 'not,' because otherwise there is no sweet and aching remorse to counterbalance what the inner type feels is the outward, visible, untrue structure.

"Can a guy like that stop? Who knows? If he has to demonstrate to himself and the world around him that he has this streak of lousy, rotten, weak, foolish, selfish, stupid and so on and so on, the tables are the way to do it rather than less symbolic acts, which would be more direct, more hurtful and forever irreparable.

"Possibly anything even more symbolic and less self-wounding would not satisfy the inner tension sufficiently. The inner fellow will never be satisfied with the knowledge that *everybody* has the lousy, rotten, sick, selfish streak in one form or another. These people, the gamblers, are idealists. They fault themselves. They can fault others on an intellectual basis, but never on an emotional basis. They think, without ever getting it up into the realm of self-knowledge, that they are the only truly rotten type there is. These are painfully honest people too. With all the world and with 90% of their own inner world. But that other ten percent they do not comprehend is a kind of self-hate which has absolutely no rational basis.

"Should he quit? Probably not unless he goes down way deep into himself and figures out *why* there is that little area inside him which makes him dislike himself. Find out what the rejection was, and when it happened, and how inaccurate it was. Then what he does is tell himself that he is, in that one tiny corner of self, an emotional cripple, and is too old for change or repair at this date, and accept the tables as the place where, from time to time, he must flagellate and purify himself, needlessly. It is the dice in the hand rather than the spike through the hand. The Roman soldier jabs the spear into the purse, not the flesh. The pain is symbolic. The incantation 'never again' is cabalistic nonsense."

I told Meyer that by God he certainly wasn't much help, and all he said was, "We are what we are and we do what we do, and the thing is to get all the way around the track without falling too many times and without running too many people into the rail." He yawned, scratched his hairy chest and went back to his damned girl-watching.

I think he is an idiot, talking all that guilt and expiation stuff. Next thing you know he will be popping off about love, truth and beauty.

Hasta Tampa
John

MacDonald to Rowan

May 21, 1968

Dear Dan'l and Elderly Campfire Girl:

I made absolutely no mention of the awards in my last letter, as I did not want to hex you. I shall treasure, always, the way you kept your cool while carrying two glittering baubles, one in either hand.

I keep wondering who produced the awards show. Possibly a joint effort by Conrad Hilton and David Susskind?

Gad, what a fantastic ballet of clout that gives you two cats! Use it. Use it all!

Look, in order to bug you to the absolute maximum extent, we two are reserved into the Hawaiian Village Motel for the night of the 7th. We are coming up with a couple we spoke about, Lee and Mary Lawrence Brown. Older than us, even, but as sourly witty, quick, skeptical and plugged into all scenes as anyone can get. They bring their 19 year old daughter, but unfortunately Lee is a hell of a wing shot.

They say they will settle for seeing the show, as that is what they had in mind in the first place and got themselves tickets. I said that we—in childish confidence and all that—were leaving our tickets up to you, friend. So if that is a faulty guess, and inconvenient for you, let me know as soon as you can and I shall mend the omission.

Last night's re-run was one of the ones we missed. And please be informed it was fresh and good and new, and astonishingly topical, particularly re De Gaulle.

I never *realized* that the mustache was going to look like *that* for Chrissake! Is it this year's thing? Anyway, I never expected Bill Cosby to end up looking like a tall, young, deeply tanned Groucho.

Best,

John

MacDonald to Rowan

June 11, 1968

Dear Group—Yes, we came drifting back through the empty night, dodging the plotzed swingers, and talking of it having been a very fine two days. Sunday was unreal, though. Did you notice?

About that idea you thought the better of my two, what if Dick is Dr. Mark Grumberger, ice cold wizard of pure math, computer technology and games theory, living under maximum security conditions because he is the genius who, through games theory, comes up with the countermoves which keep the world from being cinderized? What if, in a grotesque lab accident he manages to stick his head into an erase device they are developing to use on computer memory banks? What if you, Dr. Gus Mulligan, of impenetrable cool and the conviction all the works of man are nonsense, and who has been doing pioneer work in using electrical currents to superimpose habit patterns on the lower animals, are brought in to program the empty Grumberger skull just enough for him to get through a scientific conference in Mexico City which will be attended by his Polish alter ego on "their side," and who knows him from Cal Tech lectures? What if his younger sister, a veritable ice-maiden, thinks you are trying to make a figure of fun out of her stinker brother, the Great Genius. The program is flawed enough (like when the tapes got mixed up and you programmed him with a couple of animal tapes) so that the Pole goes back to report that Grumberger is nuts. Meanwhile Grumberger starts to regain the old synapse connections so that he begins to flicker back and forth between the stinker he once was, and the rather dear chap of your creation, the one you have become fond of despite yourself.

So, to lock in the aspects of the created creature, you give him a hell of a big and lasting jolt in the sense of humor department. Will it spoil his effectiveness when "they" try a little feint to see if the Pole is wrong, to see if they get a true Grumberger countermove.

Maybe they get a countermove so conditioned by the sense of humor that it is far more effective than any of the old moves.

And maybe you get a chance to program the ice-maiden with some tapes you record from three charmingly cooperative ladies.

Maybe the basic problem with programming Grumberger from tapes from other people is a certain lack of precise selectivity. When you try to give him math from the head of a boy genius, you also give him an overpowering urge to join the band and play the drums.

Anyway—I don't want to look pushy. I like the werewolf thing just fine. I am just farting around with an idea which could give a chance to say a couple of things about machines and people and gamesmanship.

We had a fine time and we love you both pretty good.

Cheers,

John

Rowan to MacDonald

June 30, 1968
NUGGET—Sparks, Nevada

You know, dear ones, I sometimes wish I were a diarist.

That is presumptive, I know, because it presumes you would be interested and it further presumes that what is happening is at all important or, more importantly, interesting. However, you both are often on my mind and things that happen in which you would find amusement slip my mind when I sit down to recap the fast past weeks.

The Westbury Music Fair in Long Island and the Shady Grove Music Fair in Gaithersburg, Md., were financial successes and fared fairly well critically. Neither engagement achieved what could be honestly called artistic triumphs, nor were they so designed or intended. But we all got a great measure of laughs, and that's the name of our game I suppose.

The time was spent with interviews, golf, and work. We were in Washington on the day of The March—nothing to report there that Huntley-Brinkley didn't tell you. Had a half-hour visit in his offices with the Senator from California, and Mr. Murphy called it "Insurrection City" and had several jokes about colored deacons arriving in Lincolns and Jaguars. A nice man but mind-locked, I'm afraid.

We have found a very funny man, Dave Madden, and he's now a regular with the tour and we hope to get him on the TV gang as well. Comes up with fine words like, "If Jesus was really Jewish, how come he had a Puerto Rican name?" And—"Boy, I had a big day today, went around and watched the parking meters violate themselves." He has a fetching and unusual style that goes well with his material and should have a big future. Does an insurance routine that would put you away. Oh, and he says he knew a woman who got hooked on birth control pills. Ate them like candy. One day she sneezed and sterilized her entire bridge club. Now *he's* funny!

This is a three week job, no nights off and three shows on Saturday night. The day after we close I will be off for my annual retreat to the Bohemian Grove for 10 days and then we go directly to Colorado Springs for 6 days, then two days at the Allentown Fair in Pa., then right to NBC to start taping the first show.

Got hold of a book called "Aerobics" written by an Air Force doctor and he has impressed me enough to get me running. I HATE RUNNING! I also hate to admit, as I am forced to, that I am sadly and seriously out of shape. I can't jog for a half mile. The altitude here, about 5000 feet, doesn't help, but I am going to try and run some every day and work my way up to a couple miles a day.

John, I haven't ducked the picture idea up to now, I am just disorganized, and have just now pulled your letter out and re-read it. You have a very solid idea there, and could make a helluva picture. There are opportunities for several very funny block sequences, and the plot is rich and full. Its big attraction, it seems to me, is that it is futuristic enough to be NOW, and can be suspenseful without guns and violence.

Our motion picture situation has changed to this extent since we last spoke of it. We have agreed to do two pictures with MGM with an option for a third. We are getting a big salary which we hope to defer, and 25% of the profits which, of course, we don't expect to see. One property is the werewolf idea, which when I heard developed by the writer, made more sense. Dick never, in fact, becomes a werewolf, except in a possible dream sequence, but is being brainwashed for plot purposes by a seamy, evil villain who has reasons that make *some* sense. It could be a funny picture. Have I told you all this before? The other property is one which MGM figures is its best story. They had bought it for McQueen and Lemmon, but are giving it to us. That's Butterfly McQueen and Bob Lemmon. This story is from a book "The Ballad of Dingus Magee" and is sort of Cat Ballou style western-satire-comedy with two guys.

Our schedule is such that we will finish taping and start preparing the film and plan to shoot as soon as we can in March or early April at the latest.

Strange things are happening to me, old friend, and it's as difficult to describe as it is to deal with. I am finding that I don't make a public figure very comfortably. You have no idea how rude I have become to the pushy broad who thrusts her damn napkin under my chin to sign while I am eating. They find out your room and come in without knocking or knock until you have to let them in. They are, in fact, pigs by and large. Dick, on the other hand, thrives on the attention. The mustache has saved me lots of attention but not enough. But it's strange. For instance at the theater dates, kids would stop us in the aisles for autographs and I wouldn't sign them then, but I did announce from the stage that we would sign them after the performance backstage. The crew set up a long table and Dick and I sat there and signed several hundred for two performances, then Dick said to hell with it, he didn't like it and so we quit.

At any other time, our own time, he is eager to sign and very patient; I, contrarily, feel it's an imposition and get hard to reach and want room service for food etc. I realize this situation only gets worse with additional TV exposure, and will have to get used to it, I suppose, but I don't dig it. I HATE PEOPLE AND RUNNING. But I really hate running.

How's the greatest house in the world progressing? How is Dorothy? How are the new books? Where are you? Ain't it hell in Florida in the summer? Don't you know we miss you guys entirely too much and send all our love.

As ever

Dan

MacDonald to Rowan

July 12, 1968

Dear Dan,

How come He had a Puerto Rican name? is one of the very best little bits I've heard in a long, long time. Also, like the best ones, it is a people-filter. The degree to which it is enjoyed seems to be the good old simpatico sympatico index.

Look, when you get yourself jogged up to two miles a day, let me know how you feel, and if you give it a good report, maybe I shall start jogging around my veranda, because by the time you are doing two miles, my veranda will be finished. In order to keep from losing track, I shall tote a handful of pennies and chink one into a bucket each time I pass my front door. By the time I get up to forty cents, I should be patronizingly healthy.

Tis a small small small world, man. A young man who is a friend and fan of mine named Dave Markson spent a lot of time in NY trying to make it by writing. Went to Mexico and tried to make it there. Finally came back and took job in the English Dept of the Brooklyn campus of, I think, the University of the State of New York (Not NYU) and kept plugging. His agent phoned him one evening and said, "Dave, are you sitting down? I just sold The Ballad of Dingus Magee for XXX dollars to the moom pitchers." I was so very damn glad for Dave as he had been scrambling so long. I wrote him to turn a little bit square, pretend it didn't happen, stay right in the teaching thing, and then start winging it with the next hit. But no, Dave went cruising around Europe, and from there sent me a post card at one point addressed with a pasted-on picture of me and just "Florida" for an address. I got it in five days from date of mailing, which does not mean fame, but only that somewhere in the postal department was one of My People. It got a small note in the papers, along with a photo of Wrong Mail Corrigan, my faithful route man. Dave is a good and perceptive and untemperamental guy, and if you folks ever have a chance to use him in any way on the film, he would not be a burden.

I have just had some brand new experiences. Jack Reeves mailed me the script for the first McGee movie a month ago. And one to my agent. They are doing "Amber" first. The only way I could possibly explain to Jack how cheap, ordinary, vulgar and impossible I found it was to hole up for a weekend and rewrite the entire first 40 pages of it, and send it along with a long letter of comment. CBS films had already approved it, God knows why. They (Reeves and Seltzer) had paid some chap named Ed Waters X dollars to do it. Max Wilkinson, my agent in New York, who had a couple of years orientation as right-hand man to Sam Goldwyn, pronounced it as just about the worst script he had ever read. Jack could write Max off as being old-timey and out of touch with the modrun movie, but he could not write me off. So he came down a few days ago, but he could not make it like it was *just* for that reason, so he had to improvise a visit to friends in Nassau, and came here to buy me a drink on the way home. But in five or six hard hours of talk I shook him. What happens out there is exactly the same thing that happens when people get all juiced up about some dog play that closes after two nights in Manhattan. Group hypnosis. Somehow all the people involved, from Stulberg on down were looking at the script but they were seeing my book and not the perversion of my book. Jack kept saying in defense of horrid lines that it is a director's medium, and I kept saying that a script has to stimulate directorial creative ability, not quash it by being so goddamn ordinary. Also, from a dollars and sense point of view, they were throwing away thousands on scenes which added nothing to character and did not further the plot.

Anyway, though I do not have script approval I won my major point by saying that, as it stood, they could depend upon a big fat NO from Culp. (He had been in England and did not get it until a few days ago, and they have not had his reaction yet, but they had sent him the stinker.) Now Reeves is embarking on "one last major final revision," which should eliminate, I hope, a great deal of the vulgarity and illogic and trite characterization. For example, they turned Meyer into a fat clown, clumsy and dumb. Degrade a man's closest friend and you do not enhance him by the comparison—you only degrade him too.

Also, the second point won is that if they improve it enough to actually warrant going ahead with 2 & 3, I will do for them what they should have asked me to do for this one, a simplified treatment which will retain character, retain the essence of the plot and the good visuals, but delete the things that I can get away with in a book which, by reason of their complexity, will just not come off on the screen.

Made a funny argumentation between me and Reeves—the author bitching because they had tried to stay *too* close to plot, and thus lost touch with character.

Incidentally, I find one thing hilarious. They all talk about it being a director's medium. Yet every dreary little scriptwriter puts in all this shit about ECU, POV, cut to, two shot, angle, dissolve etc. I just cannot see the Director setting up a scene and then looking at the script and seeing that the scriptwriter demands, for example, a boom shot, and then yelling, "Bring in the boom, Charlie!" A script should, I suspect, describe scene, incident, dress and dialogue on the right-hand half of the paper, and leave the left side blank for whatever directorial inventiveness a good man can come up with on the spot, and when it is of no special consequence *where* a particular establishing conversation takes place, two words "scene optional" could have a fat effect on budget and on the quality of the visuals.

Please do let me know how the briefcase telephone works.

Florida in the summer is damned great.

The house is progressing. The McGees in process are coming along. Doubleday is increasingly optimistic about "No Deadly Drug." Dorothy is dandy. And, friends, we miss you too. Come back.

Yr friend,

John

MacDonald to Rowan

21 July 1968

Dear Dan,

I do hope that you went suitably armed with the proper anecdotal materials to the Bohemian Camp, and that you stayed the hell on your own side of the river.

Could Dick say: "Did I ever tell you what my Aunt Gwendolyn said after she walked into the woods, and right into a camp full of drunken lumberjacks on Saturday night, and lost her peavey?"

Love from us, sir

John

Rowan to MacDonald

August 13, 1968

Listen, Smart Ass:

I have made a few marginal notes on your recent Playboy spread, and will be more explicit and detailed when you have moved from the "letters to the editor" to the gatefold. Your friend, Hef (that is what all of us "in" folk call him) had one of his first cameo spots on our first show. If you think he is a thrill from a writer's POV, let me tell you what a scintillating, brilliant guest he is.

The show proceeds apace. . . . I am keeping my cool. It is a copy of the one last year, and so, I understand, will be several others that will be on the air this season, but I am now assuming the posture of the man who once said, "Grab the money and run."

Adriana has been midwifing all day, and is an excited, distraught, nervous, proud, exhausted grandmother to two brand-new lively, black (with a promise to become silver) tiny toy poodles. Holly . . . she's the little silver beauty . . . gave birth today. Two males. I don't know what they weigh, because I can't get them out of Adriana's hands. This could have been solved if I had weighed her . . . then . . . what is added . . . Oh, hell, that wouldn't work, but if you are really interested in their weight, I would be terribly surprised.

Knowing your interest in graffiti, I respectfully submit:

Luther Burbank switched fruits.

Report obscene mail to an obscene female.

Capt. Christian was Jewish.

Sitting Bull died for our sins.

Show the least interest in these and I will send you more.

As Ever
Dan

Rowan to MacDonald

August 30, 1968

How are you? I really am going to have to find out when you guys generally go to bed, because I find myself starting to call you, and then realize that it's midnight or after back there.

My own feelings about the Chicago debacle [political convention] is that it may very well work to the people's advantage in the long haul. It was just possibly the most painful thing to watch and certainly one of the most obscene. The Republicans were dull and the Democrats were stupidly vicious. Not much choice there.

I am enclosing the copy of a letter written by Bob Kasmire to Ed Friendly. The correspondence was initiated by the frequent use throughout the first shows of cameo characters saying, "Look *that* up in your Funk and Wagnall's." The network objected and we asked them why, through Ed F. The letter in return is, I believe, a classic. We got around the F&W controversy to NBC's satisfaction by the simple expedient of having additional cameos taped following "Look *that* up in your Funk and Wagnall's" saying "That's a dictionary, you know."

We have just finished taping #3, and I leave this afternoon for Saratoga, N.Y., for three performances. Be back early Monday morning for the run-through for show #4 which tapes Tuesday and Wednesday. I know, I know.

Bob Culp and his attractive wife are guests on the next show and I had a conversation with him yesterday at which time I learned for the first time he's *not* going to do McGee. I told him I knew you, and he said that he loved the McGee books he read and that is the reason he told CBS he would do them. The first script he got, he said, had a great first 20 pages, and then went downhill. I suggested that scripts could be fixed and he went into some kind of mystical discussion the meat of which was, "I decided that this is the sort of mythical character I didn't believe in. It's a sort of mythology that I don't know should be perpetuated."

I don't pretend to understand that, except he seems to have seen the character like a "Shane," and I told him I thought he had passed up an opportunity to play one of the most memorable characters in contemporary fiction, and one that had a hell of a lot to say and said it well. He said that he had heard they had offered it to Rod Taylor who turned it down. I am not at all sure that these events are sad ones, but what is saddening to me is that these people, as most, tend to categorize people too quickly. I am sure they think of Trav as Matt Helm or some such, for Christ's sake. It is strange, too, because the great body of McGee fans know the man, dig his sensitive compassion, his liberality, etc. It only makes me think that these actors weren't intelligent enough to play McGee.

Of course I don't know what he's doing, nor what he looks like now, but by damn, Sterling Hayden would be a fine McGee. Well, that's the word I have heard here on that project, and thought you would find it interesting.

The Dutch kid I shack with is disgustingly healthy and pretends to being happy, but she's so damned devious I never know for sure. She is now running a mile and a half non-stop. Runs six days a week. Makes me sick! I have finally been able to knock off a few pounds and am today at 187, some 10 pounds from when you last saw me. Feel better, if you can consider a starving man as feeling well.

So, old sport, see you later. Thought you would enjoy the Kasmire letter. Haven't heard from you but realize you're building books and houses and that can take a fella's time. Our love to Dorothy and to you and drop a note when chance affords.

As ever,

Dan

[*Letter enclosed with Rowan letter of August 30, 1968*]

NATIONAL BROADCASTING COMPANY, INC.
THIRTY ROCKEFELLER PLAZA, NEW YORK, NY

Robert D. Kasmire
Vice President
Corporate Information

Aug 16, 1968

Mr. Ed Friendly
George Schlatter-Ed Friendly Productions
4425 Lakeside Drive
Burbank, California 91505

Dear Ed:

I answer my mail in achronological order (look that up in your Funk and Wagnall), so this is in response to your letter of August 7.

I know my position isn't singular because when the inquisition convenes I'll be able to produce several people who agree with me. Whether it's a minority view, neither of us can say until we measure the universe we're dealing with.

Anyhow, assuming you're serious in asking me to clarify NBC's position in standing against your plan to break comedy out of references to Funk and Wagnall, I'll try to give you a serious reply.

One point of clarification is that the problem arises when the conjunction "and" drops between the names of the two gentlemen who authored the dictionary. As George Schlatter pointed out to Travie in one of the endless communiques that issues from 4425 Lakeside Drive, when you juxtapose the names of the authors, joined by "and," you get funkand wagnall, which, as George said, sounds funny. Right. It sounds funny. It sounds funny, I submit, because in actual pronunciation the funkand gets contracted to sound like funken, and at that point it comes very close in sound to a rather crude adjective, derived from the Anglo Saxon, relating to the act of coitus. I know that you and George, as students of our language, are also aware that frequently (in the better Eastern women's colleges for example) the word funken is selected by the shy and sensitive as a euphemism for the short, direct, Anglo Saxon expression, which I understand was used frequently in the Army and Navy during World War II to describe such elements as the weather, food, officers, the enemy, etc. The Australians, as a matter of fact, achieved some rather interesting and daring effects by placing the word between syllables of other words.

I can't escape the feeling that you realize this, else why would you have raised a question involving the aspiring Japanese politician Mr. Fukuda, whose name, if mispronounced, demonstrates the versatility of the adjective by changing it into a short imperative sentence.

What I am getting at is this: however innocent the intended use of the name Funk and Wagnall might be, I and others at NBC are convinced that the effect will be a double-entendre that is objectionable because of the vulgarity of the word involved. You can think of this as my personal hang-up if you wish, but I assure you that I am going to hang right here. I'm sorry you disagree, but since NBC has sole and ultimate responsibility for everything we broadcast, I believe I am taking the only position I can in this instance.

Finally, I am happy to advise you that there is no blanket prohibition against words beginning with the letters f u. There are prohibitions against some such words, but we will continue to determine these for all shows on a case-by-case basis.

I know you'll understand that I haven't yet been able to meet your request that I check off the words on the copied pages you sent me. I will get after this just as soon as possible, and I'll try to have the checked list back in your hands before "Laugh-In" begins its fourth season, and I'm certain that given the masterful touch of you and your colleagues with sharp, clean, incisive wit and humor we will all be around for that day.

With warmest regards,

Bob

ROBERT D. KASMIRE

MacDonald to Rowan

Sept 3, 1968

Dear Dan'l,

I shall soon mail you a copy of "No Deadly Drug," from the second batch due in. It seems to be selling like wild cakes and hot fire in advance of official publication date and any reviews as yet. Mysterious.

Landed in the early afternoon a week ago today at Tampa on one of Pan Am's 727's amid thunder, squalls, gusts and funnel clouds. Fellow tried to slam it in low and fast and lost it on the first bounce. Don't know how the hell he got it back onto all its little wheels and onto the assigned runway. But we do know that all the little stewardesses, once we were at rest, forgot all their PR responsibilities and stood hugging each other, laughing and crying and kissing. As I must go on the Today Show to plug book, may start right now, afoot.

Returned and found that good old American Express had finally screwed up for good, after writing me apologetic letters about their errors and duplications of charges over the last several months. They cancelled me out, marked me lousy, refused to honor the air charges, informed my bank I was cancelled out. Took file showing my account in perfect condition to hot local attorney. We file suit in Federal Court in Tampa very soon, asking $500,000. Time people realized they cannot blame the machines, shrug and walk away.

The house is becoming spectacularly beautiful, bit by bit, and we might be in by Christmas. I found the spirit of the house in Oaxaca and it cost me about $24. It is a wooden mask made in a nearby village about 60 years ago. It is a large, bland, mild, wooden mouse—very grave and restful and somber. It has something of the look of a burro's face. When I wear it, I feel like a tall, decent, responsible, kindly, wooden mouse.

Dorothy and I would give all kinds of odds that Adriana will keep the two grandpups. And what's wrong with having four dogs? Isn't it better than splitting up a loving family? But names, of course, are the problem. How to avoid the quaints. A nice source I think is the world of the Hobbits, where you can find such as Frodo and Aragorn. Though I am still all warm inside when I think of what our cousin named his squirrel. Irving Foster Dulles.

I have a deep and everlasting interest in graffiti.

We wish you were somewhere nearby, people.

Piece,
John

MacDonald to Rowan

Sept 21, 1968

Dear Sir:

Glad your typewriter parts didn't come and so you had to use the phone.

I have a nice sneaky idea for you, one which would end the credit-grabbing for all time. You write well, you know. An article *by* you and Dick with joint byline would be grabbed anywhere you submitted it. The thing to do is make the article a *tribute* to George Schlatter!!!

Sort of . . . "We had this little old idea we'd been kicking around and we tried it the first time on an ABC show, etc etc etc." Illustrate it with stills from the first show, from the special and from the series. Tell how marvelously well George caught on and how he has managed to keep it all vital and fresh etc etc, but without committing that terrible sin so common in the Industry. George has *not* deviated from the original idea. Tell how capable and wonderful and energetic and understanding he is, but hit hard at your own backgrounds of *creating* comedy, and stake out your claim once and for all, and there is not a damn thing George can do about it, or would want to do about it. And I think it would be very very nice to see if you can do it all without using the word Friendly anywhere. As a title may I suggest GOOD OL' GEORGE ? Or GEORGE AND EMMY ? The second sneaky idea is to get yourself set up for a Playboy Interview and make damn well certain that the key question is asked, and then answered at amusing and unrefutable length.

Now gawdamnitallto hell, I have to get to the point I have been stalling about. Jesus, how I hate to ask anybody for money. Makes me feel crawly. But read the poop enclosed. Dorothy and I have known Roy and Mary Call [LeRoy Collins and his wife] for at least ten years. They are the best there is. And I am so terribly afraid that without enough funds, the forces of hate, fear, ignorance, prejudice and superstition are going to win. Would you be so kind as to send a check and also to put the extra copies of these things in the hands of people who might also lay on a little bread? I can guarantee you that there will be absolutely no publicity given to your support of Roy (assuming you want to support him) unless you give me the go-ahead to put out a press release to Florida papers, which I would send to you for your approval first. I mean, man, if you got Nixon elected by accident, how about helping me get Collins into the Senate for 6 years on purpose.

Thank God that's done. We would so love to get the Collinses and the Rowans together some day. And we shall, somehow. It is one of those situations where I know the chemistry will be very very good and rare.

But I will never really feel at ease about asking your help until, my friend, you ask me for something.

Our fingers are crossed re the sales on "No Deadly Drug." It is over 15,000 without reviews as yet, and this has enticed Doubleday into putting more $$ into advertising and promotion.

Yesterday morning I sat over my cooling coffee and brooded about my statement to you on the phone that the program seemed rigid to me, and to Dorothy.

Was I wrong?

No, by God, I was not wrong. Is such a development inevitable? Yes. Will it become more codified? Yes.

I believe that it is the inevitable cycle of any successful innovation.

Success brings in money. Money flow creates a conservative posture, so as not to upset the flow. What was once free, nimble, novel, inevitably moves closer and closer to the Establishment as it becomes an industry in itself, as more and more people become dependent upon it. Old Tom Edison was a daring and flexible guy. But you can't sit down and have a drink with Con-Ed.

But let us make what could be a useful theorem: The more freshness and innovation you can sustain *within* the tried and true, risk-diminishing formula, the longer the potential life cycle.

Second theorem: The innovator, forced to live with the increasing strictures upon his once-original concept, becomes ever more restive when forced to remain within that frame of increasing rigidity, and cannot survive on the solace of money alone, but must find independent and non-conflicting outlets for that same creativity which got him into the thing in the first place.

Third theorem: Once the innovator accepts the truth and the inevitability of theorems one and two, he can make gratifying and satisfying adjustments.

From the old pontificator:

John

Rowan to MacDonald

Sept 23, 1968

It's damned difficult to know how the Time piece will work out. A letter from the guy who shadowed me for two weeks arrived the other day and he says the cover story is now set for the October 11 issue.

This fella's name is James Easton Brodhead III. He is a very good writer, and has fine recall. He sent in several hundred words all of which to be edited, changed, culled and slanted by some faceless person in New York. I did the best I could, though, and now we'll see.

However if the shows continue to slide as badly as the one tonight, I'm not sure the race is worth the prize. I was honestly surprised last week because the show was better than I thought it would be. But tonight bears out the fears I have had. Surely the public which grasped us to their bosoms last winter will see the crap for crap and know that what once occasionally *did* glitter, now merely glows infrequently as in a mirror darkly.

Your theorems are right, of course. For those reasons, as well as for my health, I have stopped fighting. You can't sit down and have a drink with Con-Ed, but at least there *is* a Con-Ed you can't sit down with. More of last night's shit and there won't be nuthin left. The life cycle as you called it, will be a death cycle. But these are our problems, or mine, and I will now face the task of either coming to grips with them or start thinking of other directions for my own personal crew to sail for.

Now, relative to your request for my financial participation in Collins' campaign. I feel that anyone *you* boost that hard for must be all right. And I will send a check. Let me tell you why I am sending what I am. I was a contributor to the McCarthy and Rockefeller campaigns, and who knows whether the money you spend on losers is lost or not, but the fact is the money is gone. Money for everything is needed, as you know, and I don't intend to bore you with a list of my charities. And just as you feel that you have done a lot, you see pictures of those kids in Biafra. Anyway, don't think that this is a token check. I will send more if you tell me to, but I don't know what else to do, old pal.

Every copy you sent me will be given to someone else out here, and I will talk it up, but everyone I know has a candidate somewhere he is plugging. You may certainly say that I support Mr. Collins' candidacy and subscribe to his sensible civil-rights philosophy, etc. In short use the name and/or the show in any way you feel it can help. And please, for Christ's sake don't feel uncomfortable about asking for support for your man. On the other hand, don't feel upset with me if I don't send several thousand dollars. Number one, I ain't got it right now to send, and I would probably be giving it to Alan Cranston out here.

Is there anything else I can do? Maybe we could contrive to give the Flying Fickle Finger of Fate award to his detractors? We need a hook for a shot like that, and I don't know the local picture. Also, come to think of it, we are taping five weeks ahead and are at work on show 7 now. So it will have to be like tomorrow we did something. Of course the network is up so tight with every show now that the campaign is getting closer to the final weeks. They even make us soften the blows at Mayor Daley and the Chicago police.

On these past Friday nights I have been flying to Las Vegas and doing a special late show at 2:30 Saturday A.M. Believe I told you. Well, I have been chartering a twin Cessna and flying in the second pilot seat and the old urge crept in the other night and I took a turn at the wheel. It felt a little strange and I was rougher'n hell, but may give it another shot this Friday night. We have been leaving about midnight and it's a beautiful night flight. Depending on head-winds it's about an hour and a quarter to a half. No bad weather yet and I always liked night flying. Matter of fact when I was a cadet and was flying alone at night on my early training flights they would always have to almost shoot me down to get me to come back and land.

It is probably that quest of mine for solitude because I get something akin to the delight of the night flight when I am at sea on the little boat. I always wonder what would happen if I kept heading south and west. If those wonderings had happened when I was 15 and 20 years younger I would probably find out. What is it, caution? that happens at middle age?

Friend, I have sat here chatting with you and find it is now a bit after 1:30 in the morning, and tomorrow is a taping date so I better put it in the rack.

Please don't think of me as chintzy with my check of one bill, but . . . read above. I shall now go and try to make some gratifying and satisfying adjustments.

As ever

Dan

MacDonald to Rowan

October 1, 1968

Dear Dan,

For heaven's sake, that response to my plea was wonderful. I mean it. I am very grateful.

I have had one rather startling success in my one-man campaign. I sent some of the green letters with enclosure to Knox Burger at Fawcett. He talked about it to Joe McCarthy, the guy who compiled the book of Fred Allen's letters, and who has done a lot of magazine work over the years, including some work with the Kennedys. Joe suggested to Knox that Knox advise me to get in touch with Kenny O'Donnell in Boston and thus tap some of the disaffected Democrat money. I thought I had better not be the one to make the call, so I went through channels and it turned out that Roy Collins knows Kenny and the Collins people had just not thought of going to the out-of-power Democrats.

Roy leveled with O'Donnell about the critical situation down here, and O'Donnell reacted well and said he would do some scrambling. Next thing, Roy got a phone call from Ted Kennedy. Kennedy wanted to hear Roy tell the story. Roy leveled as before. Ted said that he had made a firm decision, for all the evident reasons, to stay out of everything this fall, and not campaign for anybody. But he said this was worth making an exception for. So in about ten days Roy is going to fly up to Washington where he will cut some television spots with Ted, who will say, quite correctly, that both of his brothers thought a great deal of Collins, and had considerable respect for him. He will say that he joins them in their feelings for Roy, and certainly wants him to serve with him in the U.S. Senate. Everybody is very pleased with me at this point, which is silly because it was too remote a thing to be intentional—MacDonald to Burger to McCarthy to Burger to MacDonald to Ed Price to Collins to O'Donnell to Kennedy to Collins.

Saw the first ten minutes and the last five minutes of the show last night. Goldie gets better. Liked the confetti-throwing better.

How about a switch on the dictionary? How about: "Play *that* on your Telefunken radio."

Thanks again, my friend

John

Rowan to MacDonald

October 6, 1968

What we have here is a foggy, cold, gloomy, windless Sunday. Great day for lazing around and clearing up the clutter on my desk and dash off an answer to your latest.

This John Keasler is a dandy. Do you happen to know whether or not he used to be a feature writer for the Detroit Free Press? I may have the paper wrong, but a guy with a name like that who could write interviewed us years ago, and I think it was in Chicago. I am sending the copy of his column about cop-haters to the L.A. Free Press. A beauty.

One of the request letters this week was from a committee chaired by Burt Lancaster with a board of equally well-known actors solidly endorsing ACLU attorneys without qualification, and asking for funds to finance the court cases of some several hundred people arrested in Chicago during the convention. Now the papers here have been full of the Communist-inspired revolution there, and I wasn't there and I don't know. I suspect that the majority were disenchanted kids and that there was likely a sprinkling of far-lefters egging on the confrontation.

It seems to me that the choices grow more irksome and the options more cloudy. It was some years ago that I learned that the difference in life isn't between black and white, but choosing your shade of gray. The complexities of the Chicago scene are so damn typical. The citizens of Chicago, as the citizens of Dallas post-JFK, must feel put upon to have national calumny heaped upon them. Yet, from TV and news media coverage of that event, one has to think in terms of fascisti, political machines, railroads, etc.

It isn't enough to say, as all of us will, that *all* cops aren't sadists, that there are men on that force and on police forces throughout the country who are there because they feel sincerely that they can make a contribution in that position. *They* are not pigs. The cop going down the dark alley outlined by street lights to whoever is in there, *he's* no pig.

But there are pigs on that police force, and the country has a large porcine population. I can't believe that the FBI and the investigators from the Attorney General's office all conspired in this report they issued about the Chicago riots. There *must* be some substance to it. I don't want to give the Enemy any help, but some of those well-intentioned kids need help. What the hell do you do?

The Chicago Defense Fund is to be given over to the ACLU attorneys and they will spend it at their discretion. That is a bit too general for me. I don't really give a rat's ass about maybe getting my name on someone's list for association with Reds, but I sure as hell know that we *do* have enemies and while I'm not about to go and join the Birchers or take up arms with the Minutemen, I am equally against the Communist Party and/or any group trying to overthrow this government.

Am I then a half-assed Liberal, or merely a Centrist trying to be Modern? Shit, man, I am really most against GROUPS. As soon as they start forming committees and having meetings they lose me. And the trouble, of course, is that unless you have a group you don't have the clout to get the things done you think need doing. But so often what starts out well, and has only good intentions, gets side-tracked into so many other directions that many times the original cause is obscured or forgotten, and you find yourself espousing causes in which you don't believe. Right?

Of course I have never been a joiner, and that may affect part of these feelings. But I don't want to join the Police Protective Association, and I don't want to join the Yippy movement. I don't think people should throw Molotovs into cruising police cars, and I don't think the police should roust the citizenry. But what the hell do you join that encompasses that? I don't think that the black citizen is second class, nor should he be disadvantaged because of his color; I also don't think that a white citizen should be thrown out of work and lose his job because he's white and there's a black who wants that job. What do you join in this effort?

I should hope that by now the intelligence of man would permit him to solve his territorial and ideological problems peaceably; and I am also against unilateral disarmament. What's the name of *that* group?

I honestly begin to believe that Nixon is a better man than Humphrey and that Muskie is probably the best of the lot. Can I vote for Muskie for President? This year? Could we get McCarthy in for V.P. and maybe Rockefeller for Sec'y of State? McGovern for Defense and Ted Kennedy for Attorney General? Of course not.

The system doesn't allow us to use all our best men to the best purpose, and the system also seldom allows our best men to be in government.

Well, I was called away and I'll be damned if I can remember where I was going with that. Must have been a dandy! But I have to get ready to receive a couple of guests.

Let me know how you are coming along with the American Express beef. I thought as soon as the news breaks in this part of the country I would send them my card and resign saying I didn't want to take the chances with my credit that the poor writer I been reading about did. Now there's a fun movement! I'll get all my pals to resign from Am Ex in high dudgeon. *That* will shake them up.

As ever.

Dan

MacDonald to Rowan

October 8, 1968

Dear Dan,

Pretty good last night. But I found it strangely painful not to hear a single good sound out of that long lovely tawny throat of the ageless Miss Horne. Goldie is becoming the Thing. And there should be a lot of mileage out of "blow in his ear and . . ."

Culp was a disaster. No comprehension of the touch needed. Glad he will not be McGee. Suspect he is in a stage of self-importance where he cannot take direction.

Minor quibbles—Perhaps it is a sign of being square, but I always feel the least bit queasy after I have heard myself laugh at a queer joke. It is, as far too many third raters have proven, a no-talent way to get a laugh.

Also I detected a little more action without meaning, the very fast cuts to people swimming, to a hose being carried across a lawn etc. These lasted maybe a third of a second and had no relationship to anything, thus are faked-up movement and excitement, like the spy drama cliché of the train suddenly roaring into a tunnel.

As a member of your loyal audience I deeply resented the insertion of a commercial which used the German with his "very interesting" bit. Nice that the troupe can get commercials with the residuals and all, but they should be stuffed into somebody else's program. I felt myself in the presence of half-clever greed to see a member of the cast touting a product during the commercial break.

"Your cup runneth over" was the second best moment. The karate chop on the wedding cake the best moment by far.

The Party—and how right you were—is beginning to get visibly and audibly tiresome. But there is one aspect here that one must evaluate. The "audience" is not a constant thing. My reissued books keep going because every five to six years there is almost a complete turnover of the newsstand market. And you can assume correctly that each month Laugh-In acquires X thousand brand new viewers and loses X minus Y thousand. One cannot base value judgments entirely on the freshness for Old Loyal Viewer. However, there is also a resonance factor within the company, and when a set piece becomes tiresome to the cast, they unwittingly reflect a certain tiredness.

When are you going to write the magazine tribute to George Schlatter? Or did you decide it was a bad idea?

Well, I find that Rod Taylor is going to be McGee, and they start shooting on location on Jan 15th in Lauderdale. Dorothy and I went to see him in a moom picher Sunday evening, a thing called Dark of the Sun. I have never seen so many people killed in so many ugly ways in 95 minutes. I could not tell much of anything about Taylor. He looked a bit jowly, seemed to be in good shape, but the part did not give him any chance at the light touch. My God, a murderous mercenary in the Congo who doesn't let himself get involved with people or with right and wrong doesn't have much chance to fun it up. Culp too wispy and elegant, and this one maybe too squat and hairy and direct, but if they will do lots of rewrite on that stinking script and give him some very deft and knowing direction, it could work out.

Write, dear boy. You have blown in my ear and I shall follow you anywhere.

I enclose our very best greetings to Lovely Child Bride.

Yrs,

John

Rowan to MacDonald

Oct 10, 1968

Hi Pal,

Don't really have time for much of a letter because it's a bit late and I have to be up early and away. Besides an early appearance at the office tomorrow, I have the dentist and doctor to see. The damn dentist intends me harm tomorrow, I'm afraid. Seems the teeth are okay but the gums have to go.

Your critique of last week's show was kindly. I didn't think of it in terms of last year's show or in terms of what I think we should be doing. But in terms of the competition and in terms of what we are now doing I thought it a fairly good segment. The "dirty" ones are beginning to bug hell out of me and I am having a tough time fighting them on that too. They went all the way around the block with 6 or 7 sheep black-outs to get to the sheepherder's line, "Come on, stop flocking around." I think that sort of tricky mind should amuse itself with acrostics or anagrams.

Not too surprisingly we are beginning to get some rather disappointing reviews. These are follow-up reviews from guys that are fans. They say they are disappointed, but still think it's better than anything else. It seems others feel much as I did last summer when we talked about the future of the show. As I gain in age I realize more and more that there really aren't any secrets. It's just hard to come to the realization that others still think there are. Ah, well. The show is not yet a piece of crap, so I am giving my attention to not giving it my attention.

What that means is hard to explain. It's more than "I don't want to get involved." Within a narrow boundary I am trying to function as cheerfully and without strain as possible. It would be terribly hard within the system to bull through my own concepts. It would take a hell of a lot more than I feel it's worth. Besides, there are always the ratings. If you play their game, and it's really the only one in town, you must abide by the decision of the Nielsen's and Trendex's and by their standards we are still a hit.

Nobody takes future Trendex's. If you were to attend one of those numberless committee meetings and suggest that the future of your show was dismal in the face of current high ratings, you would not be listened to with any seriousness, number one, and number two they would throw you out for injecting a pessimistic note into what must always be merry proceedings. Fie upon it. Fah!

Listen, your idea about the magazine article tribute to George suits me. But I don't feel facile enough to do it right. If I could write well, there's small doubt in my mind that's what I would be doing all this time I have been floundering. It's stronger than, "Gee, I wish *I* could play piano like that!" or "I'm really going to have to study French someday." I suppose that mixed in with my fondness for you is a great deal of envy that you write so damn well.

It's probably a good idea though, for therapeutic practice. I will try and work enough discipline into my routine to take a stab at it. If there's any chance at all that it turns out better than badly I will send you a copy for your comments. I'm afraid though it's much like several people who have urged me to sing . . . until they hear me try.

You didn't mention it, though I will, you know. About the Time piece. [Rowan and Martin were the Cover Story.] It surprised me and in a way relieved me. I didn't think they could be that bland about anybody. I feel as if I went into the doctor's fearing cancer and found out I had appendicitis. "Thank God I've got appendicitis!" You know? I think it's the sort of piece that the public may find interesting if they are fans of the show. But all in all we were treated kindly, I thought.

Dick and I had occasion yesterday to be selected to welcome Dick Nixon to Beautiful Downtown Burbank. He was every inch a winner, incidentally. Very up and high and jolly. He had quite a chat with us, considering the conditions. Said, "How do you guys get all that space in Time? I can't." He thanked us for allowing him the use of our lines. Seems he has been answering hecklers with, "Sock it to me! Sock it to me!" And he says it has the curious effect of quieting them.

I had intended to cut several articles from the Hollywood trades and send them to you regarding the announcement that Rod Taylor would be playing McGee. I, too, think he's a far better choice than Bob Culp, and I am a fan of Bob's. God, I hope they do more than make it another detective series.

The reason I haven't mentioned "No Deadly Drug," for which I thank you, incidentally, is that I haven't time yet to get into it. I started it and see that it doesn't read quickly, and will have to give it some time. So far, verry inneresting.

Goodnight, pal, it's late and I got a ball-breaker tomorrow. Wish to Christ we were sitting out in the Gulf somewhere and you were giving me a fishing lesson.

As ever

Dan

MacDonald to Rowan

October 10, 1968

Dear Dan,

GODDAMN, that is a *good* job in Time! [Cover Story on Rowan and Martin's Laugh-In.] And never again will there be any crap about whose concept it is and whose show it is. Congratulations. I bet you feel very good and you should. We are delighted.

Here is an annoying thing, dammit. Remember when I asked you how about a book for Fawcett? I got this today from a guy whose ass would be fired out of there if they knew he had finked on the Establishment. The Ralph he refers to is the editor-in-chief of all the paperback books:

I want to tell you after hours that Fawcett is putting out a book of dreadful old jokes to be called SOCK IT TO ME. The name is courtesy of Ralph, six months too late. If we get sued, it has nothing to do with you and little to do with me. I just pulled the submission off the slush pile and he put the title on, and away we went. The title has been done to death on sweatshirts et al, and NBC will write a letter. I just wanted you to know that I did make it clear that I had solicited a book from Rowan and Martin months ago through you, and this other project was quite separate and did not grow out of that offer. Ralph had never seen the show at the time I wrote you, and came up with a notion to have a gag book called that long after I had passed on their demurrer. I gather Grosset is doing the Laugh-In book, having sensibly gone to the Network and offered real money.

I hope the chaps merchandising the fragments of the show in other areas have enough muscle to show Ralph very quickly that this was a bit of a mistake. He will probably come out with another one very quickly called "Just Blow in My Ear."

Say a big hidey for us to that good-looking thang standing beside ol' funnyhat in the Time story.

Rgds

John

Rowan to MacDonald

Oct 14, 1968

In haste, amigo

Thank you, thank you for the word on the proposed gag book. The warning system is alerted and the fellas that are in charge of manning those barricades are on their way to man them.

Would like to visit but once again I'm so tired I'm about to faint. It's been that Vegas weekend, and then we taped a free TV show for some well-intentioned folk trying to get a series going for ghetto talent. It was a good idea but badly executed. The talent was poor, the production amateurish, and oh shit, just too too bad. But at least some folks are beginning to stir their asses out here and hey, they deserve some help. But now I am beat and must hit the rack.

My love to Dorothy and thanks again, Pal.

As ever

Dan

MacDonald to Rowan

October 15, 1968

Dear Dan,

Last night was, to us old followers, a very sad, tired and dreary one. Two lovely bits—"Nelson Rockefeller wakes up happy" and "Let down your hare." I did like the giving of the FFFF to the KKK also. And in-group hilarious was the series of punch lines to the old dirty ones. Otherwise a rigidity, a lot of frantic efforts within a rigid frame, with too few of them coming off.

I know you are creatively disaffiliated, my friend, but it does need one great big fat new transfusion of *something*. I have the nutty feeling it needs space. I keep remembering the slow motion balloons in the Special. It begins to feel too "studioized." I would even like to see that finale, all the opening of the doors, take place in a huge meadow, a big psychedelic cube, and the doors opening here and there all over the son of a bitch.

It might interest the network to know that local stations are, more and more, using an audio-over commercial near the end, so that if there were any sounds involved in that bear-coming-down-the-stairs bit, or right after, with somebody staring up and what looked like some sort of studio equipment, it was lost. The commercial this time was about some upcoming network movie, I believe.

I await the George Schlatter piece. Despite the Time confirmations, on second thought I think you should do it. I shall make useful comment thereon. My God, Mister Rowan, I think you have a big goddamn pressing obligation to put a lot of things down and get them into print. Who else in that enchanted industry has a clear cold eye, a way with words, and the clout to get marvelous revelations published? How else will the people find out whether the king is wearing any clothes?

I feel the same way. I think I am a sour moderate, or a humanist, or some kind of creature which doesn't lend itself to today's labeling. I suspect that Kirk Douglas is an . . . And how about *that* for identity confusion? My mind said Burt Lancaster and the fingers wrote Kirk Douglas! I mean to say that I think Lancaster an ass, politically.

Want to know something strange? In the swarms of the young in the Chicago scene there were many younguns from eastern colleges. I know a faculty type who was out there with them. It is now reported reliably to me that the biggest soft touch for the bail money in all of Chicago was Hugh Hefner, and the word is that he was made into a soft touch by being rapped across the pants with a night stick. Many things in the world come a full strange circle, no?

I do feel that 3M or Eastman Kodak may do a great deal to save our civilization. Right now the state of the art requires that the big garish glare of the television lights must go on before the actions of the mob can be recorded for 20 to 40 million viewers. I think it is a catalyst to violence, because the lights announce the presence of all those eyes, and suddenly each little pip-squeak is out on that huge national stage, and if he just stands there, his lifetime chance is lost. So pick up something and throw it, man. Yell some bad words. Bust a window, bust a cop, jump up and down and make ugly faces. The bright lights are a polarizer, like a whistle signaling the kickoff. It produces a glandular reaction. So when they get film fast enough to pick up all the action by available light, then the fun will go out of it as the signal to turn frantic will be missing.

Hope the gum doctor did not harm you overmuch. When they do their thing these days, they seem to get their jollies out of seeing how close they can get to strangling and suffocating you, to find out where you begin to panic.

Live well

John

MacDonald to Rowan

October 19, 1968

Dear Faint One,

I am now busting my tired old middle-class ass trying to get the seventeen big magazine and small book distributors in Florida to tell their route men to put rack cards in with the McGee books on every stop between now and election day. They are just card stock that stick up about four inches higher than a paperback and make my pitch for Roy Collins.

It is going to be a squeaker. My work day is now 16 to 18 hours. I enclose some stuff from the local papers to show you that the art of invective is not dead.

American Express answered my suit on the last day. They said my complaint does not properly identify American Express as a U.S. Citizen! Also that my allegations show no damages in excess of $10,000, so the Federal Court has no jurisdiction. That will result in a hearing on the plea to dismiss.

American Express !?! Not a *citizen* ?????

John

Rowan to MacDonald

October 20, 1968

Hello to whatever Hurricane Gladys left,

My disassociation from the creation of weekly programs is getting tougher and yet is even more necessary. I am getting all the old ulcer symptoms back again, and the other night with a not terribly important domestic beef, I thought I was having a coronary or something. I have been stretching myself too thin. Thinly? I'll tell you how it goes with me, pal.

Last Monday I left the office with the act of leaving two memos on Paul Keyes and George S.'s desks. Both the same and both pretty stiff. A list of "transgressions" if you will; the show's dirty, the show's mundane, the show's a piece of shit, etc. On the way home I felt remorse. These guys are both really working their asses off. They deserve better than that, I thought. I spent the rest of the night trying to get them both on the phone to apologize. It is damned hard to criticize and not get in there and show them what I mean specifically. It's not enough to rewrite monologues and news items, the show is past that kind of doctoring.

What's the answer? I don't know, John, maybe there isn't one. I see what you see on that tube, and so I know I still have a little objectivity left and that isn't as easy as it used to be either. I am not starting to believe the publicity . . . at least, not yet . . . but the goddammed thing is doing so well in the ratings and that is the standard out here.

I really don't feel like going into all this tonight. Instead I will try to give you a picture of the Richmond trip I returned from this morning.

Wednesday night in a break from taping, Dick and I read over this coming week's show with Paul K. and we took off the next morning in a Lear jet. Dick at the last moment decided to take his girl along, who is apparently a great bang, but is also out of her depth at anything else. Talks it and looks it. When Adriana found out *she* was going, A. decided to go, and with Don Saroyan our road manager, we made up a full load in that Lear. It is just a bit smaller inside than a station wagon, you know.

Left at noon from L.A. International and landed for fuel at Wichita and had a tour of the Lear plant there, and landed in Richmond an hour later than they thought we would and were met by a mob. Pictures and cameras and sweaty hands grabbing and all the time I had to go to the head with an urgency not easily denied. We were driven to the Executive Motor Inn, allowed to wash our hands and then had dinner.

The American Tobacco Company, our hosts and one of our sponsors, were gracious and warm and hospitable, but smotheringly so. They were so anxious that we have a good time they got silly about it. They paid us well to come down and our duties were all spelled out before we went. They had other things they wanted us to do, of course, and we didn't mind because they were so damned nice about it. But I have a hell of a time sleeping on twin beds. They are not long enough for me and they also seem too narrow. Consequently I tend to fall on the floor in the middle of the night and the other part of the night I am fitfully dozing, *afraid* I'm going to fall on the floor. So, I got very little sleep at any time.

A tour of the plant. Anxious to let us know *they* are integrated. "Look there. There's nigrahs working right along our own people." I didn't see any black bosses. If you have never seen the manufacture of cigarettes I can tell you that one cigarette-making machine looks almost indistinguishable from another.

Many of the workers in the plant stopped and stared, some of them asked for autographs . . . no blacks stopped, just white. At one machine there were two women working, one slim, attractive, about the color of coffee with light cream, the other a quite heavy sloppy white. The white woman wore, pinned to her drooping bulbous bosom, a WALLACE FOR PRESIDENT button. Now don't you agree that the black worker . . . who probably didn't need that hideous badge to remind her of her co-workers' feelings . . . deserved a bonus?

A parade. The rain, which was the outer fringe of Gladys and had been threatening all day, started about the time we were forming up at the Armory. A fine old southern relic, the Armory. Faded pictures of brave boys; rusted swords belonging to men long gone that *nobody* remembers.

Some man, whose name I never did understand, kindly lent and drove his own car. A Rolls convertible. When the rain started and he raised the top, Dick and I were in the back seat and were quite hidden from view. That's at all times a nice prospect for me but not near the desire of the parade people who had named us Grand Marshals. Southern charm wouldn't let them ask us to ride in the open and get wet, and only a kind Providence let them off that hook. The rain stopped to a slow, light, endurable drizzle when the parade reached the main street.

Those good people of Richmond stood out there on these streets, waving, cheering, rushing to the car to touch our hands with a desperation that suggested we were faith healers. Some parents held infants aloft and waved their hands at us, the infants screaming for warm and home and screw whoever the hell that is sitting in a Rolls waving and grinning.

Try and grin for eight miles. Facial and jaw muscles get stiff to the point where holding a pipe is a chore. It was interesting to me to see some of the black community, standing, almost defiantly, and almost invariably they waited to be waved *to* before they waved back.

When they saw you wave to them, some of the most beautiful smiles broke across their faces as they waved back.

An estimate, generous to a fault I believe, was made that some 85,000 people lined those rainy streets last Friday night. I know that some of those kids that rushed the car thrusting soggy paper at us to be signed must have nothing else to do in Richmond on a Friday night to get that much enthusiasm whipped up over us.

Saturday. Football game. Again sitting on the back seat of the Rolls as we toured around the track. Stopped and spoke into the echo mike to the crowd just as a squall hit and we all were thoroughly drenched. Watched the first half from the West Virginia spotters room, waiting for the half when we were to crown the winner of the Miss Tobacco Festival crown.

The crown of Miss Tobacco Festival is a sad article. Rhinestones taped with electrician's tape to a wire affair. And they say that Hollywood is a place of fake and make-believe. I placed it on her head and then four of us posed for all the photographers. Dick, the new Queen, and the old Queen and me. The old Queen, an antique of 20, was cute and more poised than the new one. One assumes she gained this confidence from a year's rule over her dubious kingdom. She soon learned the facts of life.

She stood next to the new one and Dick and I flanked them. The camera guys started yelling at her, "Hey, do you want to step out?"

"Who?" she tremulously asked.

"You, just step to the side there." She did, and relinquished her rule.

How long, oh mighty and fickle Nielsen, before I hear those words . . . "Step aside there, pal."

The Tobacco Festival Ball took place Saturday night in the John Marshall Hotel in the Virginia Room. An ell-shaped affair with a sound system they picked up at the auction of railroad relics when the Atlanta station was burned. R&M were not at their most effective.

Back onto the Lear and home this morning. The Lear came from Pinellas. A fine pilot, Bill O'Neal, is the manager and chief pilot there, stationed at St. Pete. He will probably be doing some more business with me, that is if and when we get some time to come back down and see Rowan's beach at Manasota Key. [On a prior visit Rowan bought a piece of residential beachfront land on Manasota Key.]

Today, Sunday, a broker came to me with an offer on the Aisling which I have accepted, so this next week will see me without a big boat. I still have the Phucoph [a Rhodes Day-Sailer], though, and will be looking for another big boat that will come closer to satisfying what we need, or think we need.

This coming week we tape not only our own show, but a Smothers Brothers, and a Hugh Hefner guest spot. Friday night the Diabetes Association honors me as Man of the Year. I haven't really done anything, it's just that so many people who have it won't admit it. Also Friday night is Vegas night and we will be flying there.

So now I think I'll go to the boat and spend my last night aboard. I sleep well there, and I can use the sleep. Deep down bone-tired.

I am having a good time with NDD and am learning a lot. That's a *good* book. How's it going? My love to Dorothy.

As ever
Dan

MacDonald to Rowan [*postcard*]

October 22, 1968

I would say last night was muffled by a paucity of sight gags. Who needs *my* opinion?

Anyway, why I write is because from the beginning of our friendship I have been aware of a nagging little fragment of memory & association in the back of my mind. Rowan? Hmmm Rowan? Hmmm.

Finally, by God, the other night I remembered. It was Lieutenant Rowan who was the hero of "A Message to Garcia." My, he was one stubborn lieutenant, that one. End of quest.

Best
John

MacDonald to Rowan

October 25, 1968

Dear Harried,

Look, don't never ask me the answer to anything, because even though I know the question is rhetorical, and even though I know I am in one of my myriad areas of ignorance, I am a compulsive advisor.

So here is what I think about the future of Laugh-In. Ratings have the unfortunate effect of giving a locked-in feeling of confidence. Show business is always essentially auto-hypnotic. To accept the format as static, and to use the ratings as the reason to keep it static, is in effect an acceptance of a limited life span for the show. I would guess right now that you are in a three season cycle.

Is this bad? Take many other high rated shows, drama included, where there have been good ratings due to initial imaginative and unusual handling. Naked City, The Defenders, etc etc. You get a first season with everybody hopped up. In the second season these shows begin to subtly parody themselves. Why? Because the creative juices cannot be sustained very long. Originality is buggered by repetition. Some of the movers and shakers of the early months leave because life is such a short trip that they do not care to spend too much of a chunk of it working at something that has become a formula chore.

Take the most successful live drama and musical comedy. Two and three years on Broadway is it. And in the last year it is usually pretty hollow, and very few of the early people are still associated with it.

But what about things that go on and on and on? Marshal Dillon, the ol' Ponderosa etc etc are in actuality the magazine serials of the contemporary era, the Scattergood Baines, Earthworm Tractor, Inchcliffe Castle things, a kind of night-time soap, half a whisper above the level of the comic strip, and definitely not as civilized as Snoopy, Pogo and BC.

What do *you* want? To be locked into Laugh-In for four years, five, six? If it gets at this time a resurgence of originality, then it will last longer. But to instill such a resurgence means going against the confirmation of the ratings, and that means going against the money and the network. Every assemblage of human beings united for a common purpose has a predictable life cycle, whether they get together to form a new religion, or make shoes, or Discuss the Great Books. In the industrial world a nice profit picture is like ratings. It leads to complacency. Profits have foundered more companies than losses. While the executives sit around beaming and shaking hands with each other, the buying habits of their customers are changing, and somebody is coming out with a more attractive product.

It comes down to what *you* want. You are suffering from the old weltschmerz of the creative person who has, by success, been painted into a corner. Now . . . do you want to spend yourself by trying to wrench the program into that shape where it will once again be a creative challenge to you, or do you want to accept the inevitable shape of the life cycle of such ventures, honor your commitments, use the money for permanent security, and start, way back in some cupboard in the back of your mind, to plan the next break-through?

Maybe you could think of Laugh-In as a published work. Inevitably it will use up its audience. People will get tired of it. Ideally, to make a transfusion of new excitement, you should fire the whole staff of writers and pick up with a new group. But a transfusion is a transfusion is a transfusion. It is not a new body, and it will never again sing and sparkle as of yore. Do not try to roll too big a stone up the mountain, particularly when all you get in the end is very large stone on top of a mountain.

That Richmond trip is classic. And kind of frightening, I bet.

The wind missed us, but not by much. We have been in some of the whirlygirls here, so we trundled off to Howard Johnson's Motor Lodge in town, with kids and grand kids in the next room. There will come a day when all the folk who have arrived during the past 10 or 12 years will ignore the evacuation warnings—as they did this time—and will drown by the hundreds when 8 and 10 foot tides sweep the beaches—and the survivors will claim they were not properly warned. It cut a couple of feet of sand off Manasota, but littoral drift should replace it slowly. Incidentally I sold my piece down there for $230 a foot, which should make you ever more certain of the value of your investment. I could have held out and gotten more, but I need the $$$ right now for other things.

Our two generations of descendants left one week ago this morning for New Zealand, and in due course we got a cable saying they were safe in Auckland, and I imagine they have set their watches back fifty years. I put a small chunk in a bank for them and waved them off and said, Have Fun. They were here for three and a half weeks. The little ones were great. Miss them.

In the December issue of Holiday I appear putting the sour mouth on the Florida Keys. We'll be in New York at the Gonk from Dec 3 thru 11th. "No Deadly Drug" moves slowly. Seventeen thousand plus copies thus far. Am once again engaged in big negotiations to unload motion picture and television rights to 33 books. Probably will fizzle out like the other things have.

I am going to think about that Richmond trip for a long time.

So afraid Roy Collins is going to get whipped. Florida is returning to the stone age.

Keep it up,
John

Rowan to MacDonald

November 3, 1968

What a wise and good man you are, sir!

That letter was a dandy. So many of the things you told me were so true and so obvious, once they were pointed out, that I feel almost silly not to have thought them out for myself. I took the liberty of showing the letter to a couple of friends who have shared my concern and it helped all of them too. I am not naive enough to think that from now on I will be at peace with these issues, but I do think that I will be able to use those words and reflect on the idiocy of fighting what is essentially an unfightable fight.

You said that I should maybe in the back of my mind start to work on something else. That is almost ESP because I have been forming the idea for a special for several months. I don't know about you, but ideas seem to bake in the unconscious for me for a time and then start to emerge and take shape. Sometimes they die when they see the light, but sometimes they grow and last long enough to amount to something.

One day on the beach at Manasota Key I was lying in the sun waiting for the Dutchman to come and take a walk in search of shark's teeth. As usual there were no people in hearing distance and it was naturally silent. A sudden loud squawk made me blink my eyes open, and peering through that red, bright haze I first saw a crab just emerging from his hole not three feet from me and his open mouth aped the sound I had heard which had come from a large blue heron. It struck me funny at the time and made me think that the relation between sight and sound is tenuous; that we are often in the midst of wondrously fascinating things and are unaware of them.

At this time the idea is being turned and worked and thought of by two writers I have hired and a possible producer. Schlatter and Friendly are not involved with this one. I haven't discussed it with anyone else, and I wanted to tell you of it and ask for opinions and, if you feel any enthusiasm, offer you a part in it.

I have several pages written, but I won't send anything at this time, just give you the "philosophy" of the show or idea. Doing that is difficult, too, because it is trying to articulate an abstract idea. There is no form or structure, really, to the show, but a collection of visual images telling the large, inarticulate story of the average man's *unawareness*.

EXAMPLE: The guard in the Metropolitan Museum, surrounded on all sides by some of the world's art treasures, reading Playboy. Bored and unseeing he spends his life with beauty and isn't aware of it.

EXAMPLE: The steelworker in the open hearth of the mill, surrounded by gigantic wonders, blazing heat and ear-splitting noise, looking at a print on a workshop wall of one of the art works at the Met.

The point of these two scenes is, of course, to start a progression of similar scenes that bring the viewer to the conclusion that if we look for it there is beauty and fascination in every job, in all locations. I am having trouble telling this.

Another part of this is to show the effect the same scene and same words can have on different people depending on their point of view. Maybe even have the classic case of an event in front of five people and get the five different views of what happened.

A small boy, crying for the light on in his room before going to sleep, is confronted in that room with large ominous shadows of obvious monsters and suddenly a large, loud, and equally frightening monster roars at him to "Stop being a sissy and get to sleep!" The parent coming into the quiet bedroom of his son, of whom he dreams rooting for as linebacker for Green Bay, despairs of this kid's alarums and wonders, "What the hell can he be scared of?" What he sees in the room is so patently reassuring.

Many things of children in this idea. The camera to be always held at the child's level showing the giant world in which he lives.

I have a guy who is a wizard with hand-held camera. I have another cameraman who is one of the most imaginative men with a lens I have met. It has long been my theory that TV isn't used visually.

What is so obviously a visual medium is most usually reduced to the level of radio. Our own show, for instance, has been drifting to that posture. I want to do a TV special that has a minimum of dialogue, not because I don't like dialogue, but because there are so many things that should be seen and not heard.

I want a guy walking through a field. He hears the whine of a Stuka and the chattering of machine guns. He looks up and there is a hawk diving on a field mouse. The sound of great earth-moving equipment draws his gaze to a couple of earth worms, etc.

Signs. And words. The effect they can have on people, depending on the connotation. Also the idea of placing ordinary signs in strange places. KEEP OFF THE GRASS. On the 18th green. DO NOT REMOVE THIS LABEL UNDER PENALTY OF LAW. On the zipper opening of a package of cigarettes.

This is just part of it, and, as I said, it is not easy to write out.

But I think we could have a pretty, and a thoughtful and maybe even a provocative TV hour and! new! And probably not too much commercial. But, as you noted, I do have some clout now. I also hear of sponsors who want something, anything, from us. Dick isn't involved at this point and there has been no casting done. We may appear in it to raise the coin or raise the rating, but only if we fit the characters that evolve. Any interest?

I have been thinking a great deal of Manasota Key. I think I will write Bill Ward and have him get a man he spoke of to clear the poison ivy and brush off the land. Then I was wondering about the possibility of long distance building. We would like to get a guest house built as soon as we could. We plan a house in back of the main house for help or guests and it would serve us as a place to use until we get the main house planned and built. This means sinking a well, and working out on which part of the lot we want what, but I should think that could be done from here. What I need is an honest and imaginative contractor to put in charge of this. Do you know of any? Should I check with Bill? [Bill Ward, a mutual friend, lived on Manasota Key.]

There is an outside chance that we may be able to get down there and visit our beach for a few short days just after the Sands gig. We close New Year's Eve and could maybe fly down New Year's Day or the day after. We could stay, if this works out right, through the week and fly home Monday morning. But it would be beautiful to get something going there before we came down.

We have been looking at beach houses and lots out here again and haven't found anything.

Goodnight, pal. Thanks again for the great letter. You really have given me some peace of mind and that's a great gift. My love to what's-her-name, and when do you move?

As ever
Dan

MacDonald to Rowan

November ?, 1968
Dear Dan,

Enclosed is a copy of a telegram phoned to me at noon on the Wednesday after *that* goddamn Tuesday. John Keasler does live on Key Biscayne and he is a great man forever.

[The vote count was so close Nixon was not declared the winner until the Wednesday after the election. At that time he had a house on Key Biscayne. Keasler's wire read WELL THERE GOES THE NEIGH-BORHOOD.]

About your idea. I like it. D likes it. I want to let it sit on one of my back shelves for a time and ripen before I make any comment. I know right now that it is a highly creative and stimulating and kind of *timeless* thing. It is what just here and there, infrequently, the best of the foreign directors will do. And there is so much scope in making visual comment on the way people anthropomorphize things.

Son, I would be right proud and happy to have something to do with a thing like that. Once upon a time Dorothy walked through the main public park in St. Pete and saw a lady on one of the benches, so withered and frail she looked a hundred and nine. She was reading, with avid concentration, a magazine called Your Future.

After saying I wouldn't comment on it, I have. So whoa, John. Don't run off at the typewriter. Think a little. Any interest, you ask? Mucho!

On the guest house project let *me* check with Bill, only because there is a good builder down there that I heard recently is jammed up somehow, and I want to get the lowdown on him.

I will get back to you soon on several things—the builder, the special, and the timing of your trip down.

Our house is to be done the end of January, we hope!

Stay uploose,

John

Rowan to MacDonald

November 14, 1968

Well, sir, Black Tuesday it was known as . . .

I tried to call you that night and find out how things were going for your man, the news coverage out here seemed to be making a point of ignoring the Florida returns, and after your phone had rung itself out I realized you were probably at some headquarters rooting for your fella. It was only the next day I found out he had lost. Was it close, at least?

The picture currently from Washington of such charming unity and smooth "transition" is just too sickening. Why anyone should be surprised at this is what is surprising. The whole point we dissenters were trying to make was that there was no choice, that both these bums were the same as we had had. However, I suppose it is true that this governmental machinery is now so burdensome and bureaucratic that maybe it *doesn't* make any difference who is in there, *nobody* can get the damn thing to move.

Happy that you both like the special idea. It is developing slowly, and the principal reason for delay seems to be that I'm having trouble getting the three guys I have working now to understand what I want. Most of them like the theme or central feeling I tell them about, but they think "linear." I don't know if that's the word I want. It's more than anthropomorphizing, it's also giving a kinetic will to park benches and telephones. It's pursuing and displaying the visual and sensory contradictions that are almost endless in their possibilities.

Before I started this or spoke to anyone else I asked Hook if he thought the network would be interested in something I had churning, and he is now telling me that not only are they interested, they want a date and where is it, etc. If it was the only thing I was doing it would be sooner, I suppose.

We have seen the first draft of the MGM picture we do first. The original title, The Incredible Werewolf Murders, a terrible name for a picture, has been changed to The Maltese Bippy which is just about as bad. It will not be the final. [But it was.] We are now thinking of two others that have been suggested. The Coogle Affair and The Strange Case of . . .

NDD is slow going for me. Unlike anything else of yours I have read, I read it a bit at a time. It's so damned comprehensive and also very impressive. The very sort of thing that makes me, and I would guess others as well, nervous around you. You know people too g.d. well, are so analytical it's awesome. I find myself being aware of everything from grammar and syntax to what my motives for saying something really are.

NBC has been after me for the boating article for a couple of months now. I wrote two. The first one was carefully correct, all about a navigational goof of mine (remember when I started for Catalina and went a bit off-course and landed in San Clemente?) that went into some detail of the hazards of trusting new instruments and checks and balances that can be used to prevent that sort of thing happening. When I read the article it seemed not at all the sort of thing that anyone would be interested in so the second one was written very simply and directly about the boat I bought, why, and how I feel about having a boat. Might have been written by a fan mag broad. NBC, of course, loved it.

Thanks to your interference I am also starting to keep a log, daily except when I forget and then have to catch up a few days at a time, and re-reading that is depressing so I am not re-reading any more. It is almost like a ship's log at first, and in the latter few days a few impressions are creeping in. I don't know what use all this is because I am afraid I'm too damned old to learn discipline, and entirely too deficient in style and talent to be a creditable writer. No false modesty, pal, these are honest fears. But I expect I won't know until I give it a more honest shot than I have up till now.

This is the second day without a cigarette and you can guess my temper/mood. Got a bit of a scare the other day. Had a physical, the treadmill job with attachments to check EKG through the various stages of fatigue and effort. Then a chest Xray and the good doctor called me back on that. Went to the radiologist yesterday for very complete chest work and today got the word. No Big C, but something he calls smoker's lungs with the bronchial branches looking fearsome. So I hold the pipe between my teeth and light it as little as I can stand, but I WANT A CIGARETTE.

My very best to Dorothy and I'm already uploose.

As ever

Dan

MacDonald to Rowan

Nov 20, 1968

Dear Sir:

I find that a good, honest and imaginative builder in the south county is one Chester A. Mayer, 301 South Harbor Drive, Venice, and that the most reputable and reliable well driller is J. C. McDonald Well Drilling Company, Harbor Lights, Venice.

About the special. I like working titles for things. Mind calling it Zonk!? Anyway, I think that once you find the way that feels right to establish an artistic unity, the bits and pieces will fall into the right places. What about making it from dawn to dawn, so that it would split roughly into ⅔rds day things and ⅓rd night things? And without trying to think linearly, I suspect there could be three unifying effects. One would be the music, a simple strong theme which could be done in a wide variety of tempos, and done on anything from a zither to 50 tubas. Another would be to pick both you and Dick up, never together, in odd and striking contrast bits throughout, without ever getting plotty. Zonk should actually have no dialogue at all, nor any purely contemporary comment in its establishing of perceptive relationships and analogies. And it should have shifting tempo from placidity to the sudden eruption of violent changing scene and action.

Sound track contrasts? Like close shot of busy ants tugging a big dead beetle along, and cut to copter shot of tugs working a big passenger ship, and use the waterfront honks and tug signals for the ants, then back to the ants and put in the huge crowd noise of sports spectacle, and cut to one of those push ball things, and then back to the ants and then the theme music reappears in dirge form and pallbearers are carrying a coffin. There should be savage things as well as the kind of fantasy you get from going from a violinist to an insect sawing his hind legs together, to Dick sawing a board, and back to the violin but with the sound of wood being sawed instead of the music, or going from a harmonica to a man eating corn on the cob, then back to the savage part like from a little boy flying his model airplane to a crash in the park, to the sound of enormous shattering smash and cutting to one of those things of rescue people milling around charred wreckage.

A texture part? Cut from the slow love-making stroke of a man's hand on woman flesh in close shot to workman plastering a wall, to pitcher massaging a new baseball, to sculptor shaping clay, to old lady stroking kitten, to blind child reading Braille, to hands shaping a sand castle, to masseur at work, to bulldozer stroking landfill, to road roller on asphalt, to body shop sanding a fender ding, to mother cat licking kitten and back to the man's love-making hand.

I think you want horror-humor-beauty-sadness-shock all so scrambled that the affinity between them is made apparent. Let me know how far off the beam my suppositions are.

Titles don't have too have much to do with a motion picture. Hell, you could call it Down the Up Escalator or Go Blow in Your Own Ear or Zonk. What difference? How about The Wolf Who Threw Confetti? Or how about Wolf! Wolf! Wolf! Hey, I sort of like that one. It resonates thrice. (And enhances Dick's image?)

Keep that log going, man. All you have to do is keep at it long enough so that you begin to feel restless when you don't. Then it will keep going on its own steam and pressure.

Cigarettes taste nasty.

What's-her-name sends love to you and Dutch.

Best
John

A FRIENDSHIP

Rowan to MacDonald

November 25, 1968

YEAH! YEAH! YEAH!

That's great stuff and right on the money. I am in the office and busy integrating these ideas into the preparation and will get back to you in more detail when I get home and have some time to answer at greater length.

Some of the stuff we wanted to do was done by someone else on a special on ABC a couple of weeks ago and the Section 8 series that S-F are going to do has a few others, so we are in the midst of shifting gears.

I have been trying to get some stuff that gives kinetic will to man's natural enemies such as the telephone, the automobile, etc. Section 8 are doing part of that, except they seem to be concentrating on conversations between phones, bananas and other fruit, etc. I had more of a picture of some human agent involved with the inanimates.

More later. Many thanks and we'll work out the proper way to use your stuff and the rest of the details of that sort later.

As ever

Dan

Rowan to MacDonald

November 21, 1968

Dear Chaplain, sir:

They're really bugging me, Chaplain. I try to remember what you told me, but sometimes it's darned hard to do, sir. I hate to think that these people I'm in business with are bad people, but the way they carry on out here makes me wonder. And I don't mean these orgiastic parties they throw neither.

Maybe I could give you a for instance and you'd get my meaning. A couple of weeks, oh maybe three weeks ago, these two young guys come up to me while I'm at work. You remember I got this job out here now? Well they came up to me and said they had some funny material for two men, and since we're always on the office for some funny material for two men, I says, "Yeah, two young men, I'm always in the market for something funny."

So the next week they carry a tape recorder into where I work and they play this funny material and I figure maybe I ought to put these two young men on the job before someone else hears about them, see? Chaplain, when I tell you that two funny young men are scarce out here, I'm not just whistling Dixie, to coin a phrase as they say. So I figure these other guys I work with out here would be happy I find these guys which are so funny with their tape recorder and all.

But it don't work out that way, Chaplain. Oh, they figure I got a right to hire these guys okay, because I'm going to bend them a little if they say I ain't . . . just joshing, sir . . . but they say some of the other guys we got writing on the job are pretty sore. Now I figure since we hired the other guys, we ain't really like working for *them*, if you get my meaning, but they are working for *us*. Anyway, everybody is kind of sore, and the new guys are getting a bum deal from the older hands, and they ain't as funny in this situation as they was when they was making the records for the tape machine. Now some of the older hands they look at me and say so okay where are these guys' funny material?

Now that's just part of my present problems, sir. You may remember me saying something about another job our partners got and it looked like ours? Called Soul? Well, we went to the big boss and we told him, like say Boss you put this other thing on here and we gonna sue your butt, and maybe stop this here job too, so the boss who is pretty smart when it comes to stuff like this backs off that other deal. Now this makes our partners a little sore and anyway they never figure they are out of line anyway, see?

So now guess what happens? They sell a show they call Section 8, which is a good title for these cuckoos, and the word is they copy us again! And I guess that's why I'm really sore, Chaplain. Don't you think, sir, they shouldn't ought to do that?

Well, anyway, that's how it goes out here. They also are working to get us off the job as much as they can. Me and my partner we like to work, not to kill ourselves you know, but too many people have been coming by and saying like, "Hey, don't see you guys much on this thing any more . . ." and "You still calling this the Rowan and Martin Show? When *they* gonna do something?" But that sounds like sour grapes, I know, sir, but since I had your ear held down I thought I may as well unlimber that beef on you too.

One thing I like about you Chaplains, you're great listeners, but I guess that's what you guys get paid for, huh? No offense, sir.

As ever

Dan

MacDonald to Rowan

November 28, 1968

Dear Dan,

We are off to NY the first (Sunday) and back here by the evening of the 11th.

So this is in a hell of a hurry because I am trying to get this desk in shape to leave it for a time.

Anyway, I had a very nutty visual idea and I do not think it would pose too tricky a problem to a good prop man.

It involves making up some giant rubber stamps that would fit on the bottom of people's shoes, and would have enough color saturation and retention, or some kind of self-inking arrangement, so they could print their way across a pale floor. You want to eliminate dialogue as much as possible. Put the camera high, aimed down at about 60 degrees. Not as a viable idea, but just to give you the feel of it, how about imagining a girl and boy crossing the pale floor, pantomiming rejection and pleading. The girl's footsteps imprint NO NEVER NO NEVER NO NEVER. The boy's steps in another color write PLEASE MARY PLEASE MARY PLEASE MARY. They stop, gesticulate, another lassie comes flaunting by, à la burlesque, leaving the legend on the white stage HI FELLA HI FELLA HI FELLA. Meanwhile you've focused on her to give yourself a chance to change the rubber stamps on the feet of the couple. Boy follows new girl saying, in footprints, HELLO! HEY! HELLO! HEY! Abandoned girl trudges slowly away but now her steps read NO? NEVER? NO? NEVER?

You could put people into the costumes of *things*, a walking tuba saying OOM PAH OOM PAH, a spider writing CURDS? WHEY? a bottle saying HIC WHEE. Or a bunch of things crossing and composing a more complex message. And if they crossed at the right time in the right place you could end up with a whole mess of messages, the earlier ones still there and visible.

Had to get this crazy thing off my mind, man. Even a fellow with a crutch, cast on one ankle, and the foot that hits the floor printing

OUCH   OUCH   OUCH. Or for a very complex message you could pan in very close to read it. Maybe it could be a repetitive thing to tie in with all the other bits.

Take care,
Yr. Chaplain

Rowan to MacDonald

December 1, 1968

Dear Absentee:

What the hell you doing in New York? Business, I suppose you'll say. Sure breaks up the picture I keep in my mind of you. See, I always see this wise old bird sitting in Paradise, thumbing his independent nose at the world of finance and hustle, saying, "If you want to talk to me, come down here and I'll meet you for ten minutes at the airport. At my house? You crazy, man? That's for me and a few close friends once in a while. Don't bug me, pal, or I'll take my business to Random House." Wrong, huh? Next thing I'll discover you eat and crap same as the rest of us slobs.

You sure have some fine notions, my friend. The other stuff was great and the rubber stamp idea is a dandy. I have added a couple of refinements to the other. Things such as: Small boy (probably same one all through film) flying a kite in the park and we follow the string up in the air and he has it attached to the Goodyear blimp. He tugs the string and the blimp bobs; he is chucking pebbles into a pond and watching the ever-widening circles and we do too . . . to the beach where they are breaking like thirty foot waves against shattering houses.

And on the theme of the plane-flying and subsequent crash; boy in bathtub with toy boat and he tips it and we see a big boat at sea sinking and people jumping, etc. You know, the idea of the rubber-stamp-footed people could make a damn fine title gimmick. For cost and expediency we would probably have to animate that part, though, and that would blow the other *real* shot, wouldn't it?

The show continues apace. We haven't lost our high ratings. If anything, they get stronger. That assures us of next season, of course. The next season I don't want to do, but will either have to or get out of the business. Can you imagine the clout a major network would hit you with for dumping their number one show? "What the hell you mean you aren't going to do it another year? What else you going to do with two broken legs? How are you going to do anything with your throat cut? And a widower at that?" Hell. I'm here until *they* are through with me. Sure would like to leave it at the top, though.

What do you hear from the New Zealanders? Guess it's really early to tell anything, either from them or about them. What we ought to do when we all get the time, is for the four of us to fly down there, visit them, let the Dutchman see her family, and get in some of the fine deep sea fishing of the world. We could do all that in three weeks, probably. Pretty country. I think you would like it. Dorothy could paint it, you could write a book about it and I could get broke.

We had my boy, Tom, down from school for Thanksgiving, and he's a fine fella. Caught a bad cold, though. He's hell-bent on working on a charter boat this summer before the Army calls him to duty, so I am looking among my friends who have that sort of operation. Would like to keep him around, but when they want to fly, man, cut 'em loose. He's one I would like to run the film backward on, just to enjoy it all over again.

Glad you are back home, and I bet you are too. Listen, I'll write again if anything happens.

As ever

Dan

MacDonald to Rowan

[*This letter to Rowan crossed Rowan's Dec. 17th letter in the mails.*]

December 15, 1968

Dear Dan,

Well, it was sure God a grim and dismal trip and once again I swear I am never going back. I guess I did okay on the main reason for going, which was to sit in on an all-day taking of depositions from American Express employees by my large rough Sarasota attorney name of Jerry Surfus. A rewarding moment was when he paused part way up the long long batch of steps at 60 Center Street, Foley Square, and said, "Hey, I feel like E. G. Marshall!" The second was when we were trying to decide on the right time for a lunch break and Jerry wanted to know how much more time we had left on one deposition and he grinned like a tiger across the dismal table at the three white-on-white staff attorneys of AmExp and with the big wristwatch gesture said, "Well, let's see what Mickey says." And he read the time on his big Mickey Mouse wristwatch, which the best one of his four small daughters— the one with the best track record for the week, gets to wear on Sundays. The look of utter, unbelieving consternation on the faces of the opposition eagles was worth it all, man. They do not know what John D. Dingaling wants and it is so simple that they can't understand it, or believe it. I want to know if a huge corporation can damage me with utter cynical impunity merely because it is big and I am small, and I want the Court to clarify this little point of citizenship, rights, damages etc in a computer-cold world.

The second thing about going up was to try to do something about my representation. Max Wilkinson is in his sixties. His partner, Ken Littauer, died last year. There is no back-stop. Hell, I do not even know if I need an agent any more. Max has gotten all dithery about forming some new alliance, and so he wanted to talk to me about it, and then he had this fellow he wants, or thinks he wants, to tie up with come winging in from the Coast to have a drink with me. He is one Marvin Josephson, and I saw him quite alone in the lobby of the Gonk, and I was not at my best having risen from my flu bed, so empty from two days of enforced fast that I dared have nothing but sherry. Perhaps he was saying to himself, "Why all the fuss about this frail old man?" I finally told him that all I want is for Max, my companion through the thin times, to be happy, adjusted and content in any relationship he cares to go into. Josephson looked puzzled and said that was what Max had said he wanted—for me.

Should piles of unsold motion picture rights begin to be an estate tax embarrassment, I shall, as I told Josephson, give them away to some worthy venture and thus take them off the appraisal list. I am not, please God, flush with money. But I do not want the constant irritating distraction of people dickering about it and using me as the fucking maypole they wind their legal tape around in an obscene dance.

Look, this is going to mess up the off-chance of seeing you and Dutch at the turn of the year, but we have decided to cleanse ourselves of New York, and take the hoke out of the holiday with a spur of the moment venture, which I ran around arranging on Thursday and Friday. (We got back here Wednesday night.) It is for us A Good Thing to Do for many reasons. New Zealand is one. The severing of oppressive local entanglements is another. Do you know what would make it perfect? If you and what's-her-name could come down there to Oaxaca. Some days there are like months elsewhere. There is no television, damned little radio, gentle people. You fly Mexican Airlines from Mexico

City to Oaxaca. I will get you wedged into the Victoria, and we can go pooting around in the little car looking at the ruins of old old civilizations, and looking at the biggest, oldest, living tree in all the world and, if our luck runs good, we could paint ourselves blue and live in the top of that tree forever. Try, will you. Itinerary attached.

We should move into the new house in February. And once I am in, I may never care to go anywhere else again—certainly not to New York.

Best

John

Rowan to MacDonald

December 17, 1968

Hello absent friend,

Did you have a roaring good time in New York? Knew you would. According to local papers you guys in Florida are freezing your cojones. You mean to tell me that after sweating out this trip back to Manasota Key that it's going to be cold and nasty? Naw! They wouldn't do that. Not to us good guys.

Haven't heard much from you, so guess when you are on the road you don't keep up with your corresponding. Difficult to answer a letter you haven't received, so will bring you up to date on the aging TV luminary and his Dutch friend.

As I may have mentioned previously, we have been house-hunting and we finally found a house that blew our minds. It isn't in the area we had thought we wanted, but it is a good, quiet neighborhood, and fairly near a freeway which in one direction will take me to work and turning in the other will take me to the water.

A Spanish Colonial built in 1927. A little over 5500 square feet, nice guest house for you folks if you ever visit, and a level acre and a third overlooking the Riviera Country Club, and a distant view from the upper bedroom window of the Pacific. Better than all that, it has dignity and charm and a lovely peaceful feeling that grabbed us both the moment we stepped inside.

Bill Ward has been a great help to us. He hired a man and I have had the Key property cleared off. He also arranged with John Lord for the use of his house again. Here's the current plan . . . if I can hold out against the importuning of some folks trying to get me to Washington for the Inaugural Ball. To entertain, of course.

We are going to try and catch a 2 A.M. Jan. 1 flight from Vegas to Tampa. This will mean running from stage to cab to airport with tux on and changing on the plane. Arriving in Tampa with little or no sleep, we will go on down to the shack and sleep a bit. Then we will call you folks and arrange a meet from there. Besides rapping with you and gathering some sun and fun I want to speak with a couple of builders and well-diggers and get that operation started. I feel certain that if we have a building down there that somehow we will make the time for a day or two now and then. And it will be something to look forward to doing.

Life Magazine is instituting something this year that amounts to an award of some kind for achievers in various fields of endeavor and it seemed that Dick and I are the only TV performers to be so honored and the network and everyone feels that we should be there for the presentation. It takes place Monday afternoon, and we fly back to L.A. that night ready to tape Tuesday and Wednesday.

We have 7 more shows to tape and then we start the picture. I am hoping that the picture goes swimmingly and ahead of time so we will have a couple of weeks between it and the summer tour, which is all set to start for 8 weeks straight June 9 in Toronto at O'Keefe Center. At the end of that we should have two weeks and we want to either go to Ireland, Holland, or someplace and get lost. Want to go?

Tom is home from Santa Clara for the holidays and is going to Vegas with us and act as helper or something so I can have an excuse to give him some money. It's not pure charade because he *is* helpful and works if I aim him at something. He has taken up photography at school. There is a credit in the subject for some reason and he is a fanatic right now and saving to buy all sorts of equipment. Wants to do some underwater stuff, etc.

We will try and get a call through to you sometime over the holidays and meanwhile I like the current posters which demand Merry Christmas or Happy Chanukah . . . PICK ONE.

as ever,
Dan

Rowan to MacDonald

Jan ?? 1969

Well,

We found it! What a great house! We peered in all the windows and can hardly wait to find out where those doors go.

The porch makes it—and such great lofty heights inside. Only great spirits such as yours wouldn't be dwarfed by this Big Beauty.

It is pouring rain today—and it was raining the last time we saw it, when we climbed the ladder to stand atop a piling at floor level. Good luck. Live in it in peace and beauty.

Much love

Dan and Adriana

1969

MacDonald to paper

[*Not mailed, copy to Rowan*]

January 22, 1969

The Editor
Sarasota Herald Tribune
801 S. Tamiami Trail
Sarasota, Florida

Dear Sir:

I wish to shed some light on recent items in your newspaper regarding Mr. Dan Rowan of Rowan and Martin's Laugh-In. I refer to Helen Griffith's column on Jan 20th, and the small paragraph appearing in today's paper.

The man everybody is wondering about is actually *Don* Rowan, a first cousin of the famous Dan Rowan. Reliable sources report that these two men have never gotten along, and it was not until Dan Rowan reached his present celebrity stature that Don Rowan has been about to cause Mr. Rowan untold irritation and embarrassment.

Apparently, in order to capitalize on a slight physical resemblance— though Don Rowan is by far the better looking of the two—Don Rowan has gained weight so to appear as portly as Mr. Rowan, and has even grown a mustache which somewhat resembles that worn by Mr. Rowan. He uses a kind of liver-mahogany pancake makeup so that his complexion is quite close to that of the famous Rowan, who achieved his coloration through many years of dissipation.

This semi-imposter cousin freely admits to being Don Rowan and he cheerfully signs autographs as Don Rowan, but he so slurs the name when he says it, and so scrawls the name when he writes it that the public is willing to accept him as the legitimate Mr. Rowan.

Thus far he has apparently taken no commercial advantage of this contrived resemblance. He travels with a female companion who bears quite a resemblance to Mrs. Dan Rowan, and passes her off as his wife. Apparently this Mr. Don Rowan merely hungers for the adulation and brisk service he receives in restaurants and hotels. But there is one thing he cannot conceal, and that is his height. The real Dan Rowan is only five foot three and a half inches tall, and his real wife, Adriana, is but four foot eleven. They are really charming little people, I am told. Hope this clears things up for you.

Cordially

John D. MacDonald

Rowan to MacDonald

February 4, 1969

Well, sir,

We had been looking forward to renewing things with you guys over our short vacation and were mighty disappointed you had gone to Mexico. It is probably better, now that the event is past, that you were not bothered on that trip with outsiders. Sounds as if that were the sort of traveling best done on one's own. Besides we had short time.

Then we went to New York, but I feel like I've told you about that disaster. Its nightmarish quality hasn't left me at this later date, so we will skip it for now and will someday analyze that, whatever it was. The sudden time off we found week before last was handled in my usual slap-dash manner. As soon as I determined that events did permit all of us to take off for almost ten days I thought of Florida, checked the weather and was told you were expecting rain with another front moving in, it was cold and cloudy here (they were to experience some of the worst rains and floods in 40 years while we were gone) and we both felt the almost urgent need for sun on our face.

A call to the handy-dandy travel service elicited the not-to-be-proven-true information that the only place the sun was shining for which we didn't have to renew our lapsed passports was the Caribbean, and deciding that it would be rather chic and extravagant to spend two or three thou on a 10 day whim, we weighed anchor, put her on the rails and went aloft mixing metaphors on the run. Reservations made for Montego Bay, St. Croix and St. John. Our agent had made an investment in our name on the island of St. Maarten and we planned to visit for a day or two there.

It started to go wrong when we landed in Montego Bay. Our travel folks hadn't advised us (called them on this and they claim it's a new rule) that I could land and stay for vacation in Jamaica as an American citizen, but that Adriana would need a valid passport. In short . . . she couldn't land there. This would be upsetting under most any other circumstances, but the immigration officer who was telling us this was telling us with such venom and unconcealed hostility that it stunned me into incoherence.

The flight of Delta's which had brought us there was due to continue its way to San Juan within a half hour and this contemptuous hating man wouldn't let us reboard, wouldn't let us pass, kept telling me to sit "over there" and wait. A passenger, a fan of the show, told me he would intervene, that he had been a resident of Jamaica for several years, and went to this Yankee-hater and came away pale. He almost avoided me when he said that "er, uh, you'll be all right" and left.

The flight left, the other passengers had cleared customs and left. I asked if I could make a phone call . . . "No. Sit over there." Well, of course, finally we were let into the country and he asked me how long we would stay and when I said I would be checking for flights leaving the next day, he said, "Good." The people at Round Hill, where we were to stay, were apologetic, but not too surprised. We spent the night at Round Hill, which for $100 a day ain't that great, and left the next afternoon on the only flight we could get, a three-stop Pan Am to San Juan. Spent the night in San Juan at the El San Juan Hotel, located at the end of the jet runway of the Puerto Rico strip.

Two full days gone and no rest, no sleep, just aggravation and further stomach upset. On to St. Croix where we stayed at Estate Carlton. A bargain the travel folders say at $80 a day. A great place if you are an octogenarian on a seafood diet and a predilection for a flat pitch-and-putt golf course. We stayed two days, sailed one day on a native sloop to an underground seaway that was too dirtied to see anything, so we swam ashore and had a picnic lunch, swatted fleas, and sailed back. On to St. Thomas by flying boat to shop and be picked up by a launch to spend the rest of the time at the Caneel Bay Plantation on St. John.

Ah! Quiet and sun and beach and no phones at last. True the folks there know the famous TV personality, but they are blasé and hip enough to wait until he finishes dinner before casually sauntering by. We *did* rest, eat pretty well, played some tennis, and managed to wash the taste of the rest of the trip out of our mouths.

The plan. We finish taping now on the 13th of this month. We begin rehearsal (we got one of *those* directors) on the flick the 17th and start principal photography on the 24th. It is set up for a 40 day schedule and we will have to give them a little time for looping and dubbing and then until the 7th of June we intend to come South and look over our building plans on the Key.

What would you think of my asking your guy to look at our floor plan and design a small house around it? Do you know some bright young man that would be better for our purpose? You can say that I will personally endorse his work from then on and you know what *that's* worth. Oh, and I *do* appreciate your help in maintaining my anonymity in your area. I had planned a splendid letter to the paper myself, but with the press of work, etc. . . .

In any case, dear boy, you will be seeing us sooner than you think, and good, dear, unmet John Lord has offered us the use of his place "while you're building," and that will be for a long time from the looks of things.

Hope all goes swimmingly with you two and you are much in our thoughts. The end of the season finds them grinding me down again, and all of a sudden I have partner trouble and that's as bad as wife trouble. More of that anon.

With all due respects, PEACE

Dan

MacDonald to Rowan

February 9, 1969

Dear Dan'l,

The four of us must spend some time here together, and we must also spend some time in Mexico together.

New York? I made the solemn vow never to return, unless under court order.

Am I rambling? Yes. But I shall cover everything sooner or later. Be patient.

Oh, about my representations and so on and all that. My agent is negotiating his absorption by Marvin Josephson, Inc. I met Marvin that last time in New York, and he seemed to me like a young man with a cool and acquisitive smile, and a shrewd outlook, and a tendency to make money. He and I agreed that, in essence, there is damned little an agent can do for a novelist, compared to what he can do for other people he represents. I told him that the biggest boon he could give me would be to keep me the hell out of any kind of negotiations going on in my behalf, except when such negotiations might require something of me.

So while this is going on, a fellow closely affiliated with CBS phoned and asked my permission and then came on down bringing one Sy Berns, now head of National General Television, to discuss a project with me which I had mentioned to said CBS affiliated guy at a long-ago lunch at The Ground Floor, memorable only because Bobby Kennedy and entourage were at a nearby table. So the idea that I style a television series using the Bahamas and surrounding other islands and places, and get the big tensions and conflicts from man against nature rather than the naughty violence of man against man. Can do, if the bread is right, and if I do not have to have any continuing connection with it. But as it comes along right during the possible agency change, I say don't bother me for a few months.

This Berns, who is president of the Television Academy I believe, is very quick and sharp, and had come over from the east coast of Florida, where, he said, all their planning had been done by Helen Keller. The bit he loved from Laugh-In was the German soldier saying to Bob Hope, "Every year I waited and waited and you never came."

If you have any comment to make on any of the above stuff, please do so.

What a dreadful goddamn thing running into that immigration type in Jamaica. Petty authority attracts such warped and evil folk. They are the kind who will smile all over themselves only if they are escorting you to the entrance to the ovens. Had it not been for Caneel Bay that would have been the world's worst vacation.

Whoa! Just reread that schedule and interpreted it. Forty days from the 24th of February means April 5th! Right? My dear people it will be wonderful to have you down here for a good long spell. How long can they lub and doop, or whatever the hell it is? Ten days? From mid-April through a week in June would give you better than seven weeks which you do not know how much you need, and it is an incomparably beautiful time of year here, to boot.

Do not let them grind you down. And, friend, partner trouble is inevitable at this stage. The whole world has been changed from one thing to something quite different, and when it moves too fast for people to sort themselves out, then it takes a rare kind of maturity to adjust a business partnership to all the new random noise. You have it and I think Dick does too—but it will take a little more time with him. Best he should cling to the arrangement, because were he ever alone he would be far more susceptible to being misused and mishandled than you, because he has a lot less awareness of who he is. Why, goddammit, do I always start pontificating in letters to you?

What do you *need* with a quarter million worth of California house? If you had a choice, would you *live* there? Lease a big one and write it off to image, entertainment, business use, etc. . . .

Best

John

Rowan to MacDonald

February 20, 1969

So anyway,

this lovely old couple still made love, only like on Sundays because Fred used the chimes on the church down the block for his stroke. You know . . . bong . . . bong . . . bong . . . bong. And like Mabel said the other day, "Dammit, Fred would still be alive today if it wasn't for that dang dang fire engine."

How are you, pal? Dorothy told A that your new house withstood all the water damage okay, so you are well built, as they used to say. Bill Ward wrote and mentioned that other keys down that way had some problems that missed him and us because of our elevation. He also said that John Lord has been using the shack and told him that we were all set for the time I can get loose, so we have a place to stay again.

We are finishing the first week of rehearsals on the flick, and shot our wardrobe tests and make-up tests today. I had a terrible scene about a week before we started with our producers and writer (Everett Freeman). They got the final to me on a Sunday and I was in their offices the next day and they said this was a hell of a time to tell them I didn't like the script and I pointed out that the day after getting the book was about as fast as I could make it.

The script they sent was really amateur night. Contrived, corny, badly built, etc. Also, and this is the actor speaking, it is a Dick Martin script and I have what amounted to a supporting role. Not just my idea but that of a couple people I had read it. Well, there have been some changes and also I couldn't see stopping the whole damn picture since they have their sets built, actors hired, etc. But it was quite an ugly scene and I wish it could have been avoided. It cleared the air, however, and ended more or less amicably the next day.

There are two men involved . . . again. This team is Robert Enders, who has some rather dubious credits as a producer and has been out here for years and is very social, knows everyone, married well, doesn't need the money, and is a smooth and brighter Ed Friendly. Everett Freeman is essentially a screen writer and has some rather good credits including The Secret Life of Walter Mitty and also has some losers lately.

Our deal is similar to the other, also. The four of us are partnered equally. We each, that is, the entities, get 25% of the profits. Dick and I are deferring our salary completely, so the next few months will be income-poor which we should make up quite well on the tour later this summer. Our deal is non-exclusive and they are making a picture right after ours finishes, with Jackie Gleason in Florida. We made a deal for two pics and an option for a third. All under the MGM aegis.

Our director, Norman Panama, is good in many ways, although he seems confused this week and somehow . . . diffident. He defers, I think, too often to my opinion. He stands in the middle of the set looking for a piece of business and so, to get the damn thing moving, I suggest something and he almost always laughs and says, "Yeah, that's it. Let's do it that way." Scares me because I know better than he how fallible my ideas are. But he is a nice man and intelligent and will probably throw most of the shit out next week when we start shooting in earnest.

After the abrasive scene with Enders-Freeman, I had to shoot the final show of our TV season and frightened the hell out of myself. Monday night I rolled and tossed and thought of many brilliant things I could have said, etc. Taped the next day and felt quite run-down and then the next night grew pretty ill. A general malaise, I figured, but slept little and poorly. The next day, Wednesday, while shooting a monologue I had a stabbing pain in my upper left chest so sharp that I gasped and caused a re-take. The pain left and then would return. After a couple of hours of this I asked Adriana to call Ray Spritzler, my doctor and pal who is an internist-cardiologist. She described my trouble and he left his office and came to the studio.

After an EKG, he said that my heart seemed normal. Then after further examination, during which I had one of these seizures, he diagnosed either an onset of shingles or something whose name I can't remember. Something to do with a nerve that causes a severe muscle spasm. Anyway it was hurtful and a drag and convinced me that I would do well to avoid these scenes. I decided, of course, to do the picture. I also decided that the best course for me was to put on a happy face and go balls out to steal this picture with the material they gave me. From now on we play results, but I think I'm on the track. The medical problem has subsided, I don't have shingles and after two days of bed rest I felt and feel much better.

And so. We hope to finish shooting the third week of April and head for Manasota Key. I intend to stay there until June 1. If at all possible we will oversee some construction of the small guest house we start with. I have an architect out here looking at my floor plans now. At least we hope to get a start by the first of May.

You are dead right about my residential investment out here. But I see no way out, really. Not the way we want to go the next couple or three years. I will buy only in a choice neighborhood where values are solid. And the demands on us socially are increasing, and we just have to recognize them. That's bullshit, of course, but that's the way it looks right now and the Dutchman would like to live in a nice house for a while, so what the hell?

If you are home Saturday night you might like the Hollywood Palace we hosted. It's a comedy concert idea we've had for some time. Nothing but comedy and altogether different from Laugh-In. Some funny people and if it cuts together right it should play. We are hoping the thing goes well because it's the first thing we have done on our own since teaming with S-F and since their efforts (Turn-On, which was cancelled after the first show, setting an industry record for failure) haven't met with great success, we hope that this may regain some ground we have lost through their publicity in the business. Ah, the fight goes on and aren't you sorry to be a raggedy old book writer and work on your own and miss all this lovely stuff?

There's more, but later. I have to hit the script to learn my lines for tomorrow. I find that by being the only actor on the set who knows his lines I can find time to discover business and ad-libs to bolster this role I don't really like. The new hours are still strange.—Go to bed early and rise early. Christ, there are people on the *streets* at 7:30 in the morning. I'm going to start stopping and asking them where the hell they're going at that hour.

Peace!

Dan

MacDonald to Rowan

March 15, 1969

Dear Dan,

I enclose for your possible amusement an account of our trip to
see Apollo 9. What I did not put in was the colorful detail of my ac-
cessories—namely one shocking pink pipe and one Swedish yachts-
man's cap. The thing is that when I happen to catch that astonishing
color out of the corner of the eye, I have a tendency to leap back away
from it. I leap out from under my Swede cap. And people have a tendency
to leap back away from me. You made me, by God, a vivid figure among
the throng.

Speaking of misleading information, I heard through my friendly
local grapevine that one Dan Rowan had written to a local politico,
a State Senator and, I might add, a damned good one, complaining
about "curious restrictions" on dredge and fill. Can this be true, sir?
For lo these past twenty years I have been breaking my ass—along
with other men of good will and conservationist attitudes, and a respect
for proper planning and zoning, to get those very restrictions made
a part of the law of this land. I have sat in endless meetings, appeared
before boards, written uncounted letters in what has often seemed a
rather vain attempt to keep this whole area from going right down the
drain as have our neighboring counties to the north.

You see, we cannot rely upon good taste and good will, because
nineteen people will be very thoughtful of their neighbors and their
neighborhood and do not need "curious restrictions" imposed upon
them, but the twentieth man will take advantage of any kind of loophole
and come in and crap the whole thing up for everybody forever. There
are many of that kind on Manasota, particularly at mid-key. They are
whining and howling about restrictions, claiming it is a left wing conspiracy to deprive good Americans of the right to do whatever they
want with their own property.

When the waterway was dredged, these chaps managed to arrange
to have the dredge sit off their bayshore and fill great long fingers of
land out into the bay, cutting off the vista and the open water and
the breeze of their neighbors. And if and when these jolly mid-key
neighbors can get the "curious restrictions" softened, their next move
will be for rezoning from R-1 residential to R-3 multiple, and they will
sell at huge profits to the builders of high-rise condominiums.

Our purpose through all these years has been to set up restrictions which will enable the property owner to obtain the necessary rights and permissions to improve his waterfront in a reasonable and attractive way, behind the established bulkhead line. Without a bulkhead line there are too many land-hungry people who will dredge and fill, dredge and fill, because it is so easy and cheap to suck up the bottom land and seawall it. The bottom lands belong to everyone, not to the upland property owner.

Whenever you have a situation as exists on many of the keys in the county where there is a broad expanse of grass flats between the upland property owners and the Intercoastal Waterway, it would be ecologically idiotic to permit each property owner to dredge a channel from his own bay frontage right out to the waterway. In a mile of frontage you might end up with 40 or more 50-foot channels across the flats. And these flats are incredibly rich, fertile and productive. They are the nursery areas. They keep the birds and the fish and the small mammals sound and healthy and numerous in our wilderness areas and on our mangrove islands.

Until very recently Tallahassee was shockingly indifferent to any kind of marine biological considerations. The restrictions we have been able to ram through have been through a constant pressuring of the Tallahassee robber barons, the so-called Internal Improvement Board, who love to sell vast reaches of bay bottom to spoilers like the Arvida Corporation.

Anyway, rather than having the fertile, valuable acres of flats bitched up by myriad parallel canals, the pattern is to have the upland owners share a common channel just off-shore running north and south to shared channels out to the waterway.

Dan, we fight such a precarious rear-guard, underfinanced action against the fast buck boys who want to dredge and fill all the "unsightly mud flats" that clout like yours can all too easily undo some of the constructive things we have done in the county. I know you must have jumped in on the basis of limited and inaccurate information. If you have inadvertently given the Wright-Hansen group on Manasota the leverage to get their "channel scouring" permits approved by the County Commission, then, dear boy, you may be in the curious position of having to award the Flying Fickle Finger of Fate to yourself.

Best to you and Dutch

John

Rowan to MacDonald

March 18, 1969

Dear John,

Just received your Special Delivery and am violating previous precedent by dictating this letter. I am on the set between takes, so this may seem disjointed as I am interrupted from time to time, but I did want to get back to you right away.

When you ream someone, I can see that old Army background shining through . . . you do a fine job of it. If I have stepped on the toes of a project you have been breaking your ass on for twenty years, you must realize that it was unintentional.

My own plans have always included the wonderful convenience of having our own boats docked at the back of our property. I want to put floating concrete piers parallel to each other and extending into the waterway from the back of my property now existing, 35 to 40 feet and something like 50 feet apart. I cannot see as a conservationist how this could possibly disturb the ecological balance. I was told that unless the restrictions are lifted, I will not be permitted a dock on my property at all. This seemed to me then, and now, as an unfair and meaningless restriction.

Subsequently, I received a letter from Bill Ward, giving me this politico's name and urging me to write him as a Manasota Key property owner, protesting the restrictions. I, of course, was totally unaware of the possible repercussions of this action.

If a further letter from me to anyone whom you might name, urging the use of all possible legislation to help preserve the natural beauty and resources of the waterway will help, I will be glad to write it. Beyond that, you can write it and send it to me, and I will sign it. This is no sop to your vanity, not meant as a crutch for our friendship, but honestly reflects the fact that I have, for a long time, been concerned about the depredations against our natural resources.

Another thing your letter has pointed out to me, which has been bothering me for some time now: As we discussed and you know, being in the same position yourself, I receive countless requests from all sorts of organizations to help them in one way or another in various causes. It is impossible to lend yourself to everything and I consider it a dereliction of duty as a responsible citizen to give a blanket no to every

request. I have adopted the practice of ignoring requests from organizations I know nothing about, sponsored by people I know nothing
about, and have, instead, given my ear and sometimes assistance to
people whom I trust. I have spent enough time talking to you and
reading you to realize we're eye to eye on almost all issues. Consequently,
when you suggest "such and such" requires and deserves support, I
don't take time to investigate personally, but act upon your word. I
did not take time upon receiving Bill Ward's request to look any further
into the matter. I have absolutely no wish to have Manasota rezoned
. . . far from it. As you know, its privacy and naturalness are qualities
of primary appeal to me, consequently I would do nothing to spoil either
one.

If I have used my so-called clout to our mutual disadvantage, I
would be pleased for you to direct my next move.

As soon as I get off this routine of up at 6:00 A.M., work all day
and flop into bed, I will sit down and write you a more personal letter.

Penitently

Dan

MacDonald to Rowan

March 27, 1969

Dear Dan,

That thing you read me about the "north county boys" getting the
severe restrictions in on account of Arvida etc, is emotional and inaccurate. [Rowan had read over the phone to MacDonald a personal
letter from a neighbor saying that the restrictions on Arvida hurt local
upland owners.] The fight with the big developers has always been
the problem of whether or not they should be entitled to buy public
bay bottom from the state and fill it and sell it to their mail-order pigeons.
The most consistent violator of the private channel rights across public
flats has been the individual resident.

Look, put the whole sorry mix-up out of your mind, and when you
and that lovely what's-her-name get down here, you and I will have
a little bull session with Jim Neville, a hard-nose you will like as much
as I do, and he will clear the air. He has a nice porch to sit on, and
a good incisive mind, and a hell of a track record as one of the most
effective conservationists in the state.

Look, what I forgot to tell you the other night was my surprise and pleasure at the bite and pace of the show Sammy Davis was on. It went right back, that one time, to the front end of the first season. And that ending, the question about relatives in Harlem etc, was delicious.

Rgds
John

Rowan to MacDonald

April 4, 1969

Dear Occupant:

We have continued a rapid pace on the movie (to them, but to me it seems long and slow) and are now a full five and a half days ahead. It would appear that I should be down there easily by the 15th, possibly sooner. The notion about the camper was prompted by the use of one on location. It is very comfortable, made by Dodge, has a big bed, a good john, a jim dandy little kitchen, etc. I thought we could use the extra john and also cool off in its air-conditioned interior if it grew too sticky for us in the house. I may, if I find one to rent, then get a scooter or Yamaha or such like to dash to town in.

Following the architect's advice I am not authorizing any work start until I speak with the building contractor. He is at present getting his sub bids. This all means, of course, that we won't see much construction while we are there, and it will be a longer time until we are in the house, but with all the other expense I have right now, it is difficult to justify the vacation house.

I'll be talking to you before we leave here.

Hurriedly,

Rowan to MacDonald

June 2, 1969

Dear John and Dorothy,

Just to show you how busy I am, my first letter after returning home is secretary-typed. The summer tour is in rehearsal and needs a lot of work; the new house is a disaster area but marvelously promising; the dogs are completely disoriented and I am harassed.

Having checked with the orthopedic man about the soreness around my rib cage . . . two broken ribs and two strained intercostal muscles plus torn triceps. There will be no water skiing for at least a month.

Thank you for helping me have a marvelous vacation . . . the best I have ever had . . . and not because it was the first in seven years.

Be happy in your new house and be well. Think kindly of us as we do so often of you.

PEACE!

Dan

MacDonald to Rowan

June 28, 1969

Dear Dan,

Well that was such a sickeningly bad book I did that it depressed me all to hell and I finally got grown up and rewrote just about the whole effing thing, and now it is medium okay, but that put me way behind schedule on the Sy Berns bit due on the 30th, and I mailed that this morning, and now I feel free as a bird for the first time in at least six months. And I am for sure pooped. Look we miss you around here. Quite much. How goest the new manse amid the flower gardens and tennis courts? It has been sick-hot here. Very unusual. Up to 94 daytime, dropping all the way down to 80 at night. Tell me about going to a premiere?

Best

J

MacDonald to Rowan

July 1, 1969

Dear Dan,

When at that final dinner we got into that charged discussion of black/white and you termed me a bigot, I was more than a little upset, first that you would so swiftly revise all former opinions, and secondly that there was not the time or the situation that would permit me to reach you with the basis of the proposition I was stating.

It is totally obvious that unless you and I and other men of good will give this area sound and good and constructive thought, the whole situation will merely worsen.

As a writer I become skeptical of contemporary fashionable attitudes, and of my own too-often automatic acceptance of those attitudes, and so I have to put them through the grinder and see what happens.

Anyway, let me hear from you sort of personally, eh? We love you both.

Cheers,

John

Rowan to MacDonald

July 8, 1969

Dear friend John,

So *many* things, mostly because I have been up to my ass on this damned tour which I shouldn't be on but am and working hardest, and have not written for that reason alone. Your letters both arrived today and I'm using my nap time before the show to answer.

Bigot to most of us is a contemporary dirty word. I asked Adriana, "My God, when did I ever call John a bigot?" and she told me what you remembered. I can only say that I have accepted our relationship so fully that I speak to you as to myself. You don't need me to tell you that you aren't. You apparently *do* need me to tell you that *I* don't think you are. You are one of the brightest people I know so you couldn't be if only because intelligence doesn't admit of bigotry. You couldn't be because I'm entirely too fond of you, and my taste is better than that. In the heat of discussion I used a shocker to grab your attention, and succeeded in having you only remember the shocker and not the following statement I needed your attention for.

My first reaction is that it would be difficult to imagine a better-intentioned but nonetheless distorted view of fact. In the first place, the "law" which you feel should never be subverted by black or white has been used to knock underprivileged citizens' brains out since Moses showed his tablets. Our country has been so abusive, brutalizing, unfair, to man of color both red and black, that if I were they and someone asked me to "respect the law" my own reaction would be violent.

I feel guilt for my white American ancestors and on my mother's side paternally we go back to at least Nathan Hale. I am also ashamed and remorseful and feel the colored races are entitled to reparations.

What else, for Christ's sweet sake, is fair? They have had their lives, their dignity, their land taken away from them. What form those reparations should take can be decided when the happy day arrives they are granted. And from the way things are going what they don't get they are bloody well going to take. My feelings are frankly emotional about this entire issue. I find it almost impossible to intellectualize the problem. This makes me a cinch for cold-blooded argument, but if you want to talk about "gut" feelings, that's mine about this mess our daddies have made. If I were black, yellow or red I would be either in jail, dead or fighting someplace for my place in the world that had been stolen from me and my people.

Yes, John, there is a difference. But there is a difference between Dan and John and between Bill and Dan, and etc. etc. Damn! We are all different. The geneticist and other scientific nit-picking about tendon and cartilage structure of feet and hands notwithstanding, I feel the issue is sociological. The drawing up of separate camps is WRONG. We are ONE. Human beings each with his own individuality, each with his own problems, own ecstasies, own dignity. We can piss it away OURSELVES, but by damn I don't see anyone *taking* it.

But as I say, pal, I need time to study your letter. It took me a long time to realize that some of my friends were "different." Some of them were darker and some did strange things at some synagogue or other, but the big differences were that I could kick a ball farther than one and that another could throw one better than I, and that most of them had a family and I didn't.

This tour, the picture, the agents, the public are all grist for future mills of ours, old buddy. Suffice it to say that both the Dutchman and I wish to hell we were driving to Sarasota tonight to see you and Dordo as opposed to facing the audience at the Garden States Art Center. We miss you both. We miss Manasota Key. And John. . . . Our differences will never be such, so far as I am concerned, that my affection and regard for you is likely to change other than deepen.

PEACE!

Dan

MacDonald to Rowan

July 15, 1969

Dear Dan,

Astoundingly, this is the very first chunk of typing I have done in this tin-roofed pagoda. Got a loaner desk in here late yesterday afternoon. Toted over the machine and the bare necessities in the early evening. Now a new day, and nothing is where it should be when I reach for it. Have to acquire a whole new set of automatic motions—like learning to brush the teeth with the left hand.

I like your letter.

Think of it this way. Here we are, two whites of better than average empathy and intelligence, and who are both concerned about what goes with the black these days. Granted we may approach the thicket from different angles, but the motivation is, as is proper, to see if there is *some* intellectual and emotional posture which can be useful in these times. We both have the public ear, and it is a fearsome responsibility. What we project will touch a few people here and there, and they will touch others.

The law is two things. It is the Law—Bill of Rights, Constitution, men created equal etc. That is the one I meant, the one that black and white must support. The other is the small "l" law, the one you point out has been used as a device by misguided men to knock out the brains of the underprivileged. Black and white must not permit the subversion of Law by lower-case law to flourish. Without the support of Law, we are nothing. We are a mob. The fabric of civilization, as has been said by many many people, is only tissue thin, and when ruptured often enough, it will all blow away, and there will be nothing to put in its place until we have lost several generations to violence and bestiality.

My personal conviction has been that all government is bad because it offers positions of power to people hungry for power, while at the same time making the paths toward that power a series of winding trails best traveled by the man with guile, hypocrisy, a talent for conspiracy, the ability to maneuver people. The man of true merit in public office is a rarity under any form of government. Some kinds are better than others—or less bad. I think ours is as good as mankind has found thus far.

I feel no guilt, shame or remorse for the social and economic oppression of the black, because I do not feel any personal responsibility for the past actions of political animals within the historic fabric of our country. I feel no guilt, shame or remorse for the gutted countryside in Kentucky and West Virginia, for the disappearance of the buffalo and passenger pigeon, for the poisoning of the soil and the water and the air. Man can always be expected to do the worst possible job with his environment, and with his relations to people of other races and of other nations. Were I to feel guilt, remorse and shame, it means that I was feeling guilt, remorse and shame for being a human being. Perhaps that *would* be a proper posture, but it is a negation of life to be ashamed of being the creature one is.

I will feel my guilt, remorse and shame for the negative anti-life acts which, consciously or unconsciously, *I* commit. I will feel guilt, remorse and shame for my failure to take any kind of action in situations where action was an ethical imperative.

At the moment I have volunteered to give help and advice and do some field work in the selection of a vastly increased percentage enrollment of blacks in the Harvard Graduate School of Business Administration. Now I know how grotesque and absurd that sounds at first look. Bear with me. The problem here is *not* to so alter the admission standards as to make the selection program susceptible of taking in a higher percentage of blacks. The problem is to find some way of being able to take the talented black entrepreneurs, who, regardless of education, are making a good track record in their own businesses, and finding good ways of enabling them to preserve the profitability and continuity of their own enterprises while at the same time giving them a chance to hone their managerial skills at the best place in the country, thus compressing the learning period and enabling them to aim higher with their own business projects. Could you say I am trying to help give them those weapons which will enable them to fight for their place in the world? But the word "giving" has a stink about it. They have earned the right to the advanced training. The problem is to find the way to make it possible for them to receive what they have earned.

Well . . . I wish I knew why people shy away from an acceptance of the reality of a very real, fundamental, ineradicable DIFFERENTNESS between the races. A thing, a person, can be different without being better or worse. The "differentness" I mean is far more than a difference in skills, abilities—it is a difference in the very climate of the mind and heart and soul. A dachshund and a terrier can breed, and will respond in quite different ways to country fields, city streets, moonlight nights and strange cats. This differentness is most marked in the pure blood lines—the pure black, the pure white. Nowadays in this country the pure black is a great rarity, so the differentness is less emphatic. (And the white is of course an interesting and complex racial mix also.)

Look. If we have gotten so screwed up by pretending that all men are ONE, that everybody is really and truly alike—if we have painted ourself into a corner with the illusion that skin color has no more significance than blonde or brunette, is it not worth the try to see what happens to race relations when we accept, boldly and without self-consciousness and without guilt, the idea that there is indeed a difference of consequence? For chrissake, where does the black find his sense of racial pride, racial identity, species identity, if we keep insisting that he is a dusky white man?

Best to your Dutchman. Raining torrents this morning. My gut is beginning to tighten up in expectation of an Apollo 11 disaster tomorrow.

Rowan, you are a good man. Come home.

Stay well,
John

Rowan to MacDonald

August 3, 1969

Picture, if you will, my friend,

your own new house while the workmen were there, or when you really needed them and they weren't there, and imagine that you are forced through circumstance and pride and stubborn willfulness to live there during the reconstruction (and it is only that I have friends in the South whom I respect or it would be a capitalized Reconstruction) and you have a faint glimmering idea of what we have had since we've been home.

When we left the assurance was that upon my return home I would be able to "play a set of tennis, take a swim, shower in my own bathroom, go downstairs and mix a drink at my new bar and shoot a game of eight-ball." By stepping over carpenters, painters and plumbers I *did* manage to get a shower. But that's it. But, of course, we love the house and if it should ever be finished and finally cleaned up and things put away, it will be the most comfortable digs I have ever had. The Dutchman is ecstatic with her new kitchen, and it is pretty and apparently functional. Except for the other night when the new 8-million-dollar sink backed up.

We arrived home last week after 8 of the worst touring weeks I can remember. Adriana preceded me by a week to start some of the unpacking and putting away in the belief that this would relieve me for some of the effort I have to expend to earn some of the money this project is going to require. She walked into a disaster area but performed heroically and when I got in last Sunday I could sleep in the new bedroom and we did have something to eat from our new kitchen. We couldn't find the china and all the cutlery, but we ate camping out in our new breakfast room which is a room for all seasons so far.

The first script for the show is some 345 pages and we will tape for three days the first week instead of the customary two. It is not in splendid shape but I feel it's better than it was when I got back and Paul Keyes and I have done several days hard work on it, paring and shoring up.

I had intended to spend the past week at the office but got hung up with the house and relative problems and the days have been crammed with action. We start at 6:30 AM and are in the sack by 10. There hasn't been time to indulge in this sort of pastime, but today being Sunday I have grabbed a few hours to catch up on part of the mail that has stacked up in my absence. Thanks for the pix, they are great and I am happy to have some of the Whaler . . . Have you got your new boat yet?

I think we can leave the discussion of black folks, don't you? We are probably on the same side approaching it for various reasons from different paths. I guess our basic difference is summed up with your asking at the end of your last words on it, where can a black find his racial identity etc "if we keep insisting he is a dusky white man?" Of course he can't and we shouldn't. I never have. Au contraire, I would be inclined to think of whites as bleached blacks.

If the pain leaves I will tell you about the summer tour at that time. I doubt if I will ever be able to report that time with objectivity, but it would be a good exercise of some sort to try, I suppose. Stay well.

Dan

MacDonald to Rowan

August 30, 1969

Dear General B. Right,

Did a rush job on an article for Life on the Everglades Jetport. Finally got a final final final treatment for a pilot in, and National General calls it "brilliant," and CBS calls it "superb" so they go with the pilot and the actual scheduling, so confident are they that happy hucksters will divvy up the tab. I call it bullshit, derivative, flat and totally without creative risk. But now I am out of it forever, with the right to ask that my name be removed should they deviate too far from my concept.

We went to Chicago and I thumped the tub for the very last time I hope. I do not like it. I do it well enough, they tell me, but I find myself becoming what They want, not what I am, and then I feel like a shifty jackass. Since my visit they have sold, I heard yesterday, 24,000 copies of "Dress Her in Indigo" in Chicago alone, which is a shame because it is, forsooth, a pretty bad book, friend.

Despite my vow of never returning to New York, we fly up there next Wednesday the 3rd, with attorney and his lady, and Jerry and I spend the 4th and 5th with the executives of American Express. They have apparently gotten disabused of trying to settle the thing through their platoons of attorneys, and are willing to pay our expenses in order to have a confrontation and explain their problems, and negotiate a settlement of some kind. We have made it clear that we are not obligating ourselves to settle by going up there, and that if we do not like their soft shoe routine, we will happily go to trial.

You sound a lot better about the show this year than last. Good. Look forward to seeing it and the new folks in it. Must have been a truly horrid summer tour. Keep notes. You could write it as it is, and call it "Eight Happy Weeks in Hell" and agitate the whole industry.

We are dandy. This house is youthening. People come and they sit and visibly slow down and smile in a dreamy way, and talk and talk and talk, and leave yawning and smiling and yawning and smiling. I get up early, pace the veranda and snuff the sea wind and say good morning to the goose, the duck, the cats, the sparrows and the palm trees.

Say hello to Homer for us. Kiss Dutch for us. Float your way into a new season, twinkling and chuckling. In a world where we are represented at the UN by Shirley Temple, everything is plausible.

Love, peace and plenty,

John

Rowan to MacDonald

September 4, 1969

Dear Market Wizard,

I haven't seen "Dress Her in Indigo" on the book stands yet but I am sure that you are too tough on yourself when you say that it is a pretty bad book. Even if you are not satisfied with it I am sure that your public is very forgiving. You have written so many good ones that they will carry you through the weak ones. If it works for Rowan & Martin, it will work for you.

We have just finished show #4 and if I sound better about the show this year it has to be because I have gotten callused and am working on the Florida-acquired attitude of "Sad's Bad." Actually, as is my custom, I think there are a lot of things that we are doing that we shouldn't and a lot of things we should do that we are not. Problems remain pretty much the same except that with time they haven't gone away and have merely become more entrenched. However, I don't think you are really as interested in these things as you have always been kind enough to pretend so I won't go into them further.

My son Tom returned from Europe Saturday night where he had a very nice two months saying that he prefers Greece and Spain to all the rest so I figure there is hope for him. I'll have him at home for the next two or three weeks and then he goes to the Army. He is commissioned a 2nd Lieutenant in the AGO and has nine weeks of officers' basic at Fort Harrison, Indiana. Expects to remain stateside for most of his first year and then it appears he will have to pull a year's duty in Vietnam. Let's hope that the Paris talks work something out before that time comes.

Our house is shaping up, getting more pleasant all the time. Tennis courts still dragging along. Bedroom currently a disaster area. We had a very large swarm of bees working in that corner of the house and in order for workmen to function we reluctantly had to have them exterminated. This was done while we were away which didn't lessen our guilt at this mass murder. Now they are having their posthumous revenge. After punishing our two poodles twice for messing on the carpet, I finally had enough sense to look up and noticed something leaking from our bedroom ceiling. Honey. I sent Dominique into the attic and he worked all day carrying out buckets of honey which, when weighed, came to something over 500 pounds. He was unable to get it all because of cramped quarters up there and what started as one little drop or two has now become twelve or fourteen different areas dripping as steadily as melting honey can drip. So it is off with the ceiling, clean out the attic, patch up the ceiling and wait for the next catastrophe.

You know what a big fan I am of your house but I don't really think you can give the house the credit for youthening your guests. I think it is the people atmosphere that has that nice effect on them, not the architectural atmosphere.

Homer grows larger and more heart-warming. Renee and Touissant have learned no more English and I am now able to order breakfast in French but I am getting tired of just drinking coffee.

We can all sleep better now that Shirley Temple is watching out for us. One thing's for sure, people who used to talk about disbanding the UN would never make a move against that establishment while *she* is there.

PEACE!

Dan

MacDonald to Rowan

September 30, 1969

Dear Chap,

Out of Chicago I think I got one pretty good interview and I have one dangling commitment to go back Nov 22nd for Bob Cromie to interview me on the Educational TV thing called Book Beat, which seems to have a lot of audience all over, mostly because every station runs the show a couple or three times the week it is released.

American Express tried to dazzle us country boys with the limousine rides and lunch at the Wall Street Club on the 59th floor of the Chase Manhattan, and finally announced that they had never settled anything for more than $2500, which includes expenses, and they were not about to start. After the final showdown, the second morning, Jerry Surfus and I went back to the hotel on the BMT. So day after tomorrow they take my deposition here, and the trial will probably be in November or December sometime.

They tried to imply throughout that I was some kind of greedy opportunist tying to use my ability to capture press coverage to hold a gun in their ribs and enrich myself.

[*MacDonald sued American Express after he had received a special delivery letter from the company apologizing for having made errors in his account, after which they then wrote to two Sarasota banks telling them his credit had been cancelled, told his travel agent over the phone they would give her fifty dollars if she could retrieve from him the "lost or stolen" American Express card, and put the non-existent debit balance in the hands of a collection agency. MacDonald settled out of court, and agreed at that time never to write a novel about credit cards.*]

I never heard such a goddamn thing as that honey dripping through the ceiling. Do you know that the way the bees keep it from melting like that is by just standing there and cooling it by fanning it with their little wings? When you slay the bees there is nobody to cool it. Right? You should think these things through before acting precipitately.

Love to Homer, Renee, Touissant and . . . uh . . . Dandeeana?

Best,

John

Rowan to MacDonald

October 16, 1969

Well, Sir:

I don't remember being this busy in quite some time. Let me tell you why. Paul Keyes, our head writer and co-producer and the fella upon whom Dick and I have relied most heavily for our personal points of view on this show, quit a week and a half ago in the middle of the day and has left the show.

He had apparently been quite upset by the way things were going on the show for some time. I was unaware of his unhappiness until it was too late. You see, Paul is a very strong Nixon man. He is one of the inner circle of Nixon friends and advisors. For whatever humor is in that campaign, Paul is the guy who wrote it. He was the first man into the suite on election night. President Nixon calls him four or five times a week and when he's in San Clemente, Paul's always there, etc. etc. He is very close to the administration on a personal and also on a political basis.

I have known for a long time that Paul was a conservative and stout Republican. I have never known his politics, however, to interfere with his judgment nor with his comedy talent. He has combined a few talents which make him an outstanding addition to any variety show. Paul is a damn good editor, he has very good taste and he is awfully funny and easy to get along with.

I like George Schlatter very much and it would be impossible to produce this show without him. He brings an energy and enthusiasm and kookiness to the show we need. George will say anything, will try anything, will do anything and when nobody agrees with him he ducks his stubborn German head and plows straight ahead. Consequently some things have been on the show which I'm certainly not proud of and statements have been made with which I don't agree.

A great deal of the edge of George's tastelessness has been blunted in the past by the tasteful negotiations Paul has been able to work out with George. The main reason Paul says he quit is that he had the title of producer but was unable to produce and had the title of head writer and was unable to head write. Suggestions he would make on certain deletions in the script were over-ridden and they were over-ridden in front of the writing staff to whom Paul gave orders. In other words his authority was undermined in front of his people and it became an intolerable situation.

Lying on the beach at Manasota Key I resolved that *sad is bad* and under that great sophomoric panoply of philosophy I included such resolves as, "this season I'm going to be Dick Martin."* I really intended to show up on read-throughs and then leave, come in, tape the show, when my section had been taped say goodbye and leave and I've been in pretty good health as a result of it. I haven't worried too much. The shows haven't been quite what I would like to have them but our ratings are still very strong. We're still number one so I wasn't going to worry too much about it. Now then Paul quit.

*[Dick Martin is one of the funniest men I know. His work habits are different from mine. I would not like the reader to get the impression that I believe his contribution to the success of the R & M Laugh-In TV show was anything other than considerable. Without him there would have been no show. Without him, it would never have succeeded.]

My schedule is back to what it was on the very first session. I tape all day Tuesday and Wednesday. When I am working as an actor on Tuesday and Wednesday it is the only time I am not standing at the executive desk with a phone to the control booth at my hand, to do an awful lot of the things that Paul had been doing. After we finish taping at 7:00 on Tuesday nights, for instance, the rest of the kids go into music rehearsal, Dick is already home or out chasing ladies, George and I go to the writers' meeting and that generally takes anywhere from 7:30 to 12:30 or 1:00 in the morning and then I have to get up again Wednesday early for a full day's taping on Wednesday. And then Thursday before the run-through we're working on fixes for the script. Thursday we have the reading with the cast. After the reading with the cast we sit and balance up the casting and do some further fixing and then later in the evening we have a production meeting on the show. If we're taping #10 we'll have a production meeting on show #13.

In addition to this change in my personal schedule on my own series, we are in the midst of producing a special for the Ford Motor Company. That special is going to be taped week after next. This week we are taping two shows for the Laugh-In series Monday, Tuesday and Wednesday. Thursday and Friday we are taping a Carol Burnett Show, part of an exchange deal because Carol is a guest on our special which will be taped Monday, Tuesday and Wednesday next week, and then Thursday and Friday we are back to work on Laugh-In.

I will certainly be ready for a nice quiet couple of weeks at Manasota Key if our schedule can be maintained and we can indeed take a hiatus.

The letter from Dordo indicates you guys may go to Mexico again this holiday season and from the way you talk about it I can hardly blame you. However, I don't believe I would want to go to Mexico because we will have that new house down on Manasota Key to get equipped and moved into and looked at.

Christmas is going to be a very quiet thing for us. The Seiberts know that we're coming down there and one of the reasons I am leaving Los Angeles is to get away from Christmas parties and the rest of the attendant bullshit and so we are not looking forward to any Christmas parties, dinners, house warmings, etc. I just want to flake-out somewhere and rest. Of course it would be great if you were going to be in Sarasota because part of the rest program is always a nice comfortable kind of session with guys like you.

Tom, my 2nd Lt. son, is now stationed somewhere in Indiana and is not very happy. From what he tells me of his Army future for the next couple of years I can't say that I blame him. He figures that inasmuch as he will be stateside for a year it would be grand if he could be stationed someplace near a law school so that he could moonlight. He is not tickled to death about the prospect of going to Vietnam next year because as he puts it the AGO folks are in charge of things like grave registration and filing clerks. It sounds pretty dull and he is quite upset about it because primarily of the loss of time.

He called me wanting to know what I could do about it. It's amazing what confidence youngsters will repose in their parents. I don't know what the hell I can do about changing his condition in the Army.

I hope that you are employed on a work of some merit which is bringing you enjoyment and I hope further that all is well in the household, everybody in good health and full of love. As usual I send you

PEACE !

Dan

Rowan to MacDonald

October 24, 1969

Dear Sir:

We are wrapping up final shots on the special today, weather permitting. We need an exterior on a high-rise rooftop and we are going to have to wait until the weather clears or else try and get it another day.

The special looks pretty good at this stage. There is really nothing innovative about it, we just hired people we thought were talented and funny and put them all together. The general premise of the show is reflected in the title Rowan and Martin Bite the Hand That Feeds Them. Just a look at various sides of the television industry. We are having a few problems with censorship.

PEACE !

Dan

MacDonald to Rowan

Nov 2, 1969

Dear Dan,

Shall write a legitimate letter very soon, about many things.

This is in haste to tell you that we shall definitely be here over Christmas.

Found that Rod Taylor is a sympatico guy—bright and witty and perceptive. Got along well enough to tell him you told me you thought he would do a hell of a job. As he is a little insecure about it, he was delighted. Said he did not know you but had the impression you are a very "ballsy guy." Hell, I had to let him go on thinking so, right? Said he knows Dick and can't quite figure him. Says he is sort of semi-visible, and said, "so he's with that image he's got, but four years from now what's he going to do about an image?" He also said, "I've found out that if I try to live the part of McGee on and off camera, I finish the picture looking like Spencer Tracy." He wants to keep the Flush as a hideaway pad, maybe bring it over when the picture is finished.

Best to you two and we look forward to seeing you soon.

John

MacDonald to Rowan

December 11, 1969

Dear General,

I have given up my naive hope of being able to write a letter-type letter.

There is no point in trying to tell you, or anyone, the horrid incredible soul-wasting complexities that seem to come jumping out at us at every curve in the trail. I keep trying to keep things simple, easy, slow-moving, restful, rewarding . . . and seem to end up going through my declining years like a continual imitation of the Marx Bros.

I cannot stand din, random noise, confusion, a lot of obligations that I don't want and didn't ask for. I think that if we have 12 parts per million DDT in our fatty tissues, and if all mother's milk in America is unfit for human consumption because of DDT content, and because it *is* a nerve poison, and because there must be some measurable amount in the brain tissue of all of us, then perhaps the little synapses and neuronic magics are being subtly poisoned and we all, every one of us, are going mad, each in his own highly personal way—whether it be by slaying Miss Sharon Tate, or snarling at one's true love.

Screw it! Enough of this tirade. It is a beautiful day and I have time to write this much, and any friend of McGee is a friend of mine.

What I would like and shall have, is a couple of nice long days when you are down here when nobody has to do or say or believe in anything constructive. Just whittle, spit and smile a lot.

See you soon!

John

1970

Rowan to MacDonald

April 3, 1970

Well, if you don't want to write to me perhaps you'd like to find out what's been going on here.

I am enclosing a copy of the event of the leg operation that I had. I have a couple of other friends who will want to know about it and rather than write it down several times I have written it in more or less diary style and sending you a copy.

You may or may not have wondered at my rather absent style during the last visit on the beach but I must confess to a certain amount of concern in the back of my mind regarding that forthcoming examination. Here now in Las Vegas working two shows a night and it has not been pleasant or much fun. I stay off the leg most of the day and use a cane on stage at night but it is a very sore and painful proposition.

I suppose that age and diabetes are preventing the prompt healing this old frame used to provide me with and the damned incision is infecting and suppurating and all sorts of nasty things. Just thought I might cheer you up for the pre-letter reading.

My son and his bride have been vacationing at Manasota Key and may or may not have called you by this time to say hello. I asked them to if they ever got near the telephone. I have spoken to him a couple of times and he told me that they ran into rather foggy and poor weather down there but don't seem at all dismayed by this. People on honeymoons certainly can overlook a lot of bad conditions, can't they?

We brought Homer and Bernie with us to Las Vegas and I have

just had to send Homer back home. We have a suite here at the hotel looking out into a little private pool and lawn area and he was gradually destroying the entire setup. He was digging up the grass, difficult to grow in the desert, and chewing up the patio furniture. I didn't feel I could afford the luxury of his company any longer.

The Dutchman is in great shape, plays tennis, sun bakes every day and tends to me in the evening. I hope all goes well with you and I am sorry to have been so late in dropping you a line.

PEACE!

Dan

Diary

During the second week of Florida vacation I noticed a swelling in my upper right thigh. At the time I thought it was a slightly larger muscle on that leg than on the other. Another week passed during which I was vaguely conscious of this—there was no pain connected with it. Adriana saw me step out of the shower one afternoon in our last week there and asked me what it was.

For the first time I took a serious and longer look at it and it was noticeably a swelling. There was still no discomfort, no pain. When we returned to Los Angeles I went in to see Dr. Cameron Hall. He is one of the best orthopedic surgeons in the country by several standards and also a very good friend. He examined it and immediately urged that I have it biopsied.

This was on a Wednesday and since we opened in Phoenix on Friday and were going to New York the following Monday and Tuesday, I asked him if it could wait until that next week and he allowed as how it could.

When I got back from New York reservations were made at St. John's Hospital for a private room and for a time in surgery. I went into the hospital on Thursday at 2:30 and was subjected to quite a few of the typical pre-operative tests. Dr. Hall told me that he had called in Dr. Donald Rockland who is, in his opinion, the best tumor man available. Dr. Rockland examined my leg late Thursday afternoon, chatted with me briefly about the different types of tumors and said he would check with

Dr. Hall who would then talk to me and that Dr. Rockland would be available in surgery at the same time to assist in any consultation.

Dr. Hall came in and examined it once more later and then sat down to discuss with me possible options depending upon what he found after opening it up. It was a tumor in his opinion and he didn't seem too hopeful. He said that if it was benign that he could have it removed almost anytime that I had some free time for convalescence. Obviously it was quite large and it would have to be scooped out and muscles would have to be resectioned and I could expect to be off the leg for two or three weeks. If it was, as he called it, a "bad one" then he had several options depending upon what kind of bad one it was. None of these options were very pleasant of course.

Since I was being operated on Friday morning and Tom was being married in Santa Clara Saturday morning I was most anxious that whatever he did I would be able to go to Santa Clara on Saturday morning. Dr. Hall said that he could not confine me to the hospital but that I wouldn't feel like going anywhere Saturday morning on the leg. Dr. LaScola, our old family friend and pediatrician and witch doctor, came in and looked at it and was the only optimistic opinion that I had. He said he believed it to be a sterile abcess caused by the insulin injections that I had given myself in that area. He then put me under hypnosis for operative suggestions to deny the possibility of traumatic action resulting from unmeaning remarks I might overhear while under anesthesia.

I accepted the entire situation quite philosophically. I was well aware of the fact that I could be in the hospital to have my leg taken off or to find out that I had a more definite terminal date than is now available but ever since the war I have felt that I have outlived my luck. I wasn't too surprised to hear a pessimistic report nor would I be too surprised to hear a final bad one.

Friday morning they prepared me for surgery. The theater became available a half hour earlier and when I was transferred from my bed to the gurney I still had the intravenous jug hanging over my head and it was carted along with me to the operating room.

When I awoke Adriana had tears in her eyes. Tears of happiness. Cam Hall had come, after an hour and half of surgery, to the room in his surgical gown with tears in his eyes and big smile yelling "it's benign, it's benign" and gave her a big hug.

I went to the wedding on Saturday having left the hospital Friday night by ambulance. Spent the night at home rather uncomfortably. The wedding went off without a hitch and we had a party at the house on Sunday. I went to the wedding on crutches and hobbled on a cane on Sunday.

The incision is six inches longitudinally on my upper thigh cut to the bone from which tissue was taken for the biopsy.

Today I went to Dr. Hall to have a fresh dressing put on the surgical wound and at that time he told me how narrow a call it had been. Dr. Rockland had told him previous to the operation that he didn't believe there was a chance in the world that it was anything other than a sarcomatous disease. He said that there was a remote possibility that it was lipoma but that in his opinion it was definitely an outside chance. Cam Hall told me today that his opinion was that it could be nothing else than cancerous and that he in fact had been prepared in surgery to remove that leg at the hip because he felt that it was the only way that I could possibly beat the rap if indeed it could be beaten. Dr. LaScola told me today that he had checked with a friend of his at Houston and described it and was told that there was a very remote chance that it could be benign because of my age and where it was and the rapidity with which it developed. There was very little chance that it was anything other than carcinoma.

So I have ducked another bullet. I didn't tell any of my friends about this while it was developing for it seemed to me then and seems to me now very good reasons. First, of course, there is absolutely nothing anyone can do for you prior to the operation and very little they can do for you after. If indeed it was the "bad one" they would be unnecessarily concerned to no purpose and if it was, as it turned out, benign they would have been worried for nothing.

Nothing has really changed for me philosophically as a result of this adventure. It reaffirms my previous feeling that life is a daily affair and should never be regarded as anything else regardless of the state of the world and the state of your health or of any of your personal situation. If you can have a good time now, have a good time now. Leave the sorrow till tomorrow because tomorrow may never come. Burma Shave.

MacDonald to Rowan

April 9, 1970

Dear Gimpy,

Now that was a very cold wind on the back of the neck. Have you noticed They are after us? Let us stay fleet of foot.

Dordo and I are both enchanted with Tom and Susan. A truly great pair. They were fun for us to be with because, unlike most people their age, they did not keep involuntarily underlining the age differential, nor are they frozen into pat attitudes and ardent conformity. Great honeymoon scene there—after all day in the Whaler, under the kind of overcast that burns you to a red cinder, the two of them were flat on their backs on a king-size bed, well apart, both spread-eagled. Bride reaches and husband screams, "My God, don't touch me!" Bride says, "I only wanted to hold your hand." And at lunch Tom said soulfully, "You know, it even hurt too much to smile."

They are so sold on the area, I think that when the Lieutenant is unsnapped from the leash, the Hook may get an earnest sales talk about the great need for a branch in this area.

About your ugly lump, I shall ever be amused by the fact that there we were, you and I, on Manasota Beach fishing, and you were bravely concealing your little worry, and being jolly, and I was bravely concealing the fact I had a brand new (and first) clot in my right leg below the knee, a son of a bitch about six inches long and ugly as sin. I was wondering how frequently they break up and start lodging in mortal places. So we were both jolly. Know what I noticed about you, pal? You were too happy and too easily amused.

All right. I have been doing the final-final-final-final on that damned #12 McGee, "The Lavender Game," and the reason I seem to go so slowly of late is that I am increasingly difficult to satisfy, I guess. Anyway, while plunging down the home stretch, in the back of my mind there was forming the belief that the Bora Bora movie proposition was like a three week trip to the dentist. I had that much excitement and anticipation about it. Talked it over with Dordo one evening. "Why do I feel that way, dammit?" What the devil would I be doing trying to fit myself to Bora Bora when I am so much involved in here and now and this place and time. Do I want to gussy up my work with smiling or unsmiling natives? No. Do I want to put myself under obligation to Mr. Fraser while finding out that it is not my thing? No. Okay, so the only feeling worth trusting is that little feeling deep down inside yourself that you are heading for a mistake. I have knocked it off.

Now I am informed by one T. Rowan that you are going to have to convalesce for longer than the time you can't stand up on the leg at all. And you should do a chunk of it down here, which is sense-making to the point where you can't hardly avoid it.

That "diary" made my blood run cold. I would miss you far too much, far more than you deserve, probably.

Yrs

Gimpy

Rowan to MacDonald

April 13, 1970

Dear Fleet-foot,

Our problem seems to be that when you think of writing to me I am thinking of writing to you and our letters get crossed. Yours are so much *neater* than mine, though. This is a shortie as opposed to a quickie, because I have to roust out in the A.M. at 6 to get to the airport for the flight to Reno where we open tomorrow night.

The plan for us is: we finish the 22nd of April in Reno, return here for two meetings which I hope to arrange on the 23rd, and then depart

24th for down there. Will stay there until somewhere around May 11.

No point in my dealing with the thrombophlebitis. You're smarter than I and can handle that situation brilliantly. I would caution you, however, to HANDLE it or I will be extremely pissed off.

PEACE

Dan

Rowan to MacDonald

June 4, 1970

Hi there,

We had two good weeks at the Sahara-Tahoe and are embarked on the theater-in-the-round tour. Opening night was a sell-out and the audience was great. The operators threw a party after that show that was replete with Washington celebs. Finally I met Sen. McGovern, of whom I've been a fan for a long time, Mrs. Melvin Laird who doesn't talk as much as Mrs. Mitchell, Jack Valenti, Sargent and Eunice Shriver, etc. We are going to have lunch and tennis with Ethel Kennedy on Saturday and with the Shrivers on Sunday. Hot stuff, huh?

The stumbling economy reveals itself in diminished houses for us. Business is down 30–40% in the D.C. area. We were sold out opening night, but ⅔ house last night and tonight. 2 years ago not one empty seat.

Time to leave for the theater. Don't like longhand writing, but will keep in touch. Next week Westbury Music Fair, Westbury, Long Island. Love to Dordo.

Peace

Dan

Rowan to MacDonald

July 10, 1970

Hey, Ol' John . . .

Are you sick? Are you sore about something? Are you just too excitingly busy to drop a note? Thanks for the birthday greetings—great picture of Homer—but I haven't had a word otherwise since we left

Florida. But then you know that, so I will get to some stuff you maybe don't know.

We got in this afternoon from our bummer summer trip. The last date was the best. Maybe because it was only three nights. Or because it was last. Business was just terrible, and the conditions on the road are not such that they make up for bad business. If it weren't happening all over and to others who are supposed to be big draws, a fella could have his confidence shaken.

The last three nights were played at the Broadmoor in Colorado Springs and we filled that theater every night. But we didn't do capacity in any other situation. Since we go into these things on a guarantee plus percentage it is necessary to do big business in order for it to pay. For us or for the promoter.

The summer circuit is made up of essentially two types of attractions. One is the typical book show, and the other is the personality show. Of the book shows this summer Man of La Mancha is doing the best and it is half filling houses that are near empty for such shows as Cabaret, How to Succeed in Business Without Really Trying with the original Broadway stars, Robert Morse and Rudy Vallee, George M, I Do, I Do with Bob Goulet and Carol Lawrence, etc. These shows are averaging 200 to 400 a night in 2500 seat houses.

It's the first summer out for La Mancha and it was expected to sell out. We have sold out the previous summers in tents and in-the-round. This year's biggest attraction is the Welsh singer Tom Jones. He is getting the giant guarantees and top scale prices. Dates are being cancelled starring him because of lack of interest and slow advance sales. Why? Because we are in a depression, my friend, and don't believe otherwise.

In New Haven, or Wallingford, Conn., which is New Haven and Hartford country, most plants still operational have cut their work force 30 to 50% and those still working get no overtime or fringe goodies. In the Baltimore-Washington area, where we worked two theaters, people are not only on short money, but are afraid to venture out of their homes at night. Parlous times, buddy, hard hard times.

We are both ecstatic to be home. We have just had a fine, quiet French dinner, will sleep tonight in our own big, comfortable bed and dress ourselves in the morning from our own closets and not from a suitcase.

Certainly hope things are okay down there and this silence is golden and not brass. You are, of course, under no obligation to write but you should know that if you don't I intend to come down with Homer and alternately do some ass-chewing.

This coming Thursday I leave for the Bohemian Grove and am looking forward to that.

So, Peace.

Dan

MacDonald to Rowan

July 20, 1970

Well now, Rowan!

Here I am back again among the living, the movers, the shakers. I got strung out something fierce on combining a batch of related short things into a novelistic structure without it being one of those things where the seams and joints show, and without it sounding as if I had hauled folk in from far left field to join the party.

I just sort of went underground because it took all available concentration to keep everything constantly sorted out in my mind. I think friend Dordo thought I'd gotten flippy. But it is now all on its way up to DogTurd City. It is the kind of thing where I do not really care now whether they want this kind of blend or not. I have learned lots about this trade by doing it in a very intensive way.

There is one in the current Playboy called "Double Hannenframmis" which is rough enough, I think, without being feral. And another one coming up in the same magazine is an okay one.

Dordo is just finishing reading proof on the October McGee. My clue to the depression you noted on the road is that my print orders go up. The unemployed read more, and when they repossess the television, there is little else to do. I am in a contracyclical trade, it seems.

I have a lot of curiosity about your bummer summer tour and other such arcane events. Sort of, what is a nice fellow like you doing in . . . etc. There is, in me, a kind of wistful feeling about trying to get involved in things that are not my dish. Now, in the closing years of my second adolescence I might even be getting smart enough to keep myself hauled back from such external idiocies, mostly by remembering that for me—sedentary though it is—this procedure of putting words together is where my action is.

Cheers,

John

A FRIENDSHIP

Rowan to MacDonald

August 10, 1970

Well, John . . .

Your welcome letter got to me at the Bohemian Grove the day before I left. We opened for a week, just ended, at the Sands in Vegas and returned home this morning. The Tour is over!!!

For two weeks at the Grove I did little other than drink, talk, listen, drink, play bridge, drink, tell bad jokes, drink, listen to worse jokes, drink, etc. Get the picture? I had a hell of a good time, met some very interesting guys and hope that I'll be able to manage my affairs to be able to go back again next summer.

Your letter had a happy, vital feeling that has been missing, and it's great to hear that your head's straight again. I read your Playboy piece (if that's what you're supposed to do with a Playboy piece) and found it a little spooky. Guilt is a bad hang-up, man. I reckon that if a fella knew how badly he was going to feel after a baddie, maybe he wouldn't have done it. Penologists will have the punitive answer to wrong-doing when they can figure a way to punish men's souls. I have always felt the Jesuits would make good wardens.

It's a very good thing to be home again. I have had a surfeit of motels, audiences, food on the road, discomfort, travel and attempting to make something different every night of routines which are endlessly the same.

Monday is the first day back at school. So . . . on Monday we start taping and will tape Monday, Tuesday, and Wednesday. Show No. 1. What's really cheering about it is that we have only 26 to do. Imagine that your correspondent just ripped off a ball-clutching scream. Not really a scream, more of a SCREAMMM !!!

The script is a good one, but could be show 17 or 29 of the past. Names have been changed . . . Goldie is gone, JoAnne is gone . . . but essentially it's the same. I have a plan. Did I tell you? Well, instead of working 5 days a week on this show, I plan to work TWO. The days we tape. The readings, meetings, rehearsals, planning, will be done without me this season. I want to accept some several dozen invites I have had to shoot at ducks, quail and other feathered game. I will sail several boats several places. I will play and practice tennis. I will get cancelled. Then I will sell everything I own and have enough to lay around for a year and a half. I will then kill myself. So as not to be a burden on the state, you know.

It is also my intention to write an account of the trip this summer, and to write an account of what Bohemia means to me. The first job may not get done because of laziness and the other may not get done because it has never gotten done yet and every summer right after the Grove I intend to write such an account and somehow never do. Why didn't somebody tell me to sit down and write every day from eight to five-thirty?

It's hotter than hell and twice as smog-polluted. Remind me to tell you of some of the interesting things heads of industry spoke of regarding ecology-environment at the Grove. Adriana is great. The dogs are thriving. My daughter, Mary, is now resident. She broke up with her boyfriend, the acid-rock drummer. I can tell you *that* was a disappointment to me. Talks now of maybe school, maybe a new job, etc. I hope your brood is well, and the pretty blonde lady you live with is even better. Love to all.

PEACE

Dan

MacDonald to Rowan

August 18, 1970

Dear Dan,

I will, of course, bug the hell out of you until you *do* write an account of the summer torment.

And I will pursue the script thing in a letter I will write to you later.

On Saturday, the 22nd, we fly to Halifax and spend a couple of days with children and grandchildren, and drive back here very very slowly in the old black station wagon they borrowed, stopping off to see relatives en route, so it will be a two week goof-off, amid the summer maniacs. But we shall be on little back roads, where people wave.

As Rod Taylor could not go to Miami to promote the film we went over for two days. Saw it the first morning, in a little viewing room with about forty newspaper people; from Florida, Texas and Boston. I was so convinced it would be utterly rotten, that I was pleased to find it only semi-rotten. They got pretty good bookings on it, like the nearly one hundred Showcase theaters in the NY area, where it opened four days ago. The sales guy told me he can fill the halls for the first night. From then on it's up to the picture to fill them. The gem part of the picture is a performance by a young heavy name of Bill Smith. He can really scare you. He is like an elemental force.

After the showing, we went aboard the cruise ship Sunward, Norwegian-Caribbean Lines, which operates out of Miami. A press party, drinks and lunch. Lovely little clean shiny ship—built in '66. I got along well with a bearded fellow name of Herbert L. Hiller, who is the Vice-President for Public Affairs of the cruise line. We turned out to have some mutual friends. He came up with a weird idea. Next May the fourth ship in their five ship fleet will be ready to join the fleet. They are built and outfitted in Genoa. They come over to Miami empty of passengers, with a crew of 100. He asked us if we would like to fly over to Genoa and come back to Miami on the empty ship. The voyage takes two weeks. I said Hey! He said he would check with the brass about it and we could invite two or three or eight or ten friends to share the experience. Imagine an absolutely empty, luxurious little ship all to ourselves. I am thinking that the MacDonalds could assemble a tidy little group for good talk and bad jokes.

Okay, so you told bad jokes at the Grove. Here is a bad joke. Man wants to shake up his golf opponent. Waits for the waggle and the beginning of the backswing. "Hey, Al, do you carry a bare-ass color picture of your wife in your wallet?" Guy stops, frowns, says, "Hell no!" Gets planted, waggles again, starts backswing. The hype artist says in a small voice, "Wanna buy one?"

Any girl who breaks up with a rock drummer can't be all bad.

No swimming, no fishing, no water sports in Sarasota Bay until further notice. During a switchover from one type sewage system to a better one, the installation people goofed and FORTY MILLION GALLONS OF RAW UNTREATED SEWAGE went directly into the bay. Folks hereabouts are terribly grim about it.

Best
John

Rowan to MacDonald

August 21, 1970

Dear Scrounger

The boat thing sounds sensational. All I have to do is figure out some way to come up with that much free time at that time of year.

Let me work on it and I'll get back to you on this thing and thanks for including us in such marvelous plans. If we *can* make it, we would love to.

Happy to hear you were not too disappointed in the film. There were a couple of trade paper reviews out here that were not too keen and they mean nothing. The ONLY thing that means a goddamn is whether or not people go to see it in sufficient numbers. I will try and see it instanter.

We taped the second of 26 (TWENTY-SIX!!! fercrissakes!!!!) this past week. My own feeling is that the deterioration I felt last season has speedily become decay. I don't think they are very funny and I don't like them and I'm not going to do a damned thing about them. Stupid? Probably. But in order to effect a change it costs too much in time and travail and maybe even $$$.

Some of our people are super, though. A new fella, Dennis Allen, is fine. Good face and funny moves. New girls: Nancie Phillips who may be as versatile as Ruth Buzzi and is prettier, Barbara Sharmer who is really playing Ruby Keeler I think. Others are there but the jury is still out on them. Some take longer to loosen enough to show us anything. Some of the new writers are funny and we should have a funny and good show. We don't. As I pointed out to Dick, who REALLY doesn't give a shit, it makes relatively little difference whether the ratings stay up or not or whether the critics like the show . . . I don't and I don't believe he does.

When we started this thing I *was* proud of it, as you remember, and didn't care then, really, whether it hit with the folks or not. *I* liked it. Seems to me a fellow . . . ahem . . . an artist, should be proud of what he does. Realizing as we both do that every goddamned thing you do can't be super, it should at least not be crap.

Mary went to an audition last week for the show. It was a cattle-call audition and she would have gotten picked no matter what, but *she* doesn't know that. Our choreographer and director were picking girls for the cocktail party sequence. She came home flying and more excited than I have ever seen her. Mark Warren told me later that she would have made it without me with no strain, that she's prettier and dances better than anyone else who showed up. Anyway she made her debut on the show and will be on show #2 which is the 21 of September, I believe. In the cocktail party, if you look quickly, she is standing alongside a man in a bowler who looks and is English. Long blonde hair and tall. Actually her hair is ash blonde and may photograph dark.

I made a new deal on a boat today, a Santana 27. It is full race-rigged and really moves through the water. It's smaller than Aisling but I should be able to sell her easily when I am ready and meanwhile she will serve admirably for getting me out on the water and also can be a fairly comfortable weekender at Catalina for the missus and me.

We LOVE this house. I guess it took the summer to bring it home to us that we love our home. It's beautiful this time of year with everything in bloom and the orange trees so heavy with fruit the limbs are near breaking.

That's the report from here, David. Hope your trip was fun and that you got some new ideas, that you and Dordo fell deeply in love with each other and yourselves, and that your troubles are minimal. Mine are, and I'm just enjoying the hell out of everything.

PEACE

Dan

Rowan to MacDonald

September 28, 1970

[*MacDonald had a heart attack twelve days earlier and was at that time in Doctors Hospital in Sarasota—an event not yet known to Rowan. It was relatively minor and MacDonald was out of the hospital and home resting by the time this letter arrived.*]

Well, ready for a surprise?

We are getting a few days off next month and are coming South. As you probably know, the Seiberts are in New Zealand or Australia or some such and on their way home are going to stop here and spend the night and we all will leave together the next day for Sarasota and that other good place a few more miles down the road.

I just watched the third show of the season with our guest star Goldie Hawn. You can say what you want about the show this year but it sure ain't funny. What it is is easy. Last week I worked one day and I am only working one day this week. George is having a BALL! No one to bug him, nobody to tell him, "That ain't funny, George" and we all go down the tubes together. Of course many folks say I am cutting nose to spite face but I seem to have this self-destruct don't give a shit attitude this year.

Nasser died today. Other considerations aside, politically and etc., the thought that hit me was . . . HE WAS 52 . . . I keep reading these items of guys in my age group popping off and I get more and more inclined to say Fuck it.

Heard a great golf joke. Don't know how it will write because when you tell it you must speak with a *very hoarse voice.*

Two guys in a locker room. Hi Fred, Hi Harry (very hoarse, etc) What's the matter with your throat? Well, Harry, this afternoon I was playing with the fellas and we came to the 13th tee and these three dames on the fairway waved us through. I smacked mine over a fence, into the field, you know, next to the 13th fairway and when I climbed the fence to look for my ball there's this broad over there looking for her ball and we both start looking together. We go around looking under cow dung and everywhere and I spot a ball right in this cow's ass. I lifted the cow's tail to get a better look and it wasn't my ball and all I said was as I held the cow's tail up, "Hey, lady, does this look like yours?" and she hit me in the throat with a five iron.

Tells better than it writes.

Haven't heard from you guys but I haven't written much either, have I? Hope you will be home during our trip. Should get there the evening of the 16th or 17th Oct. and will come home the 26th. Would like to sit and sip or whatever unless you're up to your eyeballs with work in which case you'll have to listen to my speech on what the fuck. Will call you.

                                                                          Dan

Rowan to MacDonald

                                                            November 11, 1970
Dear Sickie,

I have been meaning to write but when I've had the time I was feeling too cranky and usually I don't have the time. There is not much in the way of news. Adriana is excessively healthy, Homer is finally getting rid of his Florida chiggers and I am bravely battling my way through the miasmic swamp lands of Schlatter-Friendly Productions, Inc.

In the meantime I have been preparing my boat and myself for the Hawaiian voyage. Do the meridians of longitude run up and down or back and forth? Aw well, I'll just go to lower California and turn right. My love to Dorothy and my respect to you, sir, and I hope you're mending properly.

                                                                   PEACE!
                                                                          Dan

1971

MacDonald to Rowan

Feb 1, 1971

Dear Dan,

Life has been a confusion of late. My brother-in-law, age 49, having gone from top to bottom of civil engineering career in 3 short years due to booze, is now a brand new AA and my sister sent him down here to us to help him find employment. Dordo says it is as if somebody had thrown a sick bear into your car. His trouble is, we fear, more deep-seated than the booze bit. Anxiety, tension, the trembles, and compulsive dawn to midnight talking, all of the rambling reminiscent variety. He is in no shape, emotionally, physically, mentally—to seek work. But I have set up some appointments. IF he gets work, Dordo and I are agreed he will not keep it long—probably just long enough for my sister Dorrie to sell the house and move down here with their two kids (18 and 16) and my 78 year old mother, who despises Florida, and Bill's 72 year old mother before the roof falls in. Can and will provide money, but providing the emotional support is the kind of tension-making thing that the medics say I should try to avoid.

Sorry to have cried upon you. Anyway, Bill has his last appointment this afternoon in Tampa and then flies back tomorrow A.M. In the mail today came word a cousin arrives with her husband on Thursday for a convention here—the 5th through the 9th. But Dordo's brother and his wife arrive on the 4th with their Labrador Retriever, and we store the dog and on Monday the 8th the four of us fly off to tropical Grenada for three weeks of beach etc. I do not think I could really have taken all this other crap were it not for the thought of getting the hell and gone out of here soon.

Have sort of been marking time in some kind of professional personal sense, a fallow period of thought, appraisal, redefinition, a kind of delayed byproduct of the little coronary, and a definite product of my years, I suppose. A process of closing out all random noise and saying: What the hell am I *doing* here, and what the hell do I *want* to be doing here? I am beginning to think that it is irrational sentimentality to try to impose upon oneself this shit about walking slowly and pausing to smell the flowers. I am a worker and work is my pleasure and my nature and my way of life. So I think that what I shall do is wind myself up one notch below the spring tension of before, and get some of the exercise I despise, and stay off the weed. I shall try to stay out of doing things that bug me, but if I have to do them, if I get trapped into them, I shall extract from them the maximum amount of cash money and squirrel it away in a separate place and call it blood-sweat-and-tears money, and let it reproduce and support me in the style I would like to become accustomed to.

What am I doing? Complaining, whining and fingering myself. What a rotten letter!

We are in general agreement around here that the show where Joey Bishop was the guest was the first truly 100% dull show ever, with the following week a close second.

Please work hard these days on your navigation. Trying though you may be, we can't afford to lose you.

Oh, you might be pleased to know I came to my senses in time and cancelled that Cadillac. Back to the Fords forever. I really do not care that much about cars. If they go from here to there without drawing undue attention to themselves because of failure to perform properly, that is all I ask.

We shall be back here on March 3rd.

> Best . . .
> John

Rowan to MacDonald

> 4 Feb in the Year of the Boar

Look, John;

Don't apologize to me for a bitching letter after all the ones I have written you! Number One, or numero uno as you mexaphiles say, you got a legit beef, senor. If a deluge of family such as the one you're having, following hard on the heels of your other and more personally serious problems, isn't enough to exasperate the hardiest and most patient son, nothing ever will. Let me tell you a story which is not *necessarily* advice.

At an early state in my previous marriage I was overwhelmed with seven uninvited and unwelcome in-laws. I didn't have the space nor the funds essential to their comfort and desires, but being with a new wife and anxious to do the "right" thing by her and them, I put on a happy face and made a large effort to please one and all. It was, of course, impossible to do that. The more I tried to entertain, to listen, to laugh, to commiserate, the less satisfactory they found me and the more they demanded of me. Fair enough, I thought, nothing terribly unusual about that since I found out early on that the more you give people the more they expect and their satisfaction seems to dwindle as your efforts increase. But then I began to notice that they devoted a great deal of time to whispering behind my back . . . literally, John, whispering, and stopping when I noticed . . . and having quiet little conferences with my new wife, casting pitying glances at me the while, or, worse, stopping all conversation when I entered the room. I would ask brightly, What's up? They would give me wrenched and wintry smiles, saying, Oh nothing, we were just talking. I then knew that I had done wrong. I had let myself be used and had, indeed, become the social equivalent of the deposed stag, or the wounded shark.

I stood in the center of my living room with these people whom I *really* didn't like, nor with whom I had anything in common beyond accidental birth and marriage, and spoke firmly but quite loudly.

"Listen everybody. I want your attention. Get everyone in here. I have something to say and I want everyone here to pay attention because I am only going to say what I have to say once." This may not be total recall but is *very* near *precisely* what I said. Once the others were in the room and all silent and staring at me, I went on.

"I want you all out of my house at once." The murmur started. "At ONCE. Get your things together, don't hesitate to search for missing articles, they will be sent after you. You have five minutes, now understand this, FIVE MINUTES to get out of my house, all of you. You are never to return to this house without my express invitation, not once ever to come to see me or her."

Her mother cried, she cried, a brother who thought himself fairly handy bristled, a couple of uncles muttered, but they began to drift out of the room.

"Five minutes. That's all. Then those of you males still here will have to fight me, and I fight very dirty against these numbers. The women will be thrown out forcibly. I don't want to hurt anyone but will not be responsible for any injuries sustained in MY HOUSE four and a half minutes from now."

They left. On time, and yelling from the street and from their cars, not causing a scandal with neighbors because in those days the neighborhood I lived in made Hell's Kitchen look like Shaker Heights.

Okay. An example of invasion? An extreme reaction on my part? Possibly. But consider the alternatives, my friend. One can either "sacrifice" oneself or not, as one is disposed. But surely self-sacrifice should be thoughtfully expended and not wasted? King and country used to be sufficient cause and may still be for some folks . . . not me, anymore. The poor and downtrodden are still worthy of sacrifice for some people and I will pay my share of the burden, but *I* will be the one to name *my* share. No, no. Listen to *me*. Me the old campaigner and veteran of many private and public beefs. You pay the *big debt* for yourself, for your wife if she deserves it and yours and mine do, thank God, and sometimes for your kids but not always. That depends on your kids.

If you let yourself be invaded and used and physically abused and interfered with in the name of humanity, make damned sure it's in the name of humanity and not social convention. You have a chance, if you rest, exercise and all that other stuff the experts say you must do, to continue living, loving and enjoying. Interrupt or neglect that regimen and you make the final cop-out. And goddammit that would be stupid.

I am sure Bill is worthwhile . . . hell *everyone* is . . . and if the expense in your health and energy isn't too high, give him a shot. But only a shot. A tot. No more, no encores. It will not give him ultimate aid . . . that only comes from him to him however hard that is to believe . . . and it will cost you more than the results will be worth. The biggest problem you have, sir, is devising the word, the negative word, you lay on him. It must be clear but it also has to let *you* off *your* hook. Good luck with it and him and them. They're really *not* your final problem. *You* are.

I know how you and Dordo are looking forward to Grenada. And for three weeks. You will have at least one whole book in your head when you get back, and Dordo will have a sketch book full of ideas. Good for you both.

The outfitting of Seven continues apace, as they say. Today I dismasted her, purposefully, and have the mast at the welders for beefing up. All standing rigging is being increased in size and will be heavier and all new. The sails are ordered. I have installed a stern pulpit and helped put it in and have all stanchions backed with stout teak backing plates. All deck fittings have been torqued up and the boat in all respects I or my pal the expert can imagine will be the strongest and fittest Santana 27 in the world. I have agreed, under pressure from all quarters, to take a transmitter and a life raft. They will deny me some needed space, but will get some folks off my back. I refuse, however, to take any kind of motor because that's idiotic and unwise.

Next week after taping the 25th and 26th show of the season we wrap for the fourth time. Discussions are now on about renewal and with whom, etc. Too tiresome to discuss right now and still unsettled. And to me in this place at this time, uninteresting. We open in Vegas the 24th for three weeks and then home and Hawaii. Adriana is planning to fly to Australia and return via Hawaii to meet me there. We may then sail the Islands for a week or so and will probably come to Florida in May. I will have 5 more weeks in Nevada to work in June and July and then it's time to start next season's taping again.

Have a great time in Grenada and for crying out loud, John, shape up or you're going to be forced to ship out.

As ever . . . PEACE

Dan

Rowan to MacDonald

March 14, 1971

Hi, John,

Welcome home! The card we got from Dordo sounded ecstatic about Grenada and you must have had a fine time.

We are in our third week here at the Sands and everything is going well. Doing big business, audiences have been uniformly good, I haven't done any gambling yet, and the entire engagement is one of the better Las Vegas dates . . . so far. We did lose a pretty good friend in Jack Entratter last week, but that happened so suddenly we haven't realized yet that he's gone. I had gone to the fights with him Monday night and we all had dinner afterwards after the show, and on the following Friday we were at his funeral.

My departure date in the boat is now April 1, and I should be able to get fairly close to that. We will close here the 23rd and from the 25th on I have to get provisioned and the provisions stowed away, a final checkout with all weight and gear stowed aboard, and then if the wind is blowing, we shove off. I have been drilling myself in navigation problems, and have been able to cut my solution time from a half hour to about five minutes. Now that's on a flat desk in a level and unstressed situation. On my hands and knees, wet and cold, in a pitching boat, my time for solution is likely to escalate. I am in no doubt, now, about my ability to find my way there. If it transpires that we don't make it, we won't be lost.

I'll do more of a letter later. Love to Dordo.

PEACE!

Dan

MacDonald to Rowan

March 22, 1971

Dear Dan,

We *did* have a good unwinding time in Grenada. It even gave me a desire to improve my sorry physical condition, so as of this week I have given up smoking, drinking and eating . . . indefinitely.

You are really leaving on April Fool's Day? Do you think that old son of a bitch with the trident has that much sense of humor? We are both glad you are practicing navigation problems. Keep practicing. Pray in all known tongues. Take a fragment of the true cross. I read in Earl Wilson that Adriana is going to while away the days of tension in Saks. You may not be able to afford to make landfall, sir.

Glad the amount and quality of the audiences have been high at the Sands. I keep wondering if all the TV stuff impedes you when you and Dick have to get back to using improvisational flow and bridge materials to bring in your various set pieces.

Speaking of TV, we both bled a little for a guy we don't know, and we could only take 40 minutes of it. Arte seems like such a great little guy, sensitive and diligent and professional. How could he have let himself fall into the hands of those mechanical spooks who have never learned that television is an intimate medium, have never learned that hauling in Der Bingle, or Agnew, or Joan of Arc to save a show never does save a show, have never learned that the most sickening thing you can do to a subtle comedian is surround him with loud vulgar no-talent comedians reading bad material poorly.

I don't think he can spring back from a disaster like that Special

very quickly. It made me wonder—being of a suspicious frame of mind—
if somebody had set him up. It surely is a guarantee that he will be
still there in Laugh-In next year and the one after that.

Write. Tell Adriana not to worry about you while you are crossing
the briny because we are going to do all the worrying you can possibly
use.

Yr chicken friend

John

Rowan to MacDonald

March 24, 1971

Dear John,

We returned this morning from the four weeker in Vegas and we
are tired but happy to be finished with it. This will be a quick answer
and hopefully will be added to or another written at more length before
I sail.

Your conclusions regarding Arte's Special, which I agree with you
wasn't, are interesting. You see, Arte thought it was a great show. He
told all of us before air time . . . after shooting and editing and scoring
. . . that he finally had an opportunity to do his thing. He and his
brother wrote most of it and he personally made all creative decisions.
That's the way it should have been done, of course, because otherwise
if you are right you are right for someone else and not for yourself.
Arte was wrong. He has been wrong for some time.

He always felt that we never gave him enough time to develop his
characters on the show. I have always felt, and told him so, that these
characters on our show are cartoons, are cardboard people who cannot
tolerate longer exposure. If you walk around the back of any of our
people, there's nothing there. We designed it that way, and it works
in our particular genre very effectively, I believe. Dick and I watched
the show from our dressing room, had a group in and served Chinese
food and settled down to enjoy and were terribly embarrassed and
disappointed. Arte has said he will not come back to the show this
coming season unless George Schlatter is gone, which he won't be,
and as recently as a week before his special aired he refused any further
discussion relative to his return.

He can always change his mind, except we have to start setting
the show because we are going to have the writers start work in late

April or May and want to be ready to shoot a lot of stuff by the middle of July. The whole staff is being shifted around this coming season. More of that when we visit you in May. If you want to hear of it.

Glad you are feeling better and had such a good time down there.

Don't worry so much about this sailing trip. My God, the worst that can happen is I don't show up in Hawaii and there certainly has to be worse ways to go. I don't intend going, understand, but that thought is not so terrifying. My main concern is whether I'm taking enough to eat and drink and the right sort of equipment.

Have to get through a mountain of mail that has stacked up and Susan is sitting there at the other desk staring at me and wondering why she isn't typing this letter. Guess she figures it's dirty. Shit!— nothing dirty about it. Stay well, ol' chum, and I'll really try and bring you up to date on the boat and why I'm going and all before I leave. Love to Dordo.

PEACE!

Dan

Rowan to MacDonald

March 29, 1971

Dear John D.,

I am enclosing a copy of a note, article-type thing I have written to answer your and Dorothy's questions and a couple of other friend's questions about why I am taking this trip.

So far I am sticking pretty close to my April 1st deadline, although there are a few things which are hanging me up. If I miss it, I will miss it by a day or two and hopefully be off by the end of this week.

Very shortly after we arrive in Hawaii, we will have a short rest and will be returning home, pack a bag or two and take off for Florida. Adriana is most anxious to spend at least a month on Manasota Key, and my own anxiety to be there matches her own. We are both looking forward to seeing you both since that is always a good part of the attraction in making that trip.

Peace and love;

Dan

"WHY?" *by Dan Rowan*

Neither the boating nor the literary world is in crying need of another ocean-voyaging book, and in light of some of the courageous and seaman-like trips made single-handedly and otherwise which have been so well chronicled in the past it would be presumptuous to say "Let me tell you about my sail to Hawaii." Rather let me tell you some of the compelling reasons a man may have to attempt an encounter with physical and psychical reality by sailing a small fiber glass boat, which was not designed nor intended for such sailing, from Santa Monica Bay to Hawaii.

Modern society, in its most convenient forms, offers little to me in the way of challenge, or more properly, masculine reassertion. It doesn't help me to know that there are many men who need no such self-evaluation or confirmation. As a very young man I was stirred to patriotic fervor by the Japanese attack on Pearl Harbor and enlisted in the U.S. Air Force.

I spent something over four years there, serving my combat tour of duty as a fighter pilot in New Guinea. Although I have often said I wouldn't do it again, knowing what I do now, it would be dishonest to deny a certain thrill and visceral wrench to fly, to be shot at and to shoot at others. As a fighter pilot I depended on no navigator, gunner or other flight assistants to either get me to my destination nor help me get back to my base. There is an atavistic kick in accomplishing even that under World War II conditions in New Guinea. Hazard, personal danger, has a lasting effect indescribable to anyone who hasn't experienced it. Intellectually I *know* the insanity of killing, and the futility, waste and stupid character of War. But at a gut-level it should be recognized by those who don't have the personal information, as those who do have it know, there is a vitalizing and satisfying feeling of male-realization, of facing up to deadly situations, dealing with them, and overcoming them and your own fear of them.

War-time provides the opportunity for men to get this experience. Men playing real life cops and robbers must get it. I don't recommend it, understand, I'm simply telling you it is there for some men. If you can do without it, do without it. So the hazard involved in my trip is part of the compulsion. Maybe because 28 years ago I overcame fear, to be afraid again, to overcome it again, causes me in middle years to wonder if I've still "got it" what the hell ever "it" is. Who knows? That's part of it.

The alternatives for me are odious. They seem to me to be the choices for an old man. This trip is a hard one both physically and mentally. I expect to be cold, wet, uncomfortable and scared. Those are, somehow, necessary ingredients in the self-brewed mixture I have concocted for myself.

There are other reasons I find attractive. It is a great sailing trip. 2112 miles by Great Circle Sailing, we will probably make something nearer 2600 miles over the bottom before making landfall on the Kona Coast.

If the weather is good, we will have fine sailing with sun and warmth and quiet days and sleep-filled nights. If the weather is bad . . . we won't get as much sleep nor as deep a tan. But we will have *done* something. It will not benefit mankind at large, it will solve no international problems; it is a deeply personal, self-centered, and selfish search for a simple, honest, *real* experience. The first part of the answer has dealt with the more subjective and "hidden" motives of the trip. I have to assume that the idea of being on a boat, a sail boat, with no engine noise, no fumes and no vibration will be understood by almost everyone. There may be pollution of the ocean, as everywhere else, but there is not as much. There may be some noise there, but it is the sound of water against a hull, a bird's cry, the wind in the sails. Quiet sounds. Peaceful sounds.

My needs and requirements will become simple and direct and my filling them will hurt nobody, displace no person, disagree with no man's dissimiliar needs.

Escape? You can't. The world is going to be there, and the problems will remain for me when I return. A postponement? Why not? A prolonging of my time? Maybe.

But the really compelling reason is that I believe it is a great voyage, a beautiful trip, and, for a TV series actor and saloon performer, high adventure. We'll see.

[*Dan Rowan and two companions completed the voyage in his small boat under sail from Santa Monica to Hawaii on schedule.*]

Rowan to MacDonald

June 23, 1971

Dear Catcher,

No, don't spread your arms yet. I'm still hanging on and don't expect to get loose for a while yet.

As soon as I got home I spoke with Hook and told him of my decision to end the act with Dick. Hook said he had been expecting that but that I had told him 6 months sooner than he had expected. He was sympathetic and didn't try to talk me out of it, but suggested that when I tell Dick I should not cut him off abruptly but give him some time to adjust and I think that's fair. We have been a team for 20 years and the man should get *some* notice. We just came home from Tahoe yesterday and I didn't want to work two shows a night for two weeks with him mad, if he was going to get mad, so I waited until yesterday afternoon and then went up to his new Bel-Air home, which is a lush, well-decorated, expensive beauty, and told him my decision.

We had a long talk and he allowed as how he didn't find it a thrill anymore either, but that the money was so good he felt he could lower his head and go out and do it and collect the bread and forget it. I told him that I couldn't do that anymore, and that the money was not that compelling a reason for me to continue doing something that was distasteful to me. He knows how I feel about Vegas and suggested we pass Vegas but do some of the other things. I told him that I didn't ever want to walk on a nightclub stage again but that I would give him whatever time he thought would be fair to shut it off. That I would *not* sign the Riviera deal for the next three years, that, indeed I didn't want ever to work Vegas again.

Well, it was a long discussion and the bottom line seems to be that he will consult with Hook and determine how close he is on money and then he will ask me to play some dates to some date-certain cut-off time. In the meantime this week and part of next we will be working with Paul Keyes and some of the writers on the first few shows.

I spoke to Hook about your generous gesture of giving me the option on the three books. He says that it will be necessary that I have something from you indicating that I *do* have the options. I assured him that you and I didn't need any documents to bind what we say to each other and he shed a tear or two at such touching friendships but said that if he is asked by anybody to show them, "Oh, yeah, we've been had before by these guys who say they got this or they've got that, and it's bullshit when we get down to cases. If he's got the MacDonald options, fine, show me something."

Now this is entirely up to you. After all, it was your idea and I haven't any call on you. What we need, apparently, is a letter from you to me authorizing me, rather, telling me that I have your three books under option for film rights. Should any action from some unknown direction—other than what I stir up—show up, then I shall relinquish the rights back to you at once, of course. The terms on all or any are to be negotiated in good faith and to your satisfaction, naturally.

Both of us are well, hope you both are too. Don't remember where you are right now, but sooner or later you will be back in Sarasota, right? In the event you didn't hear . . . I won the court case. The law firm you sent me to was a winner. Thanks. Sorry for all typos but am writing this early A.M. and haven't opened my eyes all the way yet.

PEACE!

Dan

MacDonald to Rowan

June 25, 1971

Dear Dan,

That whole delayed scene must have been particularly agonizing. I bleed a little for you. We all make that special rationalization that we will take the money and use it to ease the discontent of doing something that irks. But that way, I guess, leads to the ultimate madness. I think there is such a close yet murky relationship between mind and body that if you keep on doing something psychologically distasteful, the body rebels and perhaps one stumbles and drops things. The medical wizards have been telling us for years about how emotions can create a climate of health or of illness. Years ago the French biopsied blisters induced by touching a hypnotized subject on the arm with a neutral object which the subject believed, in trance, to be white hot. The slices under the microscope disclosed specific trauma, cooked protein etc, indistinguishable from the slides of tissue actually burned. So I am wondering if it can go a step further—or step not so far—and have the body become less willing and able in responding to orders from

the brain when a person is actively and vividly discontented with the
life-vista ahead.

We finally found the magazine with One-Dish Adriana looking elegant in the elegant kitchen. And Dan, dear God, I had no idea you
kept such fat records of what is in the wine bins! Now that I am days
shy of 4 months without the weed in any form, I am able to get a
few little tingles out of the baked-out taste buds, and should the improvement continue, I may even get to think of wine as something
above and beyond a slow way to get plotzed.

I am sorry we did not find it possible to work our way loose and
fly out to Nevada. It went like this: I was presented with my medal
[The Syracuse University Ahrents Pioneer Medal], which is a big son
of a bitch about four inches across, looks bronze-like, but is doubtless
pot metal or brass. It has a strange bearded man on the front, supposed
to be a pioneer, and my name on the back. We rented a car without
brakes, took it back, and got one with brakes, and went to Utica, into
total turmoil. My mother got out of the hospital the day after we arrived.
She wrenched her back on the ice last March, tore nerves, now has
a spring lever gadget on her left shoe, is using a walker, has a nice
earnest girl who stays with her from 10 to 6:30 every day at her apartment. Actually, were she a lot younger than 79, spine surgery would
be indicated, but at that age she would be immobilized so long it is
unlikely she could ever get out of bed again. She is mighty petulant
about the whole thing because she has always been youngish and
active—playing nine holes of golf up until about two years ago—walking,
because she hates carts, toting her clubs because she hates those rotten,
smirking, lazy caddies watching her swing. Also petulant because for
the first time she is becoming a little less than sharp.

We find my brother-in-law, Bill, age 49, semi-blind with glaucoma
and cataracts, drinking far too much, yet being prodded by my sister
into negotiating (trying to negotiate) the purchase of a company that
does structural steel work and has a gross of $500,000 to $700,000
a year. At their urging I sat in on a meeting of the principals and their
lawyers, quite a Through the Looking Glass experience. Though Bill
has not worked in many many months, they have the big house, three
car, five television set kind of living they had before. Bill's widowed
mother is living in Syracuse. She has been giving them money to eat
on. We talked to her. She cannot keep laying out that thousand every
once in a while, because all she has for the rest of her life is the income
off about two hundred of them. But my sister was the most shocking
part of the whole thing. Rail-thin, with a big belly, sparrow legs, guttered

face, goggle eyes—endlessly loud, repetitious, belligerent, deteriorating in all personal habits, unwilling to comprehend that she is gone on the booze because I think that the mental damage is such she is no longer in contact with reality. She will not seek nor accept help for what is *really* wrong with her. In her view she is the martyr who is suffering all these slings and arrows, losing weight by worry etc etc etc. Their two kids are Susan 16 and Dann 19. So right now I am faced with the difficult fact that if I contribute money to them, I am merely making the day of inevitable reckoning that much more savage and merciless. The money right now would go into life-style, booze and mythology. Bill's mother is going to make any further donations contingent on my sister getting a job. That might lead to the final drop to bed-rock reality quicker than anything else. Then, when they are ready to deal with reality, Bill's mother will finance his eyes, and I will finance my sister's tour of duty at a bottle farm, get her dried out and see what's left of her. The girl Susan is staunch and good and resilient. And she might be the only survivor. Of course when the bad things happen, as they inevitably must, if they are too bad, I shall be unable to avoid the guilts and remorses. But what other way? There is no use in supporting someone's habit just to make yourself feel better.

Okay, we went on up to Piseco, to the lovely lake-shore camp in the woods which endured an indoor waterfall for many weeks last Nov-Dec when a pipe broke upstairs. Dordo's brother Sam had done endless work trying to make the place habitable. And it took us a lot of long hard days of brute labor to whip (we hope) the mold and mildew and sort stuff and throw out the ruined things, like three cases of books, etc. The idea is that we should get back up there this summer so I can be reasonably close to the deteriorating situation with my kinfolk and find the right time and the right way to step in. Aside from the damage the water caused, it was very beautiful up there, and absolutely quiet. Lots of black flies and mosquitoes. We tried to find somebody to fix the ceilings and the floor before we go back up. There is *no* depression in the north country. Every reliable builder and artisan has more than he can possibly handle, way into the winter upcoming. They are working overtime. We couldn't even find anybody to turn on the water. Sam had to come up from Albany with appropriate tools and we had to go under the camp and find the various plugs and seal the water lines, prime the pump, fix the line into the lake, then write out what we did so we can do it in reverse come fall.

When we finally left it to return here, we left it livable, if you don't look up or down. Just look straight ahead. We came back here to fix up odds and ends, find a summer home for the ducks, and pack up and drive the wagon up to the lake. I wanted enough time to do the revision pages for "A Tan and Sandy Silence" as requested by the publisher. So what happens after a week here is that my right hind leg starts to go bad on me. Long talk yesterday with the family doctor—about specialists and probabilities—leads to the conclusion I will most probably have to have the disc operation I escaped in Dec 1967. The son of a bitch *really* stings. Next week I see a neurologist, a neurosurgeon and an orthopod. Good people here, really. I have more confidence in them than I had in the specialist at Columbia Presbyterian who wanted to freeze my spine with ground-up bone out of my hip. And, after the Korp experience, I guess you would not fault local professionals, eh?

That leaves all plans in temporary limbo, and it is as if some evil genie wants to keep us away from Piseco in the summertime forever.

God *damn*, this letter reeks of cheer and joy!

What else? Oh, the red tide got so bad two days ago, leaving windrows of rotten fish on our rocks out front, causing a stench so tangible you could almost feel the waves of it—that poor Trampas, our lady duck, got to coughing. She coughed so long and so wrenchingly, that we were on the verge of bringing her inside, into the air conditioning, when the red tide began to ease. The last one that did this to us was in 1958, and the year after that, for some reason that defies logic, the fishing became very very good.

I enclose a document which should satisfy the Hook's legitimate and rational desire for documentation.

Pax & Pan

John

PS: When I returned my blue Dodge to the Hertz place at the Syracuse airport, there was a crowd at the Hertz desk. When it came my turn I told the girl that I had at last rented a car with absolutely nothing wrong with it at all. She beamed and said that was really wonderful. A man nearby was signing a car out and he said, "Hey, give me his." The girl objected. It had to be cleaned, gassed up, etc. I said it was almost full of gas, and it was dirty on the outside only. She still seemed reluctant. The man said, "Please let me share with this gentleman his unique experience." So she gave him the keys and he went happily off to take my great car out of the incoming lot instead of the outgoing lot.

Rowan to MacDonald

June 25, 1971

Hi there,

Working on the outline for the screenplay of "A Man of Affairs" with Vernon Scott, who has read and who loved the book. "I read it through the first time because I couldn't put it down and the second time to see how I thought it would translate to film." He, as I, think that it will make a good picture. There are some problems and I want you to know the way we have started to solve them, which changes your story a little and none of this will be done if you have *any* objection. Vernon and I had a short meeting yesterday, and last night and today I have been working on an outline.

When it's finished and you approve I propose to send it with a copy of the book to Ted Weiner and get an idea if he wants to finance and produce it. If not we start in another direction but I believe a book should be accompanied by either a screenplay or treatment that will show how we expect and want to make the movie from the book.

Peace,

Dan

MacDonald to Rowan

June 28, 1971

Dear Dan,

I *always* have too much going on in the books, so that if anybody tried to remain faithful to the plot they would either have a nine hour movie, or one with no time for any character development at all.

So what you have to do is jettison all the stuff that is tangential to the main line, or is not audio-visual, or is too much in tones of gray, or is a superfluity which can either be junked or combined with something else.

Very nice the way it begins to shape up, I think.

Catcherly yours,

John

Rowan to MacDonald

June 28, 1971

Jesus Christ! (That's exclamation, not salutation)

The recent litany of disaster has several Care packages, one neurologist, a Congolese witch doctor, a Navaho shaman, and three Kathryn Kuhlmann circulars on alcoholism on their several ways to you. In addition to this letter from me on my views in which I am the only one who ever seems to have much interest.

The problems your sister and her husband have must remain insoluble from the outside and you're on the outside. No way you can fix their lives for them and I imagine you will suffer the guilts because of that, but that's inescapable too. Somewhere within themselves must lie the residual strength which will defeat the booze compulsion or not, and their generally weak and ineffective approach to everything. There is always the horrible and hoped-against chance that you may be related to constitutional or psychological inadequates. Believe me, there is *nothing* anyone can do about those folks.

Now how the hell do you expect to serve as catcher if you're dragging your ass around on one bad leg? And because there is a good lawyer or two down there doesn't assure me that there's someone who can take care of your problem. I would feel much better if you were installed in a Mayo-type joint with all sorts of specialists probing, pinching, diagnosing and fixing in one place where all these great medical heads are in close huddle on each patient and not shuttling you back and forth across town and country with the corresponding lack in communication and thought. You don't need a pleasant bedside mannered gent here, nor one you rap with easily but the *best*. Don't fuck with this one, pal. Not now when the rainbow's end is in sight and the good fishing is around the corner.

I am having a longer meeting with Scott on "A Man of Affairs" and we should have the outline whipped into first draft shape soon. When that's accomplished, the circuit can be launched to see if I can get interest sufficient to form a company and get things started. Wouldn't it be grand if we could get everything in good shape by next spring and all head for a keen Bahamian island to start shooting?

Dick and I take off the end of the week for the Broadmoor date and, hopefully, that will be retirement time for the act. Incidentally

I find that I miss the beard something awful and have started it again. I am going to see how long I can manage to do the things I want and not do any of the things I don't want.

The plans for the next season are swinging and we have a chance to get back to the happy and fun stuff we used to do. Paul Keyes is great. He had a fine idea and one which he is going to be able to pull off. One of the first cameo guests he has lined up is Martha Mitchell doing telephone shticks. And he managed to get Raquel Welch for the first guest star of the season.

Thank you for the letter regarding options, it's just what the Hook needed. Take better care and I'll be in touch soon. Love to Dordo and I'm glad she's in good shape. Course you've *always* been glad she's in good shape.

Love and Peace!
Dan

MacDonald to Rowan

July 1, 1971

Dear Danroan,

I have a lot of interest in your views.

I do not need a leg for *that* kind of catching. Now if somebody dropped Lady Adriana to me from a second story window, I might manage to grasp her short of the pavement, bad leg and all, but You??? Hah.

Anyway, all of a sudden the right leg felt better, and then better and then better again. I think I am going to do nothing at all. Exercise as much as I can. We will go up to Piseco to be near the disaster area, and up there I can walk a lot and I am buying a rowing shell, and I cut a lot of wood up there usually. I have to be in shape for that Bahamian island.

You know . . . when I *did* go to the best, when I went to the Department of Neurology and Neurosurgery at Columbia Presbyterian, they wanted to freeze about four vertebrae. Lock them with bone meal from my hip bone. Twelve weeks in the hospital and then five weeks minimum in a NY hotel room before I could attempt to fly home. Screw that. I'd rather hurt now and then.

John

MacDonald to Rowan

July 3, 1971

Dear Dan,

Thought of a truly horrid name for a boat for you, based on the way people name their lakeshore cottages:

DUN ROWIN'

Incidentally, an old Hahvahd business acquaintance of mine was bugging me for a long time about how I ought to forsake this primitive village insofar as tax and accounting and estate advice is concerned, and turn all over to The Boston Company, where he is a large wheel.

So I finally told him how things are being handled and he was gracious enough to say that when he had the time he might come down and learn some useful things from the savages.

John

Rowan to MacDonald

July 13, 1971

Dear Catcher,

Dun Rowin' indeed! I knew you were cute, but I never thought you'd get the cutesies. It's better than Stop-Inn or Bide-A-Wee, but if you think I would ever put that on the transom of my boat, you have greatly misjudged me. Danada (a clever combination of the little woman's and my first names) is it and Danada it will remain, the better half's remonstrations notwithstanding. She wants to call it Adan.

Please thank Dordo for including a clipping of the victorious court case. I hadn't seen it. While thanking her for that, you might also tell her that I couldn't agree more with her estimate of your situation, and if you are as smart as I know you are, you will leave all health matters in her hands.

I am taking Tom with me to the Grove tomorrow, and although I have never been able to make you understand the Grove mystique, I'm really looking forward to getting into those redwoods.

I hope that you are on top of all situations, i.e., the bank, the relatives, the gimpy legs, and the new McGee revision. Tell me again which one is The Catcher. Every now and then after reading one of your letters, I run out into the yard, spread my arms and get ready. The rate you are going, I better hang on and get ready to catch.

The Alden Ocean Shell sounds super and if it works out, maybe we ought to have one in Florida to regale Sarasota Bay neighbors with our rowing skill. Have a good time in Piseco, hang loose and I'll be in touch with you when I get back.

PEACE!

Dan

Rowan to MacDonald

August 16, 1971

Dear Original Author,

To delay an answer to your long letter of 19 July [which was concerned only with a line by line critique of the screen treatment of "A Man of Affairs"] any further will convince you that I am 1. Lazy, 2. Disinterested, 3. On vacation, 4. Dead. Since I have given you a multiple choice, your decision won't be as easy as if it were True or False. Actually, if you answered this correctly, you would have chosen 4. Dead. I was interrupted during the Bohemian Grove with a call to tape show number 1. I then returned to the Grove for shows 2 and 3. As I told you, we have Paul Keyes back on the job, and Dick and I are anxious for him to succeed. Consequently, this has demanded more of my time than I had given last year. I have also been working hurriedly, and badly I'm afraid, on the ship's log of the trip. By the time I finish the first draft of that, I doubt that there will be any remaining interest in that trip, either on my part, or on anyone else's.

[There followed three single-spaced pages of response to Mac-Donald's detailed critique of the screen treatment.]

Now to more personal news and stuff. The Bohemian Grove was one of the best yet. I took Tom with me and he was an instant success. He has always been polite and those old guys just about ate him up. Tom has grown a beard and I was a little afraid they would consider him a "hippy" or revolutionary. He knows more members now than I, and has already been proposed for membership with plenty of men ready to sponsor him. He loved it and that makes me happy since I am so crazy about it. I can understand why you don't understand the

Grove mystique. Unless you experience the event this one is difficult to understand. Even then you might not dig it, but you would find it interesting and I would love to have you as a guest some summer when you feel you could take the time. Dordo could spend the time here with A. or could take off someplace on her own, or whatever. It costs a ton to take a guest so when you are thinking about it, don't do it for me, do it because you are interested.

I haven't any current word from you and therefore don't know where you are. I'll send this to Sarasota and also that other funny place in the event there's nobody to forward your mail. Wherever you are, I hope you are both happy and in fine health and doing what you like most.

Peace and love,
Dan

MacDonald to Rowan

August 20, 1971
Piseco, New York

Dear Dan,

This is from the remote address—and it is two full days further via airmail service, for reasons unknown.

[*There followed two single-spaced pages of comments on Rowan's comments on MacDonald's comments about the treatment.*]

It has been, Dordo tells me, seven years since we lived in this place in the warm months. The alders, swamp maple, berry bushes, etc, have turned the lake front to jungle, and up the long road, our woods are full of fallen birch and beech. To give you the visuals, until you have a chance to get up here, we have 400 feet of lake front, all rocks and evergreens, on the southwest shore of Piseco Lake which is seven miles long and averages a mile and a half wide, and sits down inside the old hills which surround it. We have 1000 feet of depth, and a narrow drive which winds downhill all the way to the camp. The camp is 20 years old this year, two stories, with heavy wavy-edge siding stained dark brown. Tiny living room, enormous native stone fireplace, long kitchen, my work room, bathroom, two bedrooms and bunk room on the first floor. Upstairs is a kind of apartment with kitchen but without bath which Dordo's brother & wife and our nephews use when we aren't here. We have electric heat, a pump under the camp which draws from the lake. We distill the lake water for drinking & ice. There is a small store and post office a mile and a half away, but any serious grocery shopping means a 16 mile trip to Speculator. It is so quiet at night it is spooky. Beau cat goes out into the brush and comes back with a shrew any time he feels the need. Marilyn cat is more circumspect.

Every day I quit work at about four to four-thirty and spend a couple of hours cutting brush and stacking it, to clear out all our old paths and picnic places. Fifty feet from camp is a tree house we had built. Actually it is a tower built on four phone poles, with two flights of stairs up to a ten by ten platform on top. It is a tree house because a nice tree grows right up through a hole in the center of the platform. It is as high as the roof peak, and a good place to drink and/or think. My Alden Ocean shell came, and it is one hell of a lot of exercise. It is great. Dordo loves it. I endure it. I would rather cut brush. That is exercise which you can look out the window later and see.

Thank you, sir, for suggesting I come as a guest to the Bohemian Grove some summer. I am going to file that good thought away and take it out for examination from time to time. I would want to make damned well certain that my motives were entirely pure. I have a reluctance to find out what it is all about. Why is that? Because it is yours, I think. I have this thing about people wearing people out. I could say this a lot better in person. People should have areas, the way wolves pee the circumference of their territory and mark it, and it is respected by other wolves. Do I get too fanciful? We feel close to you people. Closeness of any lasting value is a product of some kind of restraint, I think. I think that my fear is that if I did not react reasonably to the Grove mystique, something I cannot define would be lost.

I am a nut, forsooth. Twigs keep snapping in my psychic thickets.

Chin up,

John

MacDonald to Rowan

Sept 14, 1971

Dear Frangible Pedal Digit Type [having heard Rowan broke a toe the previous Sunday],

We saw The Show last night. I hasten to write you how delighted we are that so much of the old freshness of yore is back. And how good it was for the show to have you and Dick on for considerably more than the 8.3 seconds they had you cut to toward the end of last season.

Dorothy's brother Sam and his wife were here last evening to view it with us. In fact, he is the fellow who I enticed onto my roof to put up the 118″ aerial with which I now get NBC channels 2 in Utica and 3 in Syracuse in lovely Panasonic color. We laughed often in our tiddly fashion, slapping the thigh, saying Oh Oh Oh when the laughter was done. "The fly died." Good old Martha. Very nice.

So we got to talking about laughing and non-laughing and what causes same and so we watched Hope's labored hour, one of the weakest I've ever seen of his, the only real chuckle being when he asked the donkey about Lindsay.

Okay, so let's watch Schlatter's Wacky World. So we did. It was a perfect laboratory example of non-humor, of sad, embarrassing nothing. In fact, by comparison it made poor Arte's dreadful Special look like a rollicking joy. It was a dreadful moment for that special when they put in a little bit of the Tati movie, and people suddenly saw a fragment of genuine fun. After that, Jacques was badly misused. Trick shots are the worst thing you can do to a man who can use his body like he does. It is a matter of taste and balance, and why is it that after that funless fiasco of a couple of years back, Schlatter can be given use of the public airways to indecently expose shit like, for example, that motorcycle queen bit?

We sat around afterward and tried to decide on some group of people who might have found Wacky World funny, who enjoyed looking at it. Unless you get into the bit of retarded children who love to watch colors and motion without comprehending the meaning, there is *no* such group, not even a batch of drunken, middle-aged fags.

I can see a minor listing in future editions of the Guinness Book of Records. "In September of 1971 a television producer named George Schlatter took the final bit of fun and comedy out of people getting hit in the face with a pie."

Ah me. Life gets ever more unreal.

Speaking of same, I note in the New York Times, a notoriously unreliable sheet, that you have, or are about to be, welcomed into the family circle a simple, homespun refugee from Camelot. Those chaps seem to have the most fantastic run of luck, no? [Announcement of Peter Lawford's marriage to Rowan's daughter.]

Well, onward and upward with the arts.

All the best to you and your tennis player—

John

Rowan to MacDonald

September 28, 1971

Dear Vacationer,

Let's see. So much has been happening it's difficult to know where to start. Most of the hassle has been concerned with our old friend George Schlatter. As you know, we insisted that Paul Keyes come back this season and that George let him alone in running the show. Well, Paul has been working his ass off and the results are showing. The first show of the season put us back in the top ten, and it was a good show, and the second show was better than the first. It's better, cleaner, funnier, etc. George has been spending, rather *had* been spending his time on the shooting and editing of his TV special, Wacky World, and was not around much in the pre-production weeks. Then he launched a publicity campaign to push his special. Fine. The problem grew out of the fact that he couldn't restrict his national interviews to discussing his special, but had to start up again with the old beef about our show.

I begin to feel very Kafkaesque. For instance, Hook came over to the house one day, very excited, to tell me that he had spent the day with Bob Wood, the President of CBS, and that Wood was firing Merv Griffin and wanted R&M to replace. Offered a hell of a lot of money and a firm two year contract, pay or play. We are still under contract to NBC and can't make a deal anyplace else, but we didn't turn it down,

Hook wanting to use it as a negotiating tool with NBC. A reporter called me, in the midst of the rest of the brouhaha, and asked to have the CBS offer confirmed. As coached by Hook, I told him that we *had* been offered a deal that we were in no position to accept right now, but that we had not turned it down.

Kay Gardella, syndicated TV columnist with the Daily News, wrote about the trouble we were having on the show and said I had told the press about a big offer from CBS, and she had asked Fred Silverman, V.P. in charge of programming for CBS, and he denied any such offer had been made. Well, of course, I looked like an idiot and a terrible liar. Wood said to Hook that they would have to publicly deny it, and would continue to deal with us privately, wanted us very much for the show, but couldn't jeopardize future dealings with other people if we didn't make the deal, plus there's a restriction from the FCC prohibiting one network trying to buy an actor away from another network as long as the actor is still employed by that network.

With all this going on, we decided to withdraw from the field for a few days and let things cool and attack from a more positive approach. We hope not to mention George's name and if we do, to deal with it quickly and surgically, and then continue to talk about Paul, the cast and writers and what we are doing this season.

We are giving a huge "Hollywood" party for Dick and Dolly this Sunday and expect something over 200 people. Adriana is going bananas and is starting to get to me.

Regarding the forthcoming nuptials of my daughter Mary and Peter Lawford, I haven't much to say. There's damn little I could say that would have any effect, since the event is a month away. I hoped she would do better, but then my goals for her are different from her goals for herself. They have been going together for over 8 months and seem devoted to each other. Who the hell am I to say? I wish her well.

This letter has been too long in being written and is now too long in the writing. I trust you are both well and that your problems have eased since last writing. When do you go back to Sarasota?

Peace and love,

Dan

Rowan to MacDonald

October 15, 1971

Dear Returned One,

I am sure you remember a letter you wrote me in which you retired from the field of screen-writing, allowing as how you felt better qualified in your own department, and didn't know your ass about and didn't want to learn about writing screenplays. Well, I have retired from the arena also. Not screen-writing but producing.

The decision may have been unduly influenced by the fact that every sonofabitch in town is scrambling around trying to get a project going and all these guys have beaten me every possible way. They have the experience and many have fine track records and still can't get anything going. The situation here presently is grim and I count my blessings that I am working every week on TV. Actors, directors and writers here are selling their homes, borrowing money, and in every other way showing the attrition.

I have given a copy of "A Man of Affairs" to a bright young producer, independent, who has had success and has connections at Columbia and UA. He is going to read it over the weekend and tell me if he thinks it would make a good movie. Also what the chances are of getting something put together. He and I had a long lunch today and he filled me in on all sorts of deals, typical and unusual, and numbers and what can and cannot be done in today's film market.

There isn't time for me to go through what's necessary, and I am not at all sure that if I dropped everything else and took a year or two to develop this project that I have the necessary chutzpah and talent to bring it off. The reason to tell you all this is to let you off whatever hook you may have been on regarding these three books. If something else turns up that looks at all promising . . . swing.

Rather curious thing happened last week. Dick came over and said he thought I should make up my mind whether or not we were going to do any nightclub chores next summer, because the booking for preferential dates should be done right away. Curious because I made myself so clear when I told him earlier this year that I *didn't* want to do the act anymore. Later, a discussion with Hook revealed that Dick can use the bread because he has been pumping so much money into his new house and just before that had bought two apartment buildings and needed the cash. The income stops abruptly for both of us in January when we finish taping, and apparently his life-style calls for more income. Of course, I agreed to do it, and consequently will be doing the Lake Tahoe and Las Vegas number again sometime next summer.

If something commercially attractive doesn't develop before the time we finish taping, I think I will come to Manasota and rest for a month or two, and then take off for several weeks to Europe. The Dutchman would like to visit the tulip fields, I can try to find a dike to stick my finger in, and I would like a leisurely trip through the wine country in France and Germany. We are still intending to come down there over the holidays and if you and Dordo are in town, we will discuss this and other insanities at that time.

In the meantime, as they say on the TV talk shows, Dick and I are going about our business as all other scramblers do. We are seeking and doing interviews all over the place, and attending all sorts of gatherings to get our pictures in the paper, and generally doing the number TV folks do to keep their ratings up. And the ratings are up from the end of last season, but we are still not in the top ten. The NFL games are hurting us, but the results of the Paul Keyes change are gratifying and *we* like the show better than last year. We feel if we can keep the steam up that we can recoup a good bit of the ratings when the NFL season is over. See? I thought I would never give a shit about TV ratings, but it proves what everyone knew all the time . . . everyone can be had.

To keep from boiling over emotionally from all this crap, I am working out with a Phys Ed instructor twice a week, and doing it alone every day. I am in good physical shape and getting more fit all the time. Waist is down several inches, and weight is coming down fine, and I am moving some flab into the muscle areas. Look and feel better, so everything has a bright side, hasn't it, Uncle John?

Hope you are keeping it all together, and the time is dragging as I look forward to rapping with you. Well, just a couple of months and we can do that. My love to Dordo, and stay loose.

Peace,

Dan

MacDonald to Rowan

Nov 4, 1971

Dear Dan,

The reason this comes from northlands is because I thought I could come pounding down the home stretch on the book, but I somehow missed the clubhouse turn and galloped into the stands. So I backed up and tried again, took more time here, messed it up even worse. I have about 230 good pages which I will now humbly tote south and re-read and tread cautiously to the finish line at about 400 pages, I suspect.

We leave here Saturday, I think, and will be in residence at Ocean Place on Nov 11th.

Before I make further comment on yrs of the 15th inst, let me say that show number one hundred was splendid indeed. I was particularly knocked out by the lovely bowling ball operation thing, and the several lines about your beard when you and Dick were at your best.

I am astounded you are going to do your summer stock routine again, sir. But I *do* understand. And there is another aspect too, which I find myself prey to. It goes like this. There is something I really do not want to do, for reasons which are good, valid and comprehensible to me as well as to the people with whom I am able to communicate well. But the fellow who wants me to do this unmentionable chore cannot really and truly understand my reasons. He thinks them esoteric, self-conscious, artsy-fartsy chicken shit, and while he pretends to comprehend, and is even trying to comprehend, he is *convinced* that since a grown man couldn't possibly be that weird, there has to be some other reason which I won't tell him. So in the end I find myself doing what I vowed I would not do, just to prove to him that my original reasons were the only reasons there were, by God.

Your comment re Monday football makes me wonder how many of your audience, beginning in the Central Time Zone are refugees from Howard Cossell, who is, if you don't count Nixon, the most tiresome man in America.

We have a good yen to see you and ol' Wooden Shoes. Don't get too strong and fit. It reinforces the temptation to hit people.

Best

John

1972

Rowan to MacDonald

January 25, 1972

Well, sir:

Goddamit. I had hardly set foot off the plane after our Florida vacation when the shit hit the fan. NBC notified Romart that they would like to buy the show again for next year and although it is not spelled out in the letter, they let Hook know that they would be as much help as they could in relieving us of our onerous association with Schlatter-Friendly. That notification was also given to S-F and they have been told that the network wants the show back next year *only* if we star in it, that sole production by Romart is acceptable to them, etc. S-F realizes that we will not work with them again in any capacity and they also realize that *they* do not have a pick-up from NBC. The problem gets down to how much is it going to cost.

Hook spelled out a buy-out for the 6th season only with options for 7 or more at a quarter of a million dollars. The offer was refused and termed "ludicrous." We are still waiting for a counteroffer. So far we know from the agency representing them, they apparently want exactly what they are getting now. It is hoped that somewhere between our offer and theirs we can find a viable compromise, but we haven't reached it yet.

Meantime, we finish production this week on the final show of the original offer of 24; the writers have finished up and cleared out; and we can't make any overtures to anyone on the staff or in the cast since we don't know whether or not we have a show next year. Besides being of academic interest to you, this also means that my return to Florida is going to be delayed and might even be cancelled. It is essential that

I am on hand during all negotiations and at the completion of negotiations to be on hand in order to start an organization to work for the
next season.

We have not, repeat, have not cancelled plans for the European
trip as yet. The command performance in London at this state is iffy.
It hinges on the presentation that they want at the Palladium. It was
our understanding that it was a television variety show which we would
headline and, naturally, do a television performance. It now appears
that they want a gala variety show, parts of which they will film and
subsequently edit. This catches us in the middle because we won't
allow our nightclub act to be either photographed or edited and our
television material isn't strong enough for a stage show. We have stip-
ulated our position in a letter to the London producers and will know
more when we get their answer. If we don't do the command performance, *we* four can make our minds up about a visit to London
while we are in Spain or Portugal.

When I returned, Dick asked for a meeting with me in which he
presented a great deal of evidence he collected with aid of our agency,
APA, to explain why he did not believe the CBS deal was our best
approach to fame and fortune. We should continue doing our own TV
show combined with selected appearances at fairs, conventions, hotels,
work something like 40 weeks for the same money. Of course his argument has holes (e.g. the 40 weeks will fill the year because they
are not consecutive; the CBS deal allowed us time off during which
we would pay a replacement star à la Johnny Carson, Merv Griffin,
Dick Cavett, etc.). Since we are in the beneficial income tax years,
I have modified my position relative to doing the act to the extent that
I will take all fat, juicy dates for the next 2 years and grab as much
money as we can during that period and then head in separate directions.
I feel as if I have compromised the integrity of that fella who sailed
to Hawaii last year and who resolved on that trip not to engage in those
activities he finds unwelcome to his muse. But the here and now Dan
Rowan sees many financial obligations which must be met and the
possibility of clearing them up satisfactorily by dint of hard work and
unwelcome tasks by 1974.

This is a long letter in the writing and even longer in the delivery,
but I have just been too occupied to sit down and write sooner. Both
the Dutchman and I are looking forward to our European trip and I
trust your own ardor hasn't cooled.

Peace,

Dan

MacDonald to Rowan

February 1, 1972

Dear Sir,

You certainly are the lucky one! I have leaned back, reflected, scratched, stared at the ceiling, and damn if I can come up with one single inducement for S-F to change their demands, to lower their sights one millimeter.

Why should they? Time is working for them and against you.

What you need is for big daddy NBC to take a new stance, one that will turn them a little bit ashen and sweaty. What can that be? It can only be the End of the Show. A definite statement of intent not to renew. Then any negotiation would have to be on a new basis. (And you should *appear* to have a good place to go.)

Say, you know it might make the opposition *highly* nervous if you just up and came to Florida, wearing a mysterious smile as you leave. Chuckling a little, maybe. And brushing the lint off your CBS blazer . . .

Best

John

Rowan to MacDonald

February ?, 1972

Hey there, you with the sun in your eyes . . .

Since you asked me to tell you about the TV deal when and if finished, I will begin there. After a great deal of lengthy and sometimes quite bitter negotiations we made a deal whereby Dick and I pay S-F a substantial sum for their rights to the sixth year. This means they do not participate in the first run and re-run of any and all shows for the coming season. It doesn't affect their previous ownership. They will retain 25% ownership of the sixth season after the first re-run which means that if and when the show is sold to someone . . . all six years of the show . . . they will get half until the pro-rated 6th when they get 25%. They also get 25% of world-wide and we don't know what that amounts to but it isn't a hell of a lot since the show has never been translated and plays only in English-speaking countries.

It is tres cher, as they say, but the only and best deal we could make. It was made clear to us that we almost had to make a deal with them because the network's desire for a sixth year of Laugh-In was strong. Now we have our "back-up" deal for the 7th year. They do have an option, however, and if the unexpected happens and the show has a resurgence in the ratings they could ask for a 7th year, when we would have to negotiate again with S-F, and our own show would start on the 8th year etc. etc.

We were served public notice by Lily Tomlin that she doesn't intend to work for us next season. Neither Dick nor I feel a terrible loss, but the network feels she is essential and is fighting. We are making all the signs of vigorous pursuit but don't feel we could work in harmony with her since she has gone public with her beef. Her beef, as quoted, is that we have made inadequate use of her "extraordinary" talents and have stifled her creativity and abused the characters she brought to the show. She claims George was always very receptive to her ideas and we aren't. That is, of course, the sheerest bullshit since we are receptive to any and all ideas whether they come from her, the grip on the stage, a friend or wherever. She obviously feels she can make more dough elsewhere and wants out.

Paul Keyes and I have been looking at a great deal of new talent and have seen some very exciting people. We hope to get the cast set before another two weeks. The writers are all signed, and most of the staff. The heavy work is almost finished and I feel fairly secure about leaving.

We are sending you the itinerary as we have it planned now and should be fairly well set. Most of it will happen as we outline it in the itinerary barring accident or some such. We are going to be doing a hell of a lot of driving and one reason for A's excitement is the new car she is getting. I believe she told you she's getting the new Mercedes 350 SL.

We plan to call you and have a last chat before departure so will fill in the rest of the plans then.

Dick is recovering nicely from his hernia operation. The surgeon didn't put in the plastic pouch after all because he said that his tissues were strong enough to hold and the pouch wasn't warranted. He walks kind of funny but left the hospital two days after the operation. I am sure you will have no problem with your hernia operation and I hope you will be able to get some time off and maybe we'll get together in London or Paris or somewhere.

The damned phone has been ringing and I have to call Paul Keyes back so will wrap this, and again sorry to be so long in answering and letting you know what's happening. Love to Dordo.

Peace,

Dan

Rowan to MacDonald

March 25, 1972
Munich

Hi John,

Without a typewriter I am not only difficult to read but reluctant to write. This may surprise you but I would rather be on Manasota Key. We both caught colds yesterday. It's very difficult for me to sleep on most of these tiny beds, and the sheets—stuffed with something— are too short to cover my feet and shoulders and they also slide off all the time. The people are difficult to understand because of strange language and even when I shout a curse at them they don't seem to improve. Sometimes I don't think they really try. Part of their difficulty probably stems from the fact they eat very strange food and drink a lot. Their prices sound high but they issue funny money that can't be worth anything, so we are just scattering it around.

Yesterday we flew to Stuttgart and collected Madame's new car, removed the hard top, put on our heavy weather gear and she gave me a thrill ride to Munich.

On many occasions I have wished you two were with us because I need help in persuading A. to visit anything besides shops. That's not bad enough, but I bought her a wolf skin coat in Denmark and people stare so.

I sure wish sometimes I could write because, boy, a trip to Europe could sure make an interesting book. I'm going to have to do something to implement my income since I will have to buy an entirely new ward- robe due to a weight gain of around 25 pounds if it continues as it has started. It's time to go. *She* wants to shop for a new hand bag! I wonder? Does she know that Dachau is a suburb here. Much love to you both.

Dan

Rowan to Macdonald

March 30, 1972
Baden-Baden

Hi—

We've had four days here at this truly elegant, luxurious caravansary and have made side trips to surrounding points of interest. Leave tomorrow for Wiesbaden and then Amsterdam. Today we drove through part of the Black Forest, crossed the Rhine at Strasbourg, traveled south through Alsace and had our first 3 star lunch and the place deserves its rating. Still drinking fine local wine and beer and eating too much. I probably don't find the Germans a thrill because of residual hate from la guerre but, despite their neatness and discipline and cleanliness, I can't abide them. France looks more appealing all the time in all its dirt and inefficiency.

We've had the first service done on A's car and it was—as everything German is—too expensive. We have spent far more than anticipated in Germany and received less value. I miss you guys and Florida a lot and would love to lie on that beach in the sun. We still have our colds—some better—and are getting pale. Weather has been lousy. How are you folks?

Love
D&A

MacDonald to Rowan

April 4, 1972

Dear World Travelers,

Considering your colds (gone by now of course) and the ever lovable, charming Germans, I think it only fair to tell you that Florida has been between 2 degrees and 10 degrees ever since you left, with hard horizontal sleet storms. A huge tempest flailed the beaches, driving all the tourists inland and removing all the sand. People are choking with pneumonia and the birds are falling out of the sky. Feel better?

I don't know why you keep making these snide comments about the Germans. Who do you think made that great automobile you are riding in? Elves? The Germans are fat jolly people who dance and belch and slap their leather pants and yodel and so on. And they sing about how gemütlich they are. Well, you don't ever have to see them again, because *we* wouldn't go there even if they subsidized the whole thing.

I am pretty okay now, after having been felled by a miracle of modern medicine. It use to be that when one left the hospital the nurse put on a dressing so solidly that it was like welded in place, and it stayed there until you went to get the stitches out. Nowadays they have wonderful plastic stuff that is "ouchless," and that means it won't stick, so after the first night at home you have to hunt through the bed for your dressing, and then you find you have an infection. Three weeks from yesterday I can start picking up things. How many different smart-ass remarks can you think of in response to that, folks?

I go to Jacksonville on the 9th to give my little $500 epic speech called UNCLE TOM'S CABANA, and I do not go to New York on the 28th to get my Edgar as a (gulp) Grand Master, given by the Mystery Writers of America. Fawcett will accept for me, which breaks their tradition. So? We are both fine and we may punish ourselves by going out onto the beach and stretching out in the hot hot blinding tropical s-s-s-sleet this afternoon. We miss you. Write down funny things. I love funny things. Force yourself to think funny, Dan.

Love

J&D

Rowan to MacDonald

April 9, 1972
Avallon

Hi,

Earlier tonight we called you. The decision not to go to Italy was the result of several factors, not the least of which A. decided she would rather hear some Spanish guitar than watch Italians on strike. An eminently sensible opinion. We hope to be able to use Fielding's rental villa on Mallorca. But I'm mostly hopeful to find sun and exercise.

It has rained every day for the past 3 weeks and I have gained enormously, so look fat, puffy, pale, and am thoroughly out of sorts. I need your steady sober counsel and hope, selfishly, that you come to join us but will feel, honestly, that you'd be nuts if you did.

It's becoming more evident daily that my lady and I view life quite differently and it has opened a chasm which is sometimes past yawning and appears awesomely cavernous.

As my only catcher—the first and only I've ever had—you, or your ear, is sorely needed and *that* confrontation will have to be worked out.

Anyway—we shuffle along through these dreary days with an attempt, I promise you, an *attempt* on my part to be interested in shops, restaurants, hotels and countryside as seen from the car window. That's it—pal—no stopping at museums, galleries or such like.

Oh shit—I sound dreadful to myself and can't think what it must read like—stay well—hang on—Keep the faith, etc. etc. HELP!!

Dan

MacDonald to Rowan

April 11, 1972

Dear D&A,

I enclose a copy of the letter you didn't get in Reims. I enclose a copy of a recent letter from Nancy Fielding. It's the one I couldn't find while we were talking. I got all shook because we never got a phone call from France before, ever. It's pretty exciting, you know? That shows how secluded a life we live, I guess.

First, I will put in the kind of news I left out of my other letter. Our niece age 17 is paying us a small visit. Her father (the brother-in-law who's had the bottle problem and the eye surgery) fell down a flight of stairs and got back from the hospital a couple of days ago. He was in the process of starting a small construction business and we do not yet know how this will affect their plans. My agent, Max Wilkinson, stayed in Key West in a camper and he and his wife Mary left there over a month ago and drove back north. She got sick on the way up and she was in Columbia Presbyterian three weeks before they found out, this weekend, that she has polyarteritis nodosa, something accompanied by great pain, progressive irreversible paralysis, and, when not fatal, leaves the victim helpless. Max is really a helpless person without her. He is shattered. Though there is nothing we can do to help him, it is necessary to him to be able to phone me *very* often and weep. I just could not be tough-minded enough to place myself out of his reach at this time. It has been too long a relationship between us. And I think this is going to take every dime they have laid away.

The fates seem to be trying to tell us something this year. But a throng of kindlier wraiths seem to be saying that we shall all be together in a kindly country before too long.

Here is the way to get in touch with Temp Fielding. He keeps a staff at his place, of course. So cable FIELDING, PUERTOPOLLENSA, SPAIN, requesting phone number where you can reach him. Then call Temp. He has my letter re the four of us traveling together. Tell him we are home, sobbing. Ask about accommodations available at Mallorca this time of year, and no doubt he will offer the villa, which, after a small show of reluctance, you snatch at.

Well, damn it all, and love

J&D

Rowan to MacDonald

April 17, 1972
Geneva

Hi, there, fellow with the broad shoulders—

We drove to Geneva today and collected our mail which included, with your letter, a cable from Fielding's secretary with news to the effect that the villa has been sold and both Fieldings are away, sorry. But since both our mouths have been puckered for Spanish, we have made arrangements to board a boat in Marseilles April 25th for Mallorca. We have reservations at the Hotel Formentor. Same village where Fielding lives but in a hotel which appears to offer at slightly higher rates some of Manasota Key's advantages i.e. beach, tennis. We plan to stay there for one week, embarking for Barcelona May 4 and will drive north through Spain to France, through Bordeaux and Loire country to arrive in Paris for our rendezvous with Dick, Dolly, Hook and Pat, his wife. You are now up to date on travel plans and new itinerary.

We were both sorry to hear of the terrible tragedy which has visited itself on your friend, Max W. From so many conversations in the past which have included him we know how close you are. A terrible thing to have happen to *anybody*. When I think of the slight crap I've been concerned about and, characteristically, saddled you with, I wince.

I won't burden you with dull details, but in the event you're hanging on that last letter and possible denouement let me say that she and I had a confrontation the next day during which I gathered *my* balls firmly, stood erect, bellowed and cut off *her* balls (that never seems a permanent emasculation) and then gently listened for a spell and had subsequent and amiable reconciliation. This has eased the situation and made it livable.

This problem—and I hesitate to call it that in view of the *real* problems you're currently conversant with—is really a bit more than the jiggling, settling movements of adjustment married folks of 9 years make at times. But nothing to call forth your mighty powers for—*yet*.

Many congratulations on the Edgar. You mention it slightly, but I'm mighty proud of you. We'll have to breed my Emmy to your Edgar and get———what? A television show that's a mystery? No. Redundant. Maybe some aberrant form of mutant visual limerick? No. Too commercial. I give up. Edgar and Emmy couldn't probably have issue from union anyway being faintly hermaphroditic on both sides. I don't know what the hell that means either, John, so stop yelling at me.

We attended the grand affair April 15th I had been anticipating. A chapitre dinner at the Chateau du Clos de Vougeot in Nuits St. Georges. We were 550 at dinner which took 4 and one half hours to consume amidst much 12th Century music, 10th Century speech making, 7 courses of food, 8 wines. The dining hall was in the chateau's largest cellar, great stone arches and damp walls, gravel underfoot. Very colorful, interesting and too much for my longhand. I am so out of practice with manual writing my fingers cramp, my eyes water and I break wind a lot. It's much funnier to watch than to read.

Tomorrow we head for northern Italy and then to the South of France. These places really *sound* so much better than they are in experience. If we could somehow make Topeka, Caspar, Cleveland and Flagstaff *sound* better, we could improve the dollar balance and keep more Yankees home.

The news from Southeast Asia is too bad to discuss. Occasional glances at the Herald Tribune are distressing.

Please do all you can to stay well because you seem the psychic strength for a multitude. Don't forget something starts at home. Is it mental and physical well-being? You're a good man, John D. Don't let me nor other weaker folks over-distress you. My love to you both.

Dan

MacDonald to Rowan

April 24, 1972

Dear People,

We think about you oftener than you could imagine. We have aimed huge invisible rays in your direction saying things like Bless you, Shape up, Be happy. You are a valuable pair of people who relate and react to most things in good and similar ways, and we love you both. There is a very strange and corrosive malaise about travel in foreign places, and when it is not up to anticipation people tend to blame each other rather than the very deeply disturbing emotional trauma of travel itself. Forgive me for sounding pontifical and patronizing, but I have thought about it a great deal. Among familiar surroundings we can filter the amount of input we are willing to accept. The mind is asking a thousand questions about the environment every minute, and familiarity makes the answers so automatic that the mind can coast. But when the environment is unfamiliar, the answers do not come quickly, and we are thrust back into the overloaded input we knew in childhood. In childhood the energies are boosted to meet the great roar of input and change it into a learning process. As adults we cannot accept that total input. It is too great a strain on cognition and memory banks. So things begin to merge and blur and run together.

There is a great relentless irritability which results from the combination of great energy drain, and the awareness that one is not really coping with the input. On a subconscious level, we are violating one of the basic mechanisms of defense and survival when we can no longer handle the total flow of new impressions, regardless of whether those impressions are "good" or "bad." The ancient animal living inside keeps saying "watch out," but the conscious animal is aware of being too goddamn overloaded to cope with any more.

That is why many people who are competent in managing themselves and the things and people around them are willing and anxious to put themselves into the hands of tour directors and thus drop the whole decision-spectrum of when, where, what, food, drink, lodging, transportation, especially when many many places are to be visited in several weeks. A cruise ship takes care of the mechanics of travel also, and eases pressure.

I am not very good at going from place to place. I tend toward the savage snit. Our travel in the past several years has not been very wide-ranging. It has been, each time, a case of going somewhere and settling in and renting wheels and covering the same areas over and over until the blur is gone and you can really see the things and the people, and sit in a park and yawn, and then figure out which bar you are going to go back to this time, and which restaurant you are going to eat in. So I can find my way on wheels or afoot around Grenada, Oaxaca, Mexico City, Guatemala City . . .

Look, I am not trying to say one way is better than another way. I am just saying that the truly fantastic emotional drain of travel is not properly recognized. When you think that a full 25% of your total energy is used up in familiar environs with the act of seeing and interpreting what the eyes see, you get the idea I am trying to project.

I suppose that in one sense, an abrupt transition to another city where the language, customs, food, money, etc are all different is like suddenly falling ill with a disease characterized by fever, a sense of anxiety, a curious feeling of potential doom. So one waits the disease out, going a little further each day, staying out longer, risking a few more words.

Goddamn! I did not mean to start an essay on Travel. Maybe, analogistically, I was trying to say something about "in sickness and in health."

This week in Mallorca is going to suture the wounds inflicted back up there among the Klean Krauts. Believe me.

We decided that we would indeed come on over if the Mary Wilkinson thing got sorted out, and they said she would not live through last weekend (of the 16th). But she had a curious and unexpected remission. The pain finally stopped. She is still terminal, is hooked up to tubes for everything, and is entirely alert and aware. And talkative, despite being unable to swallow.

We are aware of your travel schedule now.

I have the dismal feeling that I not only write too much, I talk too much. My subconscious is full of dreary echoes of me, me, me, me, going on and on and on and on.

Anyway, it is *very* damned beautiful here. I had to say it.

Love

J&D

Rowan to MacDonald

April 28, 1972
Mallorca

Dear Temple Fielding (cum Santayana, Descartes, Plato etc)

The trouble with most of your philosophy is that it is so often in-arguable (unarguable?). Upon reflection, however, I am inclined to think that's probably true because it's rather general. I think that be-cause I am an arguable sort of fella. You might have said that those problems a traveler leaves home with are with him when he arrives at his destination.

Incidentally, not apropos of anything—an hour ago A. and I were sitting on the flowered terrace looking across a garden at the bay behind which a mountain was unsuccessfully trying to hide the setting Mal-lorcan sun—she sipping at the ubiquitous wine bottle—I nurturing my umpteenth cup of Spanish coffee laced with hot heavy milk when behind us from the hotel came an elderly American couple. He was wearing a bathrobe, the kind your dad used to have, flannel, red, with an em-broidered edge, over, presumably, swimming trunks—skinny varicosed legs which were whiter than your own head and she, sweet dear old tattered kindly thing—fresh from baking an apple pie—bottom crust just slightly burned—was urging him toward the swimming pool. Now we had investigated the pools. There are two of them, both beautifully tiled and both three degrees above freezing. The time was 6:30 and quite chilly with the sun going. Several locals looked at each other, grinned and rattled Spanish. A. and I remarked on his hardiness. Cu-riosity finally drove me to the pool area. This guy disrobed to his handy-dandy Sears nylon knee-length and posed, poised (I almost went for porpoise-fully but didn't) until she had snapped his slope-shouldered big-bellied skinny-legged figure for Kodak perpetuity. Then he fell for-ward with a chilly splash. He hadn't so much as dipped a *toe* in pre-viously, understand. I waited. He came to the surface—rather indig-nantly and said with a trace of hurt, "Well, Martha, the hotel brochure said it was heated." Maybe you had to be there, but it's the funniest thing that's happened on the trip.

Back to your welcome letter. The idea of overloading one's fuse with environmental change could be expanded universally to a diagnosis

of the raison d'être for violence increase—"The environment is becoming more poisonous and so is human nature." I *know* that's not
your meaning in this context. You are graciously providing a cop-out
for my ill humor and gracelessness on this trip. Incidentally, did you
read of the suicide of George Sanders? Big in the papers here as he
had been an habitué of Mallorca for years. I knew him slightly over
the years and thought him an amusing, intelligent guy. His suicide
memo said he was too bored to continue. My God! My first thought
was the high degree of complacency that would indicate. I can see
becoming bored enough to quit your job, move your residence, change
your friends, divorce, whatever. But there is so much I don't *know*—
and so many things I haven't done.

My problem primarily stems from the fact that I *knew* I couldn't
top Manasota Key. The money for this trip would have built my back
porch and bought a boat. I also shouldn't resist paying for A.'s education
of those facts.

Your letter helped. Your feelings were gratefully appreciated. After
all—you're the catcher.

Love to you both,

Dan

PS: As soon as my fingers unclench I'll write of the Mallorca Formentor—and the rest. It's 9:15 P.M. and A. is in bed. I'm going to start
Graham Greene's "The Comedians" which I have wanted to read.

Rowan to MacDonald

May 27, 1972

Hi there,

That's a very interesting flight, the one from London direct to L.A.
We took off at 2:30 P.M. and arrived at 5:30 P.M. PDT. Sunshine the
whole way for an 11 hour flight. We flew on the 747 and watched
an interminable movie, Mary Queen of Scots, and made use for the
first time of the dining room. Unless you have sat at table in the air
you don't know how uncomfortable those lap tables are. There were
also a few bridge players, so the flight went quickly.

The day before we left London Dick lost his voice, matter of fact
he lost it in the middle of the evening while on stage, but we had
finished most of our stuff and I was able to cover for the balance of

the evening. He thought it was laryngitis but it developed into a nasty cold the day they left, and Dolly got it from him, and Adriana got it from them. Fortunately someone had given Pat Hookstratten some decongestant pills which were effective, but those three have arrived home tired and with colds. I feel fine and am just starting to wade through 2 and ½ months' mail.

We have this weekend at home and the first three days of next week. During those three days I have two writer and production meetings and we introduce the new cast members to the press on Tuesday and spend Wednesday in the NBC photo gallery for pics with all the new people. Wed. night I fly to San Francisco to work on Thursday taping a thing for the Bohemian Grove Centennial and that night Dick joins me and we perform at the club in "An Evening with Dan and Dick," principally to let us rehearse with an audience and we fly to Honolulu Friday morning to perform that night and Saturday night at the Sheraton. This one is for money but not a lot. We needed a place to do the act with the new stuff and rehearse the old since we haven't done it for a long time. Fly back here for a Monday wedding of a friend and then go to Tahoe for that engagement. One day between Tahoe and Vegas coming home July 17 or 18 to tape the first show of the season. So there's the schedule.

It's too soon to really make any value judgment on that trip. It was, as is everything else I guess, good and bad. Those problems one has at home certainly travel well, remaining the same, at least with no diminution. But let me tell you of the Royal Gala Variety Performance.

Tickets are sold, or blackmailed, to the haut monde of England at exorbitant prices and is a sell-out. The Queen draws well . . . at least in London. The entire event this year was televised for the first time and there is a great deal of protocol surrounding that as indeed there is for everything else touching on the royal family. There are times when she *can* be photographed and more times when she can't. We rehearsed two days and on the day of the performance, last Monday, we went to the theater at 10:30 A.M. and were there until almost midnight. We did a dress rehearsal at 2 P.M. and the curtain went up at 9 P.M. for the show.

Curtain up. The national anthem. The opening act was a large group of British youngsters calling themselves the "Second Generation," singing and dancing and acrobatics. Sonorous Public School voice over, "Ladies and Gentlemen, Dan Rowan and Dick Martin." They enter from either side of the large stage, Rowan trying desperately *not* to look at the Royal Box wherein sits the Queen, Prince Philip, also Mountbatten, the Marquess of Exeter and assorted Royal Party invitees. He fails, but does not stare, just a fleeting glance to make sure she showed up. They do about 5 to 6 minutes of tidy appropriate material which gets far larger audience response than is warranted, and introduce "Phillipe Genty." This is an act from France in which several people dressed in black, standing in front of a black screen, manipulate various objects such as a feathered boa, etc. appearing to float in the air and is faintly received giving one the impression this audience wants more heady stuff which, following 10 minutes of the Genty troupe, R&M introduce in the form of one Larry Grayson. This is a screaming British type with very blue homosexual material which is greeted with large laughter and, granted the possibility one finds homosexuality amusing, it is funny.

R&M then introduce an act called the "Comedians," the current stage attraction at the Palladium consisting of six provincial comics who take rapid-fire turns at the mike with stand-up one-liners generic to their homes, i.e. Liverpool, Yorkshire, Lancaster, etc. They are funny, if difficult for the American ear. Following them, R&M introduce the Osmond Brothers, they of the Andy Williams Show fame. The British audience found them a little loud which worked all right since the interval followed the Osmonds, and all repaired to the several bars for hasty gulping of Guinness and such.

Not so the very nervous Mesdames Rowan and Martin who were taken to the Royal Box bar where they were introduced to Her Majesty and His Royal whatsis and were given a warm glass of champagne. This followed several agonizing decision days of what to wear besides the mandatory long white gloves. Need I say that the Dutchman was resplendent? Had her hair done by the Queen's hairdresser, had the mass of it done *up* and looked every inch the thoroughbred she is. True, she got smashed later, but was quite ladylike throughout.

Second half began with the Second Generation followed by a few R&M jollities leading to an introduction for Des O'Connor, a song and dance man of some considerable charm albeit limited talents, who stopped the show. R&M's appearance following him was interrupted by a surprise appearance of Roger Moore, he of Saint and The Persuaders fame. One of the world's most handsome men but a fun gent off-stage. He left and R&M introduced Liza Minnelli who closed the show to an ovation. There was a finale which R announced since M had lost his voice during the R&M Moore exchange. All members of the cast then standing on stage, they turned to the Box and as the audience stood the Anthem was played and all sung immediately followed by

yours truliest shouting "Three cheers for Her Majesty" and then "Hip
Hip" all the others responding "hooray" for the customary three times.
Despite feeling an idiot R delivered these directed words with verve,
you may depend. Following this there was great applause during which
Her Majesty bowed and gave that funny little restricted wave she uses.
Curtain.

Now there was pandemonium backstage as we were all lined up
according to someone's sense of importance. Well, not all, since the
acrobats and several others were on the back line craning necks, to
be introduced to ER II. Until then I was not nervous but all of a sudden
noticed a certain clamminess in the palms. Dick and I were first in
line and he was standing on the wrong side of me so that when Sir
Lew Grade, who had arranged the entire affair, came along just ahead
of H.M. he mistakenly introduced Dick as "Dan Martin" and I am
astounded to report that H.M. smiled at Dick, looked at me as she took
my hand and said to Sir Lew, "No, *this* is Dan. That's Dick Martin."
She held my hand for a time, released it and instead of moving on
as I expected, stopped and stared at me for a moment and then said,
"And you have come all this way to do this for Us?" "A pleasure, Ma'am,"
I gallantly replied. "Do you do this sort of thing often?" "No, Ma'am."
She waited. "We are usually too busy." I waited. "All this way," she
murmured. "It certainly was very kind of you." She hesitated and then
moved down the line and shook hands with others, stopping again
further down when she spoke to Richard Attenborough. A fine actor.
He had made a cameo apearance with the Comedians.

Next was Prince Philip who also held my hand a long time, and
then clapped his other hand over it and said, "What is this hideous
nonsense I hear your show is going off the air?" I was again very
surprised and stumbled in answering, "Not at all, Your Highness. We
start again this year for the sixth season." He dropped my hand and
said, "Jolly good. That show keeps me home." And from all I heard
rumored around London, the Queen would be glad of anything which
kept this playboy home. Well, there's more but it just occurred to me
that you're both commoners and couldn't understand it. Ho hum, must
buzz off now and polish my tiara. More later if you're good.

                                                                Dan

Rowan to MacDonald

June 9, 1972

Dear Catcher,

Here we are at the Sahara Tahoe and I feel as if I had been sent here for R & R instead of work. My mind is making that comfortable adjustment from the painful reality of The Trip to the fuzzier, happier moments of memory so that we can already "look back and laugh." I wonder if it is age which allows one to do this with such easy equanimity? Nothing in the event is as horrible as the before-hand apprehension of it and few things are as horrible in retrospect as they seemed at the time. But we are both tired and welcome this respite. This respite which would have formerly been called work.

When I was being persuaded to trod these same old boards again I stressed the importance to me of doing something which was new to the act and before we left for Europe Dick was most cooperative and we spent some time putting together some new monologues, then recorded them on a cassette and each took a copy of the cassette with us on the Trip. By listening to it at odd times we became familiar enough to know it fairly well and indeed used some of it in London. When we returned home we had arranged to play one night in San Francisco at the Bohemian Club to break it in and then we flew to Honolulu where we played two shows at the Waikiki Sheraton trying it some more before our opening here on the 7th.

In all we have a new half hour of stuff and it's quite different from anything we have done in person—before being more in the mold of the TV monologues. It gets less vigorous response but is better in some ways because of that. We became habituated to a form which we had, by circumstance, been forced to during our early years and never changed it. Before we became well known and were generally considered a supporting act in all but the smaller clubs, the customary situation found us opening the show for a famous singer. The audience didn't know us, had come to see the other attraction and we were seldom given more than 20 or 25 minutes to score. We soon found that it was essential to make an immediate impression and once we made it and got them laughing, to never let up for a minute. We became good enough at this to reach the point where we did indeed kick the shit out of an audience for that 25 minute period.

As we took over the headline chores ourselves and started doing more time we could never bring ourselves to allow any quiet time in the house. We started up and stayed there for the full show. Danny Thomas once told me that we left an audience too tired. He remarked that we had to learn to "play the rests." This new half hour gives us that change of pace. The material is good but is more thoughtful. Instead of hitting them with hard right hands all the way, we now have a few jabs. You have read into this that I am pleased with the way things are going and I am. Knowing myself almost as well as you know me I am aware that this may be temporary pleasure, but then temporary is better than none.

Matter of fact, it's your goddamn perception that causes so much of the problem. That, in combination with your compassion, is what gets you involved in the first place. That, of course, is why you're the sounding board and wailing wall for all your friends and is why . . . due no doubt to your friends' bungling efforts to handle their problems . . . you don't unload your own problems. Except on Dordo? I suppose none of us will ever know about *that* John D. I know *I* don't want to hear about *your* problems when it's so much more fun to discuss my own, but even I would listen, as I know others would too. Where do you go for catharsis, old buddy? Are you a closet Jesuit with a secret confessor to whom you repair with racking sobs from time to time? Interesting picture but one that doesn't focus real well.

My love to you both dear cuckoos. Stay loose indeed!

Peace!

Dan

MacDonald to Rowan

June 22, 1972

Dear Dan,

I was going to wait until I'd gone down and looked at Manasota to see what Miss Agnes did to it. But I don't know when that will be, and probably you had some kind of report on it already. You sit high enough, so probably the only casualty was your walkway.

There are better ways for us to get out of here than to leave in the cold dawn (the hot, noisy dawn, actually) with the road under about 18 inches of water starting beyond my oak tree and extending out to Ocean Blvd, with two cats loose in the camper because the two ducks were crammed into the cat carrier. We put the ducks in Howard Johnson's bath tub. They were noisy. They seemed to like it. They have been friendlier since our return. We were going to stay until it seemed that the sea might take the ducks and the automobiles. And the sea wall. It was bumping against the sea wall so hard it shook the house, and then going up into the air like half again as high as the palm trees. A very impressive sight indeed. This morning I phoned Max to find out how the hurricane was going up there. It was soon to cross Long Island. He said it was blowing very hard, and at the same time the son of a bitch was *still* blowing hard out of the west down here, covering all the windows with salt.

That is very interesting, about changing the material. Adriana told Dordo on the phone that your stomach hurts. Was that from changing the material? I wondered. Or merely the rich food and all. And thinking about the Queen. And so on.

You know, that was one fine letter too about the Queen and all. It would be for me a very difficult thing to have to introduce with any show of enthusiasm, a fellow such as that Larry Grayson. I find it so difficult to find homosexuality amusing. Also I guess I do not find it especially *dirty*, or disgusting or obnoxious. I find it inexpressibly sad. There must be a faggoty kind of loneliness which would be a very searing thing in the private moments of the heart, I would suspect.

I want to hear more about that dandy little Queen. When are you coming to tell us. We wait impatiently here (we commoners). I hope you haven't been such a fool as to wash your hand.

Well, back to the novel I am novelizing on. I go along pretty good until I read someplace about how much money Irving Robbins is making, and then I lose interest somehow.

Steady on, fellow

John

Rowan to MacDonald

August 29, 1972

Dear Catcher,

I have a further question which I had intended to ask you on the phone but the conversation was of such a different nature I didn't want to intrude it at that time. Gordon Wiles has developed a fondness for another of your works, "The Drowner." Is this committed? Would you be interested in his developing an idea about it? He has a couple of fair ideas on the handling of it. The rest of this letter needs no immediate reply, but he would like to know about the availability of that particular property as soon as possible.

We have finished taping 6 hours of the new season and although it's become increasingly difficult for me to be objective about our product, I feel that our quality this year is better than ever and that our shows will be the best we have done. Whatever the critics and/or the public think of our new season, it's a more pleasant chore this year than it's ever been. The atmosphere on the set is very friendly and warm, everyone is having a good time again, and I believe we are getting a good part of that happiness on tape.

Last night Rowan and Martin and their wives, along with Paul Keyes and his wife, were invited to attend President and Mrs. Nixon's reception at their home in San Clemente, La Casa Pacifica, or as it's termed among the Republican press, the Western White House. We picked up a pair of choppers in the NBC parking lot, flew to Camp Pendleton, and were driven by Marine sergeants down to the house. He has a beautiful spread there and the party was attended by something like 400 guests. Mostly Republicans, of course, but a substantial number of the Hollywood liberal contingent. Nothing meaningful happened politically, but it was very interesting and I'm happy we went. I was given a pair of cuff links with the Presidential Seal on them, and since I was unable to get 2 pair, I will give you one link and keep one link, since I know how anxious you are to have a Nixon souvenir.

Stay well, keep loose, and all those other unnecessary admonitions, and remember that I love you both and think of you always.

Peace,

Dan

MacDonald to Rowan

Sept 7, 1972

Dear Dan,

We are leaving tomorrow or Saturday for Piseco, taking Maria Luz with us. She will leave from up there September 30th. We will stay a while and come back down late October or early November. We are going to fly out to New Zealand from here in time to be there on or about December 15th. On December 30th we get on a boat at Auckland which delivers us to San Francisco January 20th or thereabouts.

Please excuse the delay on the news about "The Drowner," but I have been trying to find out from Max what the status is. I *thought* we got a reversion of rights after they plumbered it one time on TV, and Max is looking. Matter of fact, I shall get up from this machinery and phone him again.

Okay—he says he is of the impression we got the rights back from Universal after they did a two part TV drama. He is going to mail the proof one way or the other directly to you at Carolwood Drive.

I do hope it is free, because I think Wiles must be pretty good. I've heard nothing but good things about him.

It must be nice to work on a happy set once more. I hope you are able to delegate enough chores so that you do not overload yourself.

It kind of alarms me, you chumming about with that Nixon fellow. I would dearly love the cuff link. It would be a meaningful thing to have. I won't define the meaningfulness, however. I will buy an appropriate pair of cuff links and split them with you so that we can each wear our Nixonlink. I see one advertised which is (are) made of petrified, polished pieces of dinosaur shit. Give me your feeling about this.

I am getting over hives you wouldn't believe. A large piece of a tooth fell off yesterday. My hair is falling out. I cry a lot.

Best to your people,

John

Rowan to MacDonald

Oct 10, 1972

Well, dear friends,

Here, finally, I am. Regardless of style, mistakes and muddled thought, *this* one gets mailed.

You must surely understand why I didn't unload on you guys when this trouble began to develop. It grew very complicated and I am not sure that I, *now*, understand what and why. I did know the Dutchman was unhappy with me but I didn't know what I could do about it since it seemed to me that I had done everything within reason to make her happy and none of it was working. It was at about that time I gave up and after I gave up the attempt things came to a boil. But the night Dordo called, Monday, A and I had finished the second of two long chats on the phone and arranged for her to return the next morning from Hawaii, which she has done and we both feel much happier to be together.

Today we are planning to get in the car and start driving up the coast and have no destination but vaguely expect to see Big Sur and maybe Carmel. Depends on weather and mood. I don't have to tape this week so have the time to mend fences. I am writing this at 5 A.M. and when she wakes up and gathers a few things together we will take off.

We are losing in the ratings war this season so far. It does seem to me that we have had it. We were 28th nationally the first week, and dropped to 36th second week. Although we came up from there, I don't know the exact number yet for the third week. We were down again the fourth. And so it goes. We built a fairly solid group of fans but their numbers aren't sufficient to gather the healthy Nielsens. Nobody at the network has expressed any dissatisfaction, matter of fact they have strongly indicated they think this year's product is the best we have done in several years. That in itself is enough to convince me we have lost it. Bland and nice have set in and we could be the Nelson family doing a variety show. Why is this? Maybe because we have run out of things to say. That wouldn't be such an unlikely thing to happen, since we have done something like 130 hours of words. Within those hours we have done just about every subject, hit almost every institution, some several times, until now we are really not *saving* anything but shotgunning jokes. That in itself is not a bad thing, but it's not how we got where we are and it's not enough to keep us where we got.

This may be a faulty analysis on several grounds, but other than the obvious fact that TV shows all have their own end built into them . . . some have a life of half a season, some a little more . . . and that the public sooner or later tires of their toys, it seems a valid one to me.

It's time for breakfast, light packing, and imminent departure. This is the first letter . . . or anything . . . I have written other than jokes and sketches in a long time and it's been difficult to gather my thoughts. Everything I have touched on has something else to be said about it and I can't pull it together this morning. But for a long overdue letter it does put you in the picture a little and maybe I can loosen my head enough to write more later, if not . . . when I see you. You know of course how much I appreciate your concern and so does A. You're very lovely friends to have.

Dan

199

MacDonald to Rowan

Oct 16, 1972
Piseco

Dear Friends,

This is a quick dumb letter because I am trying to finish this book so we can get the hell out of here. It is too cold. This is an October they should have sent back.

We hope you had a good trip up the coast. I saw the NBC news this A.M. and it showed great big ugly mud-slides blocking the coast road at Big Sur. And I said to myself, wow, that is pretty neat for Dan and Adriana, getting to see those mud-slides first hand, right?

I think you guys are going to be okay. It is just that everybody gets some kind of fixation on exactly what his or her life is going to be, and love is trying to project for that other person that hoped-for version of existence. Then when stress diverts people, it is hard to sustain the continuing gift, and somebody says, "Hey, you're somebody else!" Nuts. You are the same person who did try, and can now try again, but from a better base of reality.

I have wanted to say something about the show this year, but I did not dare because I had the feeling you had bet too much on it to want to listen to amateur diagnostics, and I did not want to sap your strength in any way. You have not run out of things today that need saying. They are all around us. But the show is kind of gumming at the things it used to bite. And the "takes a look at . . . " is too much variety show musicale, sort of, without skit things with real real bite. I think that if you take some good bites, that word of mouth will swing back that section of the audience which has departed because they like to see the mess when myths are exploded.

Would it take a new writer or two? I don't know. But how about the absolutely impenetrable, disinterested, jargon infested little bureaucrats who are supposed to help people with problems? Some of the very worst, of course, are the dough-faced old broads who won't let you into the hospital until they get the whole form filled out. If she could be persuaded not to overdo it, Tomlin could do a good bit on delaying the admission of Dick to the emergency room. Exaggeration makes the point. Have him on a stretcher, bleeding to death. Have him give her a great wad of cash when she asks for credit references.

How long have you had this illness? When were you last a patient?

Another scab that needs picking is the corporation which has unctuous institutional ads about their clean clean production facilities, and then when nailed for dirtying the air and water, brings in experts who give the corporation lawyers their chance to get the whole thing thrown out. (Suppose the plaintiff's house and yard have been filled with hot tar up to the second floor windows) "I have taken samples of the substance to my laboratory and I am unable to state with any certainty (1.) How long the substance has been there, (2.) The source of the substance, (3.) The reason why persons unknown have stored the substance at its present location, or how they intend to use it."

How about the loan companies who want to "solve all your credit by letting us consolidate all your loans into a single easy monthly payment"?

I guess that what I am saying is there was a kind of laugh that you used to get from the kind of nervous shock which comes from having some monstrous inequity or great irritation exposed in public, when people thought it taboo to talk about it. And there are still lots of those around, waiting for Quixote. There are lots of kings who wear no clothes.

How about the savage tensions of living in a "retirement colony" which has the day to day mortality rate of an infantry regiment, where people don't dare make friends, only acquaintances.

How about the fact that the colleges which made a maximum effort to recruit bright black students on the grounds that the interracial mix would be beneficial to both races, now find that the blacks refuse to mingle with the whites, forming their own closed enclaves? This is sad and funny.

How about a TV interview where the lady interviewer does not realize that she is holding the wrong book and interviewing the wrong author, but is so intent on being charming and talkative, she rides right over the man's efforts to set things straight.

How about the primitive, organic-type commune which cannot exist without all the highly sophisticated products of an industrial culture. "How can I light a fire without a lighter, dummy?"

I think there are a lot of fat targets and you have to start to take some good savage bites at them. Anyway, I would like the program better than I do right now, but I do not know how typical I am anyway. We send love.

Best

John

MacDonald to Rowan

October 17, 1972

Dan, last night we saw the show and this morning I went up to the mailbox and grabbed back this letter to add comments.

That was a *dandy* show. That was the best we've ever seen this year. Really.

Overwhelmed by my own perspicacity, I watched it with note pad at hand.

Opening: All those shouted introductions by Gary something were once upon a time a parody of the way other shows open, and it was ironic and funny. But the parody is now long forgotten and so it has all become exactly what was laughed at on old Laugh-Ins. In these days of audio-visual trickeries, cannot some new way, or some new parody be devised?

Dandy gags the first five minutes.

Then why all those clown suits? What for? Production numbers. Bah. Humbug.

8:09—Another shouted introduction. Why the shouting, for God's sake? It merely irritates.

8:13 to 8:15—More good gags, some with a nice cutting edge.

8:15—Edith Ann [Lily Tomlin]. Gag, retch. No point to the monologue.

8:16—Three girls and the lion tamer bit. Very nice idea, except that apparently nobody was able to figure out a useful ending. So it went flat right when it should have been up.

8:18—My God, *more* clown suits. Did I miss something? Production numbers used to be parodies of over-produced shows. Now Laugh-In is getting that same kind of pansy elegance, that cutie-cute choreography that it used to make fun of. I do not think there are more than 17 or 18 people in America who want to turn on their TV set and see production numbers. Laugh-In *used* to know this.

8:20—Nice Jack Benny, Oral Roberts line.

8:22—And here are Dan and Dick all dressed up in early American with lace cuffs and all. There is something way off about that. Something wrong and out of balance. It comes off like kids dressing up for a party they are not terribly anxious to go to. Why? Because it is not necessary. Anything unnecessary is bad art. Could it have been done with just the powdered wigs? Yes. Would it have looked cheap? No. Would this policy make some costume people and prop people redundant if carried to its logical extreme? Probably. And then when we get to the party and see everybody in that Colonial rayon shit, it turns legitimate humor into *strained* humor. At a party a man can say a very very witty thing. But what if he is wearing a lampshade hat at the time and a diaper made out of a tablecloth? And he jumps up and down. It gets hard to laugh at.

8:25—Betsy Ross. The white flag line is beautiful.

8:29—All of America said "Sock it to me!" All of America said "You bet your bippy." Practically none of America is going to go around wiggling their fingers and saying "Pookey Pookey Pookey." The times Rowan has said it, he has looked as if somewhere inside he was dying a little.

8:32—Something went diagonally by. Printing. Princess Rose is rising, or some such crud. Paradox department. When it was unusual it beefed up a weak gag. Now it has become so tiresome-ordinary it turns a medium gag into practically nothing. They made you stop running it across the bottom of the screen because that is supposed to be used for emergency messages. But they didn't say anything about *carrying* it across the bottom. If they got some great girls, or people in animal suits or whatever, and had them (double camera thing, reduced size) walk across with the gag on a stick, or on a banner two of them carry, why, by God, once again we are beefing up a weak line through the means of presentation. Try it. They'll like it. (A guy on a tricycle in yellow rain gear about three inches high could pedal across with a short gag towed behind on a wagon.)

8:35—What's the news across the nation? The format makes it less endearing through familiarity. Needs some kind of permanent revamp. Don't know what. Think, think, think.

8:37—Canary Islands and Virgin Islands. Very good.

8:39—As with the lion tamer, more often than not this has no bite, which is a shame with such a fine springboard.

8:41—Bill Cosby imitation—beautiful.

8:44—Tasteless and dull bit with deaf old folks.

8:45—"Rochester, what have they done to you?!" Lovely.

8:46—Agent and talent, Old Man River. Okay.

8:48—Strip Poker—a gem indeed.

No comment about the continuing bits, hospital bed, etc.

But let me say that Angel Goode is a damn sight better than good. She is wonderful, and the material is like unlimited.

JDM

Rowan to MacDonald

October 20, 1972

Dear Catcher,

Your critique arrived today. I feel very lucky to have such a perceptive friend, and one who is willing to tell me the truth and then make suggestions. Possibly one of the reasons I like the letter and the suggestions is that most of them have occurred to me and have been made part of next season's plan. I will quote to you from my own notes about this season and also some of the ideas I have and will try to sell Dick and the network for next year.

First of all, and I know this will sound like cop-out time but can't help that, there are some of the things you suggest we explode lying on the editor's floor because the network won't let us do them for one reason or the other. The censor's philosophy is not a constant one; old people have suddenly become sacrosanct for instance. We are once again in that eerie area of broadcasting when 50 letters of approval can be outweighed by 4 strongly against. Especially if those four threaten boycotts of sponsors' products, or threaten petitions against the show. Many of the cranks know that this works and use it with great effectiveness. God knows that for a time the networks said, "Screw that group, let's get something said on the air," and we were allowed more freedom. Agnew maybe made the difference, I don't know. I do know that the news department is scared to death of him. But onward to your letter.

We did a salute 2 years ago to hospitals and I was very happy with it because we did the whole number on emergency admissions, ladies having their kids in the halls, wrong people being operated on, others lying forgotten etc. We caught hell from the AMA, from hospitals and also, happily, drew some fine mail from members of the profession.

I quote from a memo from me to Paul Keyes dated Sept. 24: "Must we *always* open the show with Gary and the billboard? Isn't there a visually effective way to billboard cast and guests? We have been doing it this way for a long time now, pal, and I would like to see a change."

Since then we have had several discussions about it and the problem arises from the fact that the actors and their unions insist on billing "on air" and translate that to mean "no" to the last few ideas I have had.

Re the clown suits. I asked Paul Wednesday where they were stored and when he asked my reasons for wanting to know I admitted that I intended to burn them. He understands that they are not to be used again. I have never liked productions and everyone knows it and for some reason I have *never* been successful in getting rid of them, unless you realize that I really have no right to unilateral decisions and haven't been able to convince Dick of this. His attitude is that everyone seems to like them so much . . . *he* doesn't . . . there must be some value to them. I have gone along with this but have written in my presentation for next season these words, ". . . production numbers will be parodies of production numbers and will not be a weekly feature at that. If there is a song number it will be used to kid that style of 'old variety' format."

Costumes. In a desperate search for a "new look" I do permit myself to be talked into them from time to time and always regret it. I will stiffen my opposition because I agree with your analysis.

I think, incidentally, I am going to have the MacDonald aphorism painted on several art cards and hung in the writers' offices. "THIS IS AN ART FORM. ANYTHING UNNECESSARY IS BAD ART."

Pookey pookey pookey is Paul's line and he loves it. Hell, I don't know. I grew very sick of "Sock it to me" but it caught on and I felt unnecessarily foolish.

The news *has* gotten predictable and familiar and I *have* thunk and thunk thunk and here's what I came up with for next year. There will be no news song nor dancing ahead of it. We will have a serious O.S. announcement and it will go "And now to the R&M news desk for a look at the week's news in review." There will be a blank time period of maybe five minutes left in the taping schedule each week and the deadline, 9 days before air (that's as close as we can get to live because of Canada where they air the show earlier than we do and it represents a big income for network sales) will be taped with an honest look at the *real* not fictional news.

"President Nixon denies any knowledge of the Watergate case." We go to *two* desks where both sides give their views, as funnily as possible of course, of this case. The two sides will be given on *all* controversy hopefully getting around the network fiat against political comment because of equal time.

I would like to see a minority look at the world's news, a youth desk, manned by somebody from the Free Press or Rolling Stones paper or some campus paper for *their* views . . . not *generally* but of a specific and real news item.

In a general sense I have thought our *average* was high for quality because you must believe me when I tell you that it is IMPOSSIBLE to throw a winner every week, week after week. The system is wrong and nobody should be expected nor contracted to do the same show once a week for year after year. It becomes more and more difficult to *do* the show, much less continue the weekly fight for something unusual and different. It becomes a fight to simply fill the hour, deadline by deadline. In discussion within the industry with other producers and creators I find that everyone has the same problem. Nobody *wants* to do shit, and as somebody very very wise said about TV, "They don't want it good, they want it Tuesday." Within that truism there is room and reason for everyone worthy of the time space to *try* to do better all the time and with the restrictions of network, sponsor censorship and dictates, it's remarkable anything gets done.

Okay. If you can't stand the heat, etc. etc. But I can't quit, I'm a star, he said. It's very funky and difficult for me to ride herd on Paul Keyes who gets to the office every morning at 7:30, works every night late and takes work home. He invests his guts. He is a proud man in addition to being a work horse, and if I lean over his shoulder, as is my wont, he would be justified in getting less done than he does and he could also tell me to shove it and we would be in serious trouble because *I* don't want to work that hard anymore and Dick never did.

This is a fast ball game and one must commit . . . over and over again. If your instincts are right and you've been faked out enough to learn the right moves there's a chance that 7 out of 10 times you will hire the right people, make the right choice, do the proper thing . . . but you must ACT. Then it's essential you let the play roll or you find that you have waited too long and the boat has sailed. That's a terrible mixture of metaphor, but I hope you get my thought. Once a season is under way, especially when there's as much content as on our show, it's disaster to try and change . . . at least to make any deep change.

I certainly have never thought to call you and say, "Hey, watch this one, it's my best." But we have done 128 hours of these jocosities and, man, that's a lot of one-liners and black-outs. This is not meant as an excuse for trashy shows, but I don't truly feel we have done any BAD ones. We have failed on many occasions to measure up to our best and every point you make in criticism is well taken and agreed with. No question about it, our fangs have become blunted and our look has gotten tattered. Maybe the next season will be better. Maybe we can refurbish slowly through the end of this season to bring it up a tot. We try.

Listen. I thank you for the time, for the thought, and for the love it takes to tell a friend he needs a deodorant. Not because *you* can't stand the smell but because he's going out in front of strangers. And it's helpful. How can I reciprocate?

Hope the book goes well and we'll see you in a month, God willing.

Again, Peace

Dan

1973

Rowan to MacDonald

May 16, 1973

Dear Catcher,

I really am sorry to have had to spurt away from the Key so precipitately because I had been anticipating a long chat with you both about my personal life and my career. Both these matters and my mood have improved considerably since that time of departure.

The situation on the show is still fluid due to the Writers' Guild strike. I have just learned that there is a strong possibility that the strike will be ended this week. The networks will then have to decide what date they prefer or can best manage for the new season's start. It looks now as if that will be the first of October. Historically the season always starts the middle of September.

The morning after my return Dick and I taped a bit of dialogue for the RCA people in which we were very vague in our plans for the special. Following the tape session, Paul, Dick and I had a long meeting during which the final decision was reached that we were going to use a straight vaudeville format in the special with a rundown starting with a Dan and Dick monologue into a big headline act, flash act, headline act, flash act, etc. We are trying to assemble a very high caliber, exciting talent roster, e.g., Jack Lemmon playing piano and singing, Carroll O'Connor and Jean Stapleton singing a tune from their new album, Steve Lawrence and Eydie Gorme, possibly the Smothers Bros. We are going to try very seriously to avoid shooting the show at the studio and have scouted several locations. If it can be worked out our choice at the present time is a beautiful new room in the Beverly Wilshire Hotel. We are trying to achieve razzmatazz amidst elegance.

There has been no abatement of enthusiasm on either Dick's or Paul's part about the format, so either I have stewed too long on it and am wrong or am dead right and we are all doomed.

The balance of my times before the Vegas opening May 29th will be spent with meeting and discussing problems with Keyes, playing tennis every day and maybe even getting out on the boat for short cruise. That pretty well brings you up to date and as soon as we know more about the series and/or special I will let you know. Please pay my fervent respects to Dordo and stay loose, old sport.

Peace,

Dan

MacDonald to Rowan

May 20, 1973

Dear Dan,

The way it is around here, the weather is absolutely great and there is a new creature in the house here name of Luz, pronounced in the Mexican fashion Loose. Fellow named Reb has a place where he raises exotic animals, found an egg that had rolled out of a nest, picked it up to toss in trash barrel on way to the house, except a bill pecked a hole in the egg and tapped him on the hand. That was last Tuesday. Luz is a goose. A Chinese White Fancy, sex unknown. All the inputs are open. It rides happily in any deep skirt pocket Dordo has.

I am plugging along on the Lippincott book, trying hard to get it done this upcoming week. Thus we go nowhere, do nothing. We stay home and goose-sit. The roster for the special is most impressive. I think that the way you and I spell DOOM is due to the totally professional awareness that when the marketplace is clogged with a certain kind of product, the thin chance of survival depends upon doing it either very different, or a lot better. And the one thing you have which is unique is Dan'n'Dick, a plus which must be utilized with a view to doing it better and doing it differently. All the agonizing was based upon that very simple equation of survival. I just hope to Christ you can change the insipid patterns of host-guest intercourse. Maybe I am alone in being totally sick of (1.) Scripted jocular banter, (2.) Jokes based upon the private life or public image of guest, (3.) Fanfare, hushed voice, forced sincerity—AND NOW WE PRESENT THE GREATEST TALENT IN THE HISTORY OF THE WORLD . . . One yearns for people to *talk*. Oh well . . . Glad you got your household help set up so fast. Maybe they will work out, even. New subject—Educational Television has been broadcasting unedited Watergate, 8 P.M. until the end of the tape. Great! It fascinates because it is a morality play and man has never tired of those. Also, it is a detective story. I found Mister Odle a likeable and persuasive young man, with a rare air of total competence. But I could not believe he would not have peeked at that file folder he was asked to take home. McCord becomes totally plausible only when you realize that his whole life has been styled to the retention rather than the dissemination of classified information. It is brutally difficult for him to wrench himself all the way around and aim in the other direction. He lets loose of the bits very reluctantly, not out of guile, I suspect, but out of habit.

You sound better in the letter, certainly. Take the best care, my friend. Keep me up on all.

Stay Luz

John

MacDonald to Rowan

June 21, 1973

Dear Dan,

I mailed "The Turquoise Lament" to Lippincott yesterday. Soon we shall prepare for the tub-thumping trip which begins in Detroit on July 8th and ends in San Francisco on the 25th or thereabouts. It includes Minneapolis, Chicago, San Diego, Los Angeles, Portland and Seattle, the last two optional. I shall send you the firm schedules when they send me one. I shall be at the beck and call of eager idiots, of course, but hope to be able to break free once in a while.

I have been thinking about you and hope that things are working out okay professionally. I thought of a good story idea for Rowan & Martin, but as you know, I am on strike. I will give you a hint. This would be a half hour or one hour depending on how they wanted to do it. The thing is that you are a team which researches and writes a popular Travel Guide. You are the good business head which keeps the enterprise going. Dick is the chief tester, researcher, taster, bed tester. If the bastards wouldn't be too cheap to make it all on location, it could be a fine series because it could be comedy, drama, and great visuals. You could go check on complaints, incognito. Go for scripting as apt and telling as, for example, Maude, and there could be a lot of things to say about travel, people who travel, service hang-ups, etc. etc.

What else is there to tell you? Oh, that Luz, the new goose, is taller than Duck.

Keep on beaming,

John

Rowan to MacDonald

June 25, 1973

Well Sir,

You will be in San Francisco at the same time I am at the Bohemian Grove which is not all that far away (about a 3 hour drive). If you are going to have any time in the city and feel like company it would be nice if you were to call me at the Grove and I will try and make arrangements to come in and visit.

The special at this time is still fuzzy because of booking problems and the lack of a total concept. I still seem to be the only one in the group pessimistic about this whole situation. None of us have come up with a great new or innovative idea on this presentation, so at the present time we are simply making an attempt to have a one hour special with big name exciting performers, e.g., Harry Belafonte, Goldie Hawn, Smothers Bros, Johnny Cash and several acts of the Rudy Cardenas type. I fought a good but losing battle to have this presented live from a beautiful Beverly Hills Hotel hoping to capture the excitement and spontaneity that is only present during a live show but our sponsors, RCA, felt the risk was too great and our network, not unnaturally, sided with the sponsors. There isn't really very much left to say about the television picture. I wish I could report to you that I had dreamed up a whole new concept that I was excited about but I am afraid that my mind has been channeled to Laugh-In ideas for so long that they're the only type I get. I thought of opening with the Music Hall Rockettes who miss a high kick and give us all a very graphic visualization of the domino theory with the last girl clutching the stage runners to bring them down, the stage runners attached to the curtain bringing it down, the curtain catching on the side of some set flats, bringing them down, over which a nervous announcer stammers "And here they are . . . " And Dick and I picking our way over the debris and the fallen bodies to say welcome to our show. Whether or not it looks funny on the tube it immediately smacks of Laugh-In. I am beginning to realize that what we did for 6 seasons wasn't Laugh-In but every fucking comedy idea in the world and I nor any of us will ever think of any new ones.

Your story idea of the travel guide researchers does not hit me. That has nothing to do with whether or not it's a good idea, it's just that at this point in time I can't get my head into any ideas for a scripted situation show about two guys writing a tour guide. It is certainly an elastic enough idea to be able to cover broad areas of entertainment and does have fine possibilities for visuals.

Vegas was as usual. I played poker and won for the trip. Adriana spent a total of 3 days and so we got along fine. I am currently in the process of trying to sell 3 Chesapeake pups and a Rolls-Royce convertible, having two teeth extracted and hobbling around on a cane from sprained ligaments suffered on the tennis court over the weekend. What else is new? Don't ask.

Dan

MacDonald to Rowan

August 16, 1973

Dear Dan,

This is an unplanned letter. My head is full of confusions due to trying to clean up and get out of here by Sunday, in the van, to drive to Piseco.

The new goose is great. I shall never again be without a goose.

I can guess that you are up to your hocks in confusions and alarums also. Hope thee has unfuzzed the concept for the special.

I explained to Adriana over the phone why I did not think it would be very useful to haul you out of the deep woods for six hours' time in an automobile just so I could gaze upon you in wonder and all that. It was one of your typical rotten publicity tours. The good part was the early morning talking to the drivers and the route men. The bad part was everything else. We went from Seattle to New York and I was pre-interviewed (!) for the Cavett show. I kept yawning.

Some of the newspaper things have come in and I find that in San

Diego I am five foot eight, have sharp blue eyes and a high-pitched chuckle. I *knew* it was a long trip, but . . .

Had four crashing migraines, and several fits of the uglies. Sarasota to Atlanta to Syracuse to Utica to Detroit to Minneapolis to Chicago to San Diego to Los Angeles to San Francisco to Portland to Seattle to New York to Sarasota makes for a shit trip. I bought us a lot of twenty dollar apiece lunches and thirty dollar apiece dinners to get even, but they haven't come through with the expense money yet. They did get so many reorders and in such quantities that after the initial 600,000 they are going back for 300,000 more next month. But I know damned well that would have happened anyway. "The Turquoise Lament," Lippincott, October, is an Alternate BOMC selection in January, and it is the choice of the Detective Book Club in January, and it is a selection of the Book Find Club in November. So McGee is a bit more respectable than I would like to have him, for the nonce.

I will not go into the weird maneuverings we indulged in in order to trap Reeves, Filmways et al into giving up the rights to McGee. Now I have them back, as of last Saturday the 11th, all movie and TV rights.

Now the people are lining up and we are hanging back wondering what kind of a deal to ask for, or even if we should make one.

I'm not really anxious to sell my boy to the Mafia because they might hurt him. But can they hurt him that bad, I wonder? I am sick of golden futures. I want some walkaround money now, while I am here to spend it.

Dordo says Hi, and she says All the Best, and Love and so on. Take care of yourself. Don't let them agitate you too much. Tell them that you are inclined to bite.

Stay with it

John

Rowan to MacDonald

August 22, 1973

Well, let's see . . .

I looked at the final edit of the Special yesterday morning and am satisfied we did it right. Better than that. I really feel that it could be said with some truth that we may have done for the TV variety show what we did for the TV comedy show six years ago. In a different sense, of course. That is although we haven't come up with a new type show, we have produced a show we feel indicates the way a *television* variety show should be done. I recommend it to you.

Not so incidentally, I am delighted, happy and unsurprised that "Scarlet Ruse" has been so well-honored. That's just super news. And I shouldn't worry about McGee respectability. It doesn't always go with popularity, e.g. Christine Keeler and all kinds of exotic humping.

Your trip for the publishers sounds fairly routine. Those are expected to be shit trips, old sport. I will be as surprised as you at your agreeing to the next one. I am sorry you didn't let me know when you were to be in SFO because I wouldn't have hesitated at the trip into the city to rap. There are several things we never got to on the last visit and are still hanging and these particular things are not easily discussed telephonically or through the mails. Later for that jazz.

Re: the selling of the McGee. Generally I am reluctant to accept or to recommend friends accepting participating percentages in movie deals. The bookkeeping is shady, the gamble usually not commensurate with the effort, and isn't a viable option when the future gold isn't as attractive as the "now" type. Beyond that, a total sell-out of *all* rights is okay with the exception for *future* works. That implies an obligation which can get heavy and reduces your own incentive for production. Such a deal may be a tough sale, as well.

The Dutchman and I are having our problems. As you know, she's currently on her way home from Australia. Should be back here this coming weekend. I have to say that I have enjoyed my bachelorhood these past weeks. More than that. I have *loved* my bachelorhood and haven't been as happy for some years. It's quite nice to have a free head when I go to work in the morning and have total freedom to do just whatever I want *when* I want and not to *argue*. Jesus Christ! I am so sick of fighting over bullshit.

But DAMN, old buddy. There's a lot of good, attractive, painless life out there and I feel age and shadows looming on the horizon and would rather have less hassle in my life. Well, as I said, she returns this weekend and we'll have to get some things sorted out when she gets home. Don't fret. For either of us. I'm happy as a clam and she's got herself together . . . she says. She tells me that she has found her "identity."

Let's see. I have a club date in San Diego next week and then open in Vegas the 1st for 10 days. Then I have a Dean Martin to do, another week in November at the Sahara and in the meantime hope to do a

whole lot of wing-shooting, tennis, laughing and loving, and start planning the start of our TV season in December for the January start.

My love to Dordo and have a great summer up there.

The same but more liberated

Dan

MacDonald to Rowan

August 28, 1973

Dear Dan,

Glad to hear about the Show. I kept being worried about it and
wondering how it was coming along. If you are reasonably satisfied
with it, then it must be okay, as you certainly are not the easiest man
to please I have ever met. Television is an intimate medium and they
have been trying to make it into Big Stage and Cast of Thousands for
years. Whatever you have done, they will begin the theft of it immediately, and all begin talking about intimacy, and personalized television, and coziness etc.

I am certain that it would have been a long wasted ride for you
to have come into SF to see a man who had been taken in tow by
idiots and wastrels, and who by then had become badly frayed at the
edges, and was concealing his condition by being terribly loud and
smartass and so on. All my defenses were raised high, and I was cow-
ering behind them, wishing I was home, safe and warm.

I value the words on the selling of the McGee. It seems to me to
be a useful approach.

Yesterday Dordo's brother Sam and I put together the old electric
chain saw and got it working. We fixed the heater on the Dodge van.
Changed a tire on the van. Fixed the Sears refrigerator by reading the
wiring diagram and rendering inoperative the two heaters that are
supposed to keep it frost free, but instead were keeping it warm. I got
my trail bike finished in Sarasota. I was going to put a big husky carrier
on the front bumper of the van. But that didn't seem to be too great
of an idea. I could see it bounding up through the windshield in case
of weird accident. I felt disconsolate and then suddenly I realized, "John,
for chrissake, if you *want* one at Piseco, you can ride in the van down
to Utica and *buy* one and have it licensed and put it inside the empty
van and take it up to the lake. And then you will have two bikes, so
what?" It was a sense of liberation that I could indeed do that if I

wished. But now I have remembered I promised one Rowan that I would buy no more toys. So I am asking you. Have you bought any? If you have, you rotten traitor, I can go buy the Utica machine. (Remember, sir, I had the trail bike kit long before the agreement. I had it a year before I took it out of the box. It got shipped to Florida by error. It was suposed to be sent up here.)

About all that other stuff, I just don't know. I will not get fretful. I get all tangled up in my endemic Calvinism which always says that for things to be good they have to be bad, and if they are effortlessly good, then it is some kind of self-indulgence which, in time, can corrode.

It is hot and humid and now we are going to go up to Speculator and see what is available at Charley John's Big Store. Then I am going to design a work bench for the new boathouse and go buy the lumber and *build* the ugly son of a bitch.

Oh yes, and start a book.

Have fun in San Diego, Las Vegas, Burbank,

Las Vegas and Burbank.

John

Rowan to MacDonald

September 27, 1973

Hi,

While glancing through the evening paper I saw your name in connection with an item about John Huston going to do a number on McGee. Sounds as if you're getting it together.

About the show. I won't cop out in retrospect. I think we did what we decided to do, i.e. produce an entertaining, colorful and tasty variety hour. We set out to build a car and didn't think it should look like a boat when we finished. I liked the show and still do. I no longer think it's as good an idea now as I did then, and if I were a single voice in the matter and could make that sort of unilateral decision there's little doubt that I would not do it as a series come January. Our ratings were not good and we got some bad reviews . . . also some damn good ones . . . and I feel it's not commercial and can't, therefore, be successful. This past Monday we had a 3 hour meeting here, at my instigation, with the four writers, Paul Keyes, Dick and me.

I pointed out that I wasn't interested in being a Monday morning quarterback and that I liked what we did but didn't think it was a success and wondered if anyone shared my opinion that we should maybe go in another direction. At first nobody did. Dick in particular. He has a big hard-on against NBC, not without justification, and said that we have a deal to do 16 shows and we should do them, save as much money as we can in production to get big profits, take the money and run. He said that we could then make a deal at CBS where they might appreciate us more and would stand a better chance. That there are so few people that they can get to front a variety show we are a cinch to stay in action. That we can count on getting a bad time spot and it won't make a fucking bit of difference what we do in the form of content, we don't have a chance with this network. And many other negative words to that effect.

My views, as I so stated, are that whatever treatment we get at NBC there's little evidence to support the view it would be any better at another network and that all corporate thinking is fairly well patterned the same. That when we decide that what we are going to do is "screw them" we may as well decide also to get out of the business. I reminded him and them that when we went on the air with Laugh-In they put us in the worst time spot they had, one with a 15 year history of failure for NBC and that we knocked off Number One spot in that time slot. It was then pointed out that we had a "new" show then and one that set everybody talking and that we have now done all we know to do in a provocative and spicy way and therefore there's nothing new to do. I said that there are other directions to go with TV variety than the simple presentation of acts. That we could enlarge on the concept and open it up and make it more interesting and more human. At this stage Paul said, "Well, you sound as if you have an idea of a different way to go. What is it?" And I laid out the Plan, using the people we had on the Special.

I suggested we could have a 2nd unit who would film and record the run-through and rehearsals. All of it. The money for this would be available if we only taped one time as opposed to taping a dress rehearsal and "air." That uses four cameras and my idea would use one on a crane that can shoot long, medium and close. And STAY OUT OF SIGHT OF THE ACTORS. It would not be long before people forget the thing was there and we would get spontaneity and the ad-lib quality we need. That we would talk to the performers about themselves, what they do, how they do it, why they do it, etc. etc. Outtake would roll, and we would splice this material into the show in editing. We would still have a performance from everyone but the audience would know more about the performer and what he was doing, and in my view, be more interested in it. Everybody began to get enthusiastic except Dick who allowed as how it sounded like a dull talk show messing up a vaudeville presentation and would slow it down to a crawl.

The discussion became a little heated and I sat back and let them run. But Dick was so negative about it I finally said, "Hell, there's no question that this will be harder and more work, so fuck it. Let's do the 16 and run." The others didn't go along with that. Dick said, "What the hell, I'll do anything you want, it isn't going to make any difference anyway." I was a little pissed off and haven't been ecstatic with the way things have been going for me lately and blew my cool and he blew his and the guys got embarrassed and he said, "What the hell did you ask my opinion for anyway?" I said, "Because you've got half the action and half the say." And he said, "Well, shit, go ahead, it's not going to make a bit of difference." And I said "Screw that! I don't *know* that this is a good idea that will work. It's chancy because nobody else has done it. Vaudeville is safe. You want to play it safe? We do vaudeville." He said . . . I said . . . they said . . . The bottom line is that Paul and the writers are going to kick it around and come back with opinions and technical problems, if any, e.g. union dues for stage crews who will be on camera? Do we have to hire actors to act like stagehands? And all that ridiculous bullshit. It's in the works.

You sound as if you're enjoying your trip to the lake. In answer to your ???'s about bikes and new toys . . . no. I haven't bought anything. I am bearish, as you may have guessed. You go buy the bike in Utica. And anything else you fancy. Anything you find fun, pleasant or even whimsical. You've got it all together well enough and deserve it all. I'm feeling shitty and getting sophomoric and that's a drag for you and worse for me so will knock it off. Stay well, love to Dordo . . .

Dan

MacDonald to Rowan

October 2, 1973

Dear Dan,

Got your letter yesterday. I hasten to get this into the mail. I don't know why I hasten to tell you something you already know. Maybe because you sound kind of eerie in this letter I have here from you. So the old saw I inflict upon you is that you are quite unable to eat more than one meal at a time, breathe more than one breath at a time, spend more than one day or sleep more than one night at a time. Also, to extend the old saw even further, I cannot imagine a degree of calculated mismanagement which would leave you with only one roof, one set of wheels, one bottle of wine etc. Always there will be choices. Even which tennis racket to use.

Interesting look at the conference. It all goes back to the basic idea that people *are* interested in the nuts and bolts of any profession. Remember The Violent World of Sam Huff?? I imagine that if you strapped the same kind of recording device to a prima ballerina doing Swan Lake, you'd get the same huffing, grunting, straining, thumping around. Everything requires effort to make it look easy. (Not that Sam ever made it look easy.)

The idea will work, especially if it generates a lot of enthusiasm within the group. And I suppose these past few years have been pretty abrasive on ol' Dick too.

One thing—well, more than one, confused me. If you are going to live in a house, why sell the great house? Looking for less upkeep and operating expense? I think that the uptrend of land prices and the cost of building would mean it would be worthwhile dragging your feet. Vague feelings that you ought to do this or ought to do that are pulled down to earth with a pencil and paper, right?

About John Huston I don't know anything about that at all. Three parties are remotely interested in McGee. One of them is a chap named Bautzer who is supposed to have some kind of connection with Huston. The Huston mention is probably some flack earning his bread. (What will I say about Huston today, dammit?)

I bought a beautiful blue bike in Utica. It is a World Voyageur, a Jap Schwinn, and it has toe clips and straps. I wish to report that if you come to a sandy road and wish to stop and get off, and forget that you have fastened your toe straps nice and tight, you end up exactly like the unknown fellow in the yellow slicker riding the trike in Laugh-In. It is slow, majestic, slightly painful and totally humiliating.

Stop sounding so bleak, will you? *These* are the good old days.

Best

John

Rowan to MacDonald

October 20 (?), 1973

Hey, Catcher,

How's it going. Two Jews and two Arabs were riding on a train together and the two Arabs had a ticket each and the two Jews had one ticket between them. The Arabs said, "How are you going ride two for one?" and the Jews said, "Just watch." When the ticket collector started through the car the two Jews went into the men's room and locked the door. The collector knocked on the door and they slid the one ticket under the door, the collector punched it and went on to the next car. When the two Jews returned to their seats the Arabs allowed as how that was very clever.

On the return trip the same two Jews and the two Arabs found themselves traveling together again. This time the two Arabs had one ticket between them and the two Jews didn't have any tickets. The Arabs said, "How are you going to do it this time?" and the Jews said, "Watch." When the collector started through the car the two Arabs went into the men's room and locked the door. One of the Jews went to the door and knocked and they slid the ticket under the door.

James Caan, he who played Sonny in The Godfather but did a better job in Brian's Song on TV, is our guest this week and a good one. A little stiff, as we have found most straight actors to be, but a nice fella. I had never met him previously and was surprised, as I often am, to discover how small he is. Motion picture actors always *look* so big on the screen. They also seem to receive more respect from the public. I have noticed for a long time that whenever I am in company with picture folks the public comes up to me and says, "Hey, Dan. How are you, Mr. Heston" or whatever. I know, I know. It's because they see me in their home and the other guys they go buy a ticket to see.

I have been sitting here at the machine writing down ideas for next season's show, which presentation will have to be made sooner or later to the network people who are really begining to wonder what we are going to do next year. I needed the break and thought I would chat to you for a bit.

What I am looking for is more comment and also something that will give folks out there a chance to talk about what we said or did the night before. We have become terribly bland and part of the fault is Paul Keyes, who is a sweet but non-confrontation type, and also the network has gotten very skittish. Little doubt it's the result of Agnew's attacks and the possibility of FCC's licensing control. We are becoming a vanilla custard and it bothers me, but there are so many things we can't talk about because they are running so damned scared. We have been trying to get a gun control piece on since the beginning of the season and they are so afraid of the NRA lobby we haven't been able to. Now I don't know one solid argument against the control of hand guns and we will keep trying but that's just one example of the problem. The network and TV critics scream for originality and would like to see something different but when one tries, there's no way they will help. I have suggested we take a one year hiatus at the end of this season but I am the only one who thinks it's a good idea. Dick doesn't want to, the network is afraid we would be in danger of losing our audience, etc. We have already lost a hell of a lot of our audience if Mr. Nielsen is to be believed. Variety shows are getting killed this season. Flip Wilson is the top rated variety show and is 15th.

We have been running second in the category and our high was 28 and we are currently like 37th. Never been so low and it's better when you're high. In the glowing words of Joe E. Lewis, "I've been rich and I've been poor and believe me, rich is better."

My mind is wandering from this letter back to my business and I will end up doing a bad job of both so will wrap this and go back to work.

I am going dove shooting in Mexico next week with some pals and looking forward to it since I've never shot dove and hear it's great game. Will let you know. Looking forward to Florida, I am. And you guys.

Peace and love and stuff.

Dan

MacDonald to Rowan

December 11, 1973

Dear Fellow!

What goes? I understand you are out slaying feathered friends.

We got back here a few days ago. Stayed too long. All the damned work I did up there at the lake this year, you could insert in a gnat's anus without discomfiting him a damned bit. I filled the circular file with deathless deadly prose, and returned empty-handed and more than a bit anxious about my lit'ry future. Like it has been turned off, maybe.

I understand further that you have sold or are selling the Carolwood house and moving to more open country.

Why don't you write me a lot of interesting stuff like you used to? Cat got your pen?

We saw the Carroll O'Connor thing. You and Dick were good, of course. And so was the guy who did the PR man bit, but I think he would wear that routine out after about 4 shots at it. What is the matter with Rickles? Is he some sort of psychotic? Is he coming unwound in some way? Goldwater is a nice gentleman, isn't he? Would that he had been elec . . . The hell with it. He wasn't and won't be. Would you settle for Ford? Or are you still under the Spell of the Cufflink?

Old friend, the world seems to be going to hell in a hand basket, to coin a phrase. Don't sell Manasota. Don't sell those two motorbikes that get 100 mi per gallon. You could become the tennis pro at the Club, right? The whole financial fiasco began to give me sweaty hands until I realized that by some careful calculation I can arrange to live well and die broke, if the timing is right.

Merry merry for now. Joyous yool.

John

Rowan to MacDonald

December 13, 1973

Has the cat got my pen? . . .

Shit, I don't know. I'm so fucked up in so many ways I thought it would be more appreciated if I *didn't* write for a spell, or until I had something cheerful, up and positive. Your letter has touched the nerve which needed touching to sit down and tell you what's going on here in the land of tinsel and magic. This may take a little time. Because first I answer your letter.

How can you stay too long in a place you like? (Piseco) Empty-handed or not that period of time had to have been fruitful. Your literary future is assured whether you ever want to write another line, but you know that. You will stop writing . . . and improving . . . I would imagine about the same time you stop breathing, so bullshit to all that being turned off crap.

We have not sold Carolwood but are gearing up to do so. Why?

Because I don't feel I can afford it anymore. Moving to the country? Maybe. The domestic situation here is so uneven that the move might be in two different directions. In that event I wouldn't be moving to the country, more likely to the water. Don't sell Manasota? I don't want to, but the lady says she doesn't want to spend time there and in the event of a split it would, along with many other things, have to be sold to get liquid.

Why don't I write you some interesting stuff? Would that I could. Rickles *is* psychotic but that shouldn't deter comics, never has. Settle for Ford? Of course, although I really think the country needed a Lincoln. I have never been under the Spell of the Cufflink, you asshole. I voted McGovern. I voted *against* Humphrey. I didn't campaign nor contribute beyond some money I sent to McGovern before his nomination. He would have been better than Nixon, but so would Attila the Hun.

Okay, that's *your* letter. Before I forget, thanks for it. I needed to hear from you.

My feelings about the variety show were simply that *if* it hit and would prove just what the country needed, great! The people around me were high on it and I was too in the sense that *if* it worked, my work load would be not only tolerable but desirable. Go in two days a week and rehearse and tape and all the other work done by others. We had some interesting ideas later about how to improve it and make it more provocative and interesting for a series, but the network never heard those ideas.

The network at the time said they liked the show. They never said otherwise, matter of fact, to this date. We kept hearing a lot of rumors near option time for current shows, rumors ranging from time periods for our show to which show we would replace, and we asked repeatedly for an order so we could start booking the show. Finally they came to Hook and said the only time period available was Thursday night 10 to 11. That's about like putting the Flintstones on at midnight. They knew we could not make that time work for us and it became apparent in subsequent discussion they didn't really want our show. They had bombed out with their own variety show NBC Follies and didn't have any confidence in ours. Whether or not they are right is moot. We are not going on the air this winter. We have negotiated a release in which they gave us some money and we will have to spread some of that around to people to whom we had made commitments. But we still end up with a couple of hundred thou each for our efforts.

We are satisfied with that but for different reasons. Dick is happy because he hates NBC, my argument that all networks are alike not-withstanding. I am happy because I didn't have the necessary faith and enthusiasm for the project anyway. We are currently arranging our coming work year into what appears to be 10 to 12 weeks in Nevada for which we will receive too much money, but will keep us from dipping into reserves.

In the meantime Paul Keyes has come up with a solid idea for a situation show which I am working on with him and it is a *good* idea we believe should be well received at CBS. Simply, I am a conservative Senator and Dick is a liberal Congressman from the same district and state. So we have the same constituency and problems. How they are approached from either side of the aisle provides the meat of the episodes. This will be written into a presentation and delivered to Bob Wood at CBS when the papers from NBC are finalized. We don't dare discuss the project with *anyone* yet because we have found that when you have any meetings out here it may as well be done in open forum because everybody knows of it by that afternoon and NBC could balk on our settlement. So, shhh!

What else. I don't believe you should be subjected to the domestic beef for several reasons. Not the least of which being your reluctance to know about it. We've found ourselves further and further apart on most things and I'm really trying to hang on and disregard the ir-rationality and crap that's coming down. The residual damage is going to be hard to estimate. The original deal I had with this lady is fond memory now. The good day is the one we don't have a knock-down drag out. One reason for my looking for things to do away from home. We are both happier apart. Just trying to be nice to each other right now is effort. Ain't that the shits? It may change and I hope it does, because she's a good lady somewhere in there. And I don't need another failure in my life.

I have to go and wrap some booze for the mailman, the trash col-lectors, milkman, 3 newspaper delivery men, gardener, some market people etc. I don't know many of these folks personally but they all seem to know me because I get Christmas cards well in advance of the season. Strange.

Are you staying nearby for the holidays? What are you going to power the van with [because of gas shortage]? Want to swap for a couple of Hondas?

Stay well and give my respectful love to Dordo. Merry merry right back at you.

Dan

1974

MacDonald to Rowan

February 20, 1974

Dear Dan,

This is in great haste. It looks as if Eleuthera is out for us. Very sorry. Seems I have developed some sort of skin crud. ("The heartbreak of . . .") Am having regular treatments, sleeping with hands in baggies, rubbing gunk on bad places here and there 7 times a day, must stay out of the sun and not sweat says the Dermatologist, also telling me that the best I can hope for is getting it under control.

I am going to go around tinkling a little bell and crying, "Unclean! Unclean!"

Sorry about all this. I had a sneaking desire to cavort with the billionaires, but maybe I would have grown too accustomed to it.

Looking forward to seeing you people.

Yr scabrous friend,

John

Rowan to MacDonald [six months later]

August 27, 1974

Hello again!

As I mentioned somewhere along the line, I would write when I knew what to say. If I wait much longer there is every chance I would *never* know. There is so goddamned much going on and none of it is good and there's no joy nor pleasure in dumping on friends. Let's see how objective I can be about all this crap.

You know that A has brought action against me. Against me, Dick, Hook and our corporations. She says that I wanted the divorce and so she took the initiative. A divorce is nothing anyone *wants*. It came to be the sanest answer to our situation for several reasons. When a marriage is over . . . as ours has been for a couple of years . . . both parties must share "blame." I believe it just didn't work. She has changed a great deal from the girl I married and I couldn't handle her new "identity." I didn't want a divorce. I wanted my female, willing, compliant, non-combative, dependent, absorbed-in-me girl back. As A. said very forcibly, that girl is gone and there's a "woman" in her place who knows her mind and is fiercely her own person. I am strongly in favor of everyone being their own person. I just made a different deal. I really feel that she's got a great deal going for her in her new role and there's undoubtedly thousands of men who need that type. I don't.

That's all pretty general, but without going into gross detail I believe that's a fair summary of what happened. I also believe I tried, tried very hard. It didn't work. Having no wish to remarry, not being in love with anyone else, for that matter not seeing anyone else regularly, a separate maintenance would have done for me. Not fair for her, though, since she's only 32, young and healthy and wants kids. So . . . divorce. But it's turned very ugly, I am sorry to say. Extremely ugly.

She's trying to injure me. Where it counts, economically. I instructed counsel that I would give her a lump sum for a quit claim on my life with no future or further claims. For that I would expect her to settle with no arguments, fights, splitting dishes and chairs, etc. I also don't want anyone to have a lien on my future. She has sued for half of everything I own separately and for substantial alimony with no cut-off date, as well as a large *down payment* toward her attorney's fees and court costs. She claims I had no real estate and $5000 when she married me and that as a result of her help and guidance I had a successful career and became a millionaire.

The facts are: When I married her I moved her into a house in Beverly Hills—in my name—and owned a house in Hollywood which I had leased out—in my name—and a net worth of something over $250,000. I had spent 12 years with Mr. Martin during which time we had progressed through our training and apprenticeship in this business to the point where we were headlined at the Copa, at Vegas and getting top fees as guest stars on TV variety shows. Had made a picture at Universal, starring, and were on our way quite nicely. She has never done a day's work nor wanted for anything materially since the marriage, and as you know we have had no children.

When I bought my next house after the marriage, I had the deed made in my name as a married man and as my sole and personal property. I told her at the time I wouldn't put real property in her name because of my feelings about California divorce laws and she, at that time, agreed with me completely and said she deplored what "American" wives did to their men. She had no interest in taking anything from me, just my love, etc. The signing of quit claims became a pattern in our lives. No matter whether the property was residential or later, on the apartment buildings, I was careful to get a quit claim signed each and every time. She read these carefully and the first one Hook presented her, she asked *him* why I wanted them and he said that he understood I would not put anything in her name because I was afraid of losing property in a divorce. He also told her explicitly what they were and she said she understood. This explanation in some detail took place on other occasions.

The last one Hook tells me that she said, just before signing, "When is he going to have faith in me?" Hook said she should know that I had made a new will adding these properties and she would get them as chief beneficiary. That, barring divorce, the property I was accumulating would one day be hers. She now makes the claim that he misrepresented quit claim deeds to her, that she *never* knew what she was signing, and that we (Hook and I) conspired to cheat her. This didn't surprise me as much as it has angered him. He is a tough little bastard but dead straight, and his integrity and honesty has been challenged. He *was* one of her biggest fans, but now wants her hide. As she wants mine. Or, as she tells it to me, "I'm going to take you for everything I can legally get."

She hasn't had a drink for over a year and a half and is suing for half my wine collection.

She has engaged the services, incidentally, of her analyst's son. He, Mason Rose V, is an anxious, very ambitious young man working in a very prestigious firm. This is, according to my counsel Harry Fain, his first fat account and he's damn well firm on not only winning a big case but bringing big fees into the firm. Makes it tougher to deal. They have the first hearing set for when I'm working Vegas. We are trying to get it continued for when I am home. Mason V says she is willing to do so, but would like me to agree to give her a membership in the Beverly Hills Tennis Club for doing this favor.

If two people marry, same age or nearly, and he is getting his law or med degree and she works to support him and she works in the office for him until he gets going, and they have kids and she grows older and he falls for a younger lady and dumps her, the law provides . . . rightfully . . . that that lady is entitled to ½ of the property they have acquired and support for the kids. Ours is nowhere near that case and yet the law can be read to apply to both women equally. Not fair, sir.

I am 52. As you know, diabetic. As you may not know but may have guessed, my career is in the shit house. We now have trouble getting dates and no chance of getting the money we used to. We have no deal in Tahoe or anywhere else right now. We have *had* our success. I am *not* saying that it is over for R&M. But it's reduced a great deal.

You are a bright man and can be much more objective than I. Where am I wrong? Is she right? I know that on our last visit you and Dordo were very much on her side, feeling I was abusing her. I was behaving as I would always do in front of you two people, in other words as I would at home. She and I had been beefing and I was unwilling to pretend that everything was all right. A sore ass. That's me. But what you see is what you get. I have never pretended with my friends to be other than I am. I realize I would have more friends if I did, but I would lose one important one. ME.

Answer when and as you see fit. Or if. I know that I have been wrong in not writing. I was miffed, you see. It seemed to me that day in Sarasota that not only was my wife gone but two damn good friends as well. At least one. I suppose Dordo must by nature opt for A. Maybe you too. It's dreadful to be involved in this sort of problem. I wish you weren't. But I am afraid that the way things are, the way I feel about this lady, a good friend of hers must care less for me, and that's the way people such as I end up lonely, I suppose. Make your own decision, and if you don't answer . . . and I won't blame you . . . I will understand what the decision is. When you offered to be the catcher, I know you didn't mean from a fall like this.

Dan

MacDonald to Rowan

September 8, 1974

Dear Dan,

Note change in the Adirondack address. The same house but they shuffled post offices and somehow shifted us 31 zip codes away from the prior number.

We were about ready to come up here in late July, had begun packing etc, when my sister in Utica went into the hospital with bleeding due to back pressure from cirrhosis. She went in by ambulance on the morning of August 1st, and when they couldn't stop the bleeding they did a portal shunt, a 4½ hour operation on the third of August. She was in a coma in intensive care for nine days. We flew up and got to Utica on Labor Day. What she is right now, Dan, is a creature of certainly no more than 70 pounds, skeletal, with a terrible restless energy, strange starey eyes, and a whole set of delusions. One doctor says it is his belief that her irrationality will persist, that the brain damage is permanent. Another expects her to recover her wits in six or seven weeks. The first doctor believes she will go once again into kidney failure and will not survive. My mother is in her eighties, has an apartment and, because of two bad falls, a part-time nurse-housekeeper. She and my sister Dorrie were very close, talking each day, etc. My mother is in complete despair at this turn of events. Bill, Dorrie's husband, died of a heart attack last year. He was an only child. His mother, age 73, lives nearby and has no other relatives except my sister and my sister's two adopted children, age 20 and 22, neither of them sufficiently mature to be of any help in coping with events here. I am handling monetary affairs for my sister, and there are a lot of very tough decisions to be made, depending on how things work out.

The reason I am boring you with all this is because it cannot help but have an effect upon my reaction to the problems you cite in the letter I got the day before yesterday.

It makes me quite willing to bear down and tell you exactly what is in my head re you and Adriana. Understand, one does not "take sides." That is an assinine simplification. If two friends are struck down by the same disease, one does not arbitrarily say that one is sick and the other is well. And once the disease has struck it seems a forlorn exercise to place any importance upon which person first announces the presence of the illness.

Your yearning for a willing, dependent, compliant girl-wife seems to me to be an adolescent dream. There are nothing-people who can remain forever twenty in their minds and hearts, with all the vapidity and silliness of a musical comedy springtime. The something-people grow and change and mature, become more valuable and stimulating as time goes on. On the title page of the upcoming McGee I have a quote from Santayana: "Life is not a spectacle or a feast; it is a predicament." To want an eternal girl-bride at the expense of not having the experience of sharing life with a mature woman would seem to be a desire unworthy of a grownup fella.

Had you not written me as you did, I would never have had the chance to express to you my dismay at the Dan Rowan we met at the airplane the very last time we have ever seen you.

I should have been warned by the very first exchange. The previous time I'd seen you, you had looked a bit puffy and out of condition. But you were tanned and fit and so I said, "Hey, you look great." You snapped your head around and looked at me with raised eyebrows and said, "Is there any reason I shouldn't?"

So much for taking pleasure in the well-being of a friend.

Then the lunch. Do you really have any idea of what you were like? You were a total embarrassment. You were loud, crude, vulgar and a total disaster. Nobody was inciting you. You had never been like that before in anybody's living room when we were around, much less in a public restaurant. Regardless of the public place, I think that hacking at the mate is not something one does in front of anyone else. It is tasteless. It lacks empathy. And you had to *know* that you had been way out of line because the Dan Rowan we have known for so long could not help but know when he had been an ass.

Third item. You told me that anecdote about the fellow who plays Jesus parts (Can't come up with his name at the moment) and the line about who gets the chair for the lady, when you were over at a tennis tournament. Jesus, Dan, I am not a prissy person. I had my six years in the army. But I had a hell of a difficult time coming up with an obligatory chuckle. Don't tell me that show folks is different. Unfunny vulgarity is unfunny wherever and whenever it happens. IT WAS NOT LIKE YOU. That's the strange part. Why should Dan Rowan go around being Don Rickles? Dan Rowan is a bright, sensitive, perceptive person. He has empathy and awareness. After telling me the anecdote you said, as though in some kind of explanation, "Being a comedian you can get away with more than you could otherwise. They expect it." They? I saw a lot of people lolling around the set of Darker Than Amber who would have screamed their skulls off at that line, but who wants them around? And who wants to tickle their particular sycophantic funny bone?

Fourth item. At that same time, that same day, you told me you have a new philosophy of life. You said, "I am not going to do anything that does not please me. I am never again going to do anything I don't want to do." It shocked me because that is not a philosophy. It is a childish hedonism. It is counter-growth because it presumes that you will know in advance exactly what any experience will be and how it will affect you. There is a frictive factor in the affairs of men which stimulates insight. It is an empty rationalization to say Life is so short I am not going to waste my time etc. . . . But acceptance of life means an openness, a willing response to experience good and bad. You always knew this before? Why the need for this new and demeaning philosophy? And I would point out that by following it, you condemn yourself to the company of only those people who are willing to do what *you* want to do. In other words, you impose your will upon them in the pursuit of your pleasures, and thus deprive yourself of even the constructive abrasion of having people about you who are willing and ready to disagree with you.

Then you did the next un-Danlike thing. You left Manasota and went trundling off with some strange rich fat man and other assorted hustlers. As you no doubt may have suspected, we used my scabrous ailment as an excuse not to go. We found it unthinkable to accept the hospitality of some stranger playing suckalong with the celebrity circuit. And this is not a contradiction of the concept that one must be open to experience. You do not know how gladly we would and could have joined you and Adriana had it been like the Haiti thing, where we all took care of it by ourselves. (Though you did make Haiti somewhat awkward by deciding too obviously and abruptly you wanted no more to do with the General. It could have been done in a more kindly and emphathetic manner. It is wicked to wound when it is unnecessary and merely self-gratification.)

Okay, I have beat on you, but I am your friend. I think it gives me the right. Friendship is not something that has to be earned by good behavior. We were very troubled about you. We talked about you quite a lot after the whirlwind disaster visit. We decided that it was the combination of the anxiety about the career, and the male climacteric, and perhaps some other factor of which we were unaware.

As to your letter, Dan, you know and I know it is special pleading. It presents one side of a mutual problem. You are both good people. Good people can act in emotional situations in ways that are unfortunate. But they do not turn into monsters. The opposite of love is not hate and rancor, but indifference. Hate and rancor are some of the other faces of love.

I know nothing of the law. I did not know that in a divorce action the California law awarded people on the basis of performance. I thought that if you were married for thirty-five years or thirty-five minutes, in the absence of a marital contract arranged before the actual marriage, everything was owned jointly. Insofar as your net worth in any given past year is concerned, I would suspect that with the accounting and legal help you have had, it would be easy to establish it beyond doubt. I would guess that the difference between what she wants and what she gets is up to the courts. Insofar as her never doing a day's work, come *on*. We saw you two over quite a few years. Being married to you is a very demanding occupation. It took one hell of a lot of work, strain, tension and understanding, and to her I am sure it was worth it. She was not sitting on a satin cushion being hand fed, surely. About those quit claim deeds, I can tell you exactly what transpired between Adriana, Dordo and me some four years ago. On at least two separate occcasions she asked our advice. She said she was being asked to sign quit claim deeds on everything you acquired, and that you and Hook had told her that it was for the purpose of making it easier to switch various pieces of tangible and intangible property around. She knew of my business background. She said she could not really pin you down about it because you blew up each time she tried. She said it made her feel as if she was not trusted, as if she was only a conditional partner in the marriage. I suggested to her that if she was really troubled about it, then she should go to Hookstratten and sit down with him and ask him exactly what it meant to her to be signing these quit claims, and if his answers did not satisfy her, then she should seek out legal advice and find out precisely what the consequences were. She seemed to accept this as a reasonable course of action. I do not think that four years ago she was laying any groundwork for divorce. I could never believe that. She was (and I am afraid she still is) in love with you.

About the wine collection. Tom gave me the same pert little line. She wants half the wine collection and she doesn't even drink. I think you told me once that the wine collection is worth thirty or forty thousand dollars. It is an investment vehicle for many people who do not drink. It has worked out well for them. I would suspect that if she were having assets appraised, it would be dumb to leave out the wine, right?

Enough of this picking of nit. We do not opt for anybody. We are merely saddened by the whole sorry mess.

You are 52. My damaged sister is 53. You say your career is in the shit house. I say her life is in the shit house. When you talk of trouble getting dates and filling houses, I suspect that you are talking about economic conditions in this U S of A, and not of the professional condition of Rowan and Martin. You are a bright, creative man, and if you sit down and say your career is in the shit house, doubtless, in time, that will come to be true. But if you happen to get off your ass and go to work on your career, you may well overcome the malaise of the times and do very well. I think you should take stock. As you know, a certain tendency toward black depression is often a byproduct of diabetes. In addition you have always been inclined to look upon the fates with the feeling that they conspire to hammer you flat. So you have a double whammy. But the blessing is the intelligence which can work you out of it.

We are so sorry that you two are clawing at each other. And our hearts and best wishes go out to *both* of you.

Yr friend

John

MacDonald to Rowan

Sept 19, 1974

JUST HOME BETWEEN RENO AND LAS VEGAS TO GET YOUR ASTONISHING LETTER OF 8 SEPTEMBER DO NOT WANT YOU TO HARBOR ANY THOUGHTS I WILL NOT ANSWER IF I CAN FIND A TYPEWRITER IN VEGAS I WILL WRITE FROM THERE OTHERWISE WHEN NEXT AT HOME I WAS DISTRESSED TO HEAR OF YOUR FAMILY CRISIS AND I HOPE EVERYTHING IS MUCH IMPROVED SANTAYANA ALSO SAID QUOTE VALUE JUDGMENTS OF GOOD FRIENDS SHOULD BE MADE CAREFULLY MERCIFULLY AND HARDLY EVER UNQUOTE THATS HARRY SANTAYANA YOU DON'T KNOW HIM

DAN

Rowan to MacDonald

24 September 1974

Dear John,

Since your letter was so provocative it will take me some time to answer it all. I also have to use a small portable non-electric which takes time and causes mistakes. However your letter is much on my mind and I am going to deal with it as time and opportunity permits. One of the sad qualities of your letter, and perplexing, is its note of *anger.* In my circle of friends and acquaintances, none use words more efficiently and thoughtfully than you, consequently I must believe you meant literally what you wrote and you wrote as a very pissed off gent.

You refer to me variously as "assinine"; "adolescent"; "a total embarrassment"; "loud, crude, vulgar, a total disaster"; "tasteless"; "an ass"; "childish hedonist"; "wicked"; and also mention special pleading, and general unfairness in my attitude regarding the court's view of divorce, etc. The only out options you seem to make available to me in exculpation of my total shittiness is the male climacteric, needless career anxiety, or possibly my diabetes. Wow!

As I said, you sound so damned *angry*. Your letter makes me wonder at many things. Over the years you have known me, through personal contact and correspondence, you have made me feel that you really liked me a lot and was indeed a stout friend. It sounds now as if you have been suffering strong pangs of distaste. (I have no idea, for instance, of your honest attitude . . . if your letter truly reflects it . . . regarding the Haitian trip.) It is difficult for me to believe that a man of your perception and understanding could reassess his entire range of opinion concerning a friend based on *one*—or were there others you didn't have time to mention—incident. The last visit of ours to Sarasota, following the Houston debacle, is something I would like to forget but will not be able to. You are both fortunate and heroic not to have such incidents in your own past. Until receipt of your letter I could at least say to myself, as indeed I did, that "thank God I slipped that wheel in front of John and Dordo instead of . . . etc."

There is never a credible defense or excuse for such aberrant behavior and I will not attempt one. There are usually some *reasons*, however, and you should know them. I have been on a downer for months due to domestic and career problems. It seemed to me then, and now, that the "hills and valleys of life" idea was being rendered invalid because of the unending parade of valleys. I had grown increasingly desperate in my attempts to cope and becoming a basket case emotionally. I needed some "good" news and there wasn't any. It's one thing to intellectualize positive, good thoughts to promote positive action, but it was proving impossible for me to do practically. I was in a funk. I felt that if A. and I had one more scatching, bitter fight I'd go bananas. She has the ability, which I envy, of fighting in private and then turning it off completely when somebody walks into the room. We had a terrible time in Houston, and had had a beef just before landing at Sarasota. I had not recovered from that and was seething and sore as a boil when we landed. Remember, this is not to excuse my behavior, there is none. This is the emotional background and the mental climate I was living in at the time.

Have you ever found it necessary to change your speech patterns, your conversational style and/or humor, topics or manner when you leave one group and enter another? For instance, the talk and style of your writers' lunches would be different in tone and form from a board of regents meeting, right? Well, I usually have no great difficulty doing that, but I hadn't made any change or adaptation that trip. For instance: Paul Keyes and I have had a silly habit of saying "Thanks for the warning" when the other would say "See you in the morning" or whatever. "How's your wife?" "As compared to what?" "What time is it?" "I don't care." And we laugh at this shit. Okay, it's not Mark Twain, but to us after heavy days it's silly and funny. "Hey, you're looking great." "Why shouldn't I?" or "Why are you so surprised?" or "Don't I always?" It was in that frame of reference I answered your greeting at the airport. If I had known that it was a question from you spurred by the background of concern the response would have been different. So much for taking pleasure in the well-being of a friend.

The anecdote you took exception to, I don't intend to defend. I thought, and think, it was funny AT THE TIME. Maybe you had to be there. Maybe you had to know the people. Maybe you are totally right and I am totally wrong about it. I certainly meant no offense and apologize if I gave any.

It would seem to me that we have talked our philosophies over many times on many occasions. "I am never going to do anything that does not please me. I am never going to do what I don't want to do," is not mine, as stated. It was part of resolving to do what I think is right. If you *do*, it will, as Mark Twain said, gratify some and astonish others. It will also make me less regretful and regret is an indulgence I no longer feel able to afford. I was saying also, "Enough of guilt. Give me no more." But I have rattled around too much and scrambled too much to believe that I still only do what I want or what is always pleasing.

Regarding my ". . . trundling off with some strange rich fat man and other assorted hustlers." ". . . some stranger playing suckalong with the celebrity circuit." I resent your blanket denial of my right and ability to choose friends. I resent your calling a pal of mine a hustler. You never met the man. Right? You really know nothing about him, right? How dare you? You may resent, rightfully, my abuse of your friends, but by Christ I never called your pals down without having ever met them. To call *this* dude a suckalong is so laughable as to be ridiculous. In a sense the whole world is a star-fucker as you know. But after initial contact with someone who may have wanted to meet you because you wrote books they liked, I am positive *some* of them have become friends. We once had a long talk about the few *new* friends I had made after gaining my celebrity *because* of that fact of resenting people who wanted to be around only because I had celebrity. Further, there were no "assorted hustlers." The party consisted of our host, his wife, the owner of the boat, the skipper and mate, A. and I.

I am not going to argue the merits of community property laws as written in California. I feel one way and you apparently feel another. As in the case of your out-of-hand condemnation of friends you haven't met, how in HELL can you presume to judge my property situation, not having been present at: A—The pre-nuptial discussion A. and I had in Australia before the marriage. B—The various signings and discussions which accompanied the signing of the quit claims. C—The discussions and explanations Hook had made to A. ??? The fact she discussed her concern over them with you and Dordo is a little perplexing. You will not believe me . . . as you *know* you won't, but neither Hook nor I *ever* told her it was to make property easier to switch around. Do you believe Ed Hookstratten is a liar and a crook? If you believe such of me, it would be difficult to say so of him, not knowing him. He does have a very good reputation for honesty and A. was crazy about him until she brought suit. Would you also call Ed's wife Pat a liar and a crook? Not if you knew her. She's the original Goody two-shoes. She was present at one of the meetings Ed had with her and wondered to Ed later why A. was willing to sign the quit claims after his detailed explanation of *precisely* what they were. You are, in order to maintain your posture that I and my lawyer have done her dirt, going to have to stretch credulity very far indeed.

I truly bear you no malice for the things you have said about me, for the names you have called me, for the position you take vis à vis Dan and A. I really truly don't. I do wonder at the route you took to arrive at your judgments and am sorry indeed that you seem to have shaken out your noose based on one rotten afternoon with me at my worst. Did we never have good afternoons? Did you never find more than one occasion to think well of me? Must your friends be totally perfect at all times? That's a heavy load of responsibility, old friend. Maybe I should have told you what I thought too evident. I ain't a saint.

Ah, yes. The wine collection. An asset, surely. But my hobby, actually. I was clumsy in what I said. It seems to me that I have no claim on her cameras or dark room equipment, not using that stuff nor very interested in it. She isn't interested in wine. Possibly I should recognize that both the wine and the lenses have value, it's community etc. I was looking at it more subjectively. Sorry. The wine has been put into a bonded locker for the court to distribute and I have told her I intend no claim on her stuff. As you say, enough picking of nit.

Possibly the cruelest and most unjust part of your letter has to do with your comments regarding my career as opposed to your sister's problems. I don't see the relevancy. I didn't say nor do I think there is a qualitative comparison available. I am sorry about her because she's a person, but more because she's yours. If the slump in my career has anything to do with any other person's dilemma of any kind, I fail to see it. I am not complaining about the nail in my shoe to a person with no feet, pal. What I did say, and what is fact, is that I am earning much less. I have had a TV hit and *nobody* has had two. It is reasonable in the face of those odds to suppose that my peak earnings have been had. I will get off my fat ass, as you suggest, old chum, and work on my career. Always have. Whatever I got . . . I GOT. No raffles, no gifties. The reality of life is something I swear to you is familiar to me.

Painfully,

Yr friend

Dan

MacDonald to Rowan

September 30, 1974

Dear Dan,

Never fear. I like you a lot and am your stout friend.

I should not want us to get into a yes-I-did   no-you-didn't kind of non-productive dialogue.

Perhaps a word on basic posture is necessary. I have the feeling that valuable human relationships can and must become abrasive from time to time. Else they are vapid. The avoidance of significant friction, no matter what, is a game for tea parties.

I have never written a rougher letter. Now why in God's name would I want to shake up good old Dan?

Who am I to set myself up as the paragon able to determine when the other fellow needs a jolt?

Step back in time. I meet a bright, honest, complicated, ambitious, talented, troubled guy at a time when his career was going very well and due soon to really take off. What about this Rowan? He has a sharp eye for human frailties, for the ludicrous. He has positive but not overbearing opinions. He has a considerable empathy about other people and he is quite able and willing to laugh at himself. We become friends. We have many good times. I am aware all along of deep insecurities in Dan Rowan, due to confusions of acceptance-rejection when he was a kid. Also I am aware of the neuroses which creative personalities seem to nurture.

Okay, so during a few years of Laugh-In there is no essential change in Dan Rowan. But there is at work the odd corruption of power. Status, money, decision-making, fame. I suppose that if a veritable saint were surrounded by obedient, sycophantic, non-contentious, yea-saying people for several years, and if said saint were likewise aware that his work was changing some of the fabric and mores of the society in which he lived, it is *possible* but not probable that the saint would survive those exposures with his basic humility intact.

I would not expect you to experience all that without it having some effect upon you, and it certainly did have. I can put my finger on the precise change which did occur, which I could see. Prior to those exposures, Dan, you were willing to concede that in most matters in this brief and harried existence, there are two or more acceptable points of view, open to discussion, and you believed that reasonable men's opinions are responsive to change through discussion and experience and time. What you came gradually to believe, and to accept as immutable, was the myth of the total and absolute correctness of your opinion on all matters large and small. No argument permitted. In fact, it got to the point where even the shadow of dissent became an affront to you because it seemed to smack of some kind of disloyalty, or some kind of personal criticism.

It sure limits conversation, having to sidestep all divergent opinions in order to avoid making you unhappy.

Perhaps the most destructive aspect of this iron insistence upon being totally right in all things is that it has let you paint yourself into too many corners. Perhaps you are defining manhood improperly. To adopt a point of view and then cast it in concrete and charge ahead no matter what, is not the quintessence of manliness. Life gives no rewards for an unthinking constancy. A person to be truly alive must be open to change, to persuasion, to self-doubt.

With this rigidity of being always totally right goes, somehow, the suspicious quickness to take affront. A year ago Tom did a wicked and hilarious imitation. He would walk away, being you, and feed himself the line, "Hello, Dad!," and then spin around, stern, scowling, ap-

prehensive, head-cocked, and say, "What does he mean by *that?*" I
hasten to say Tom meant no harm at all by that. It was and is funny.
But, Dan, if it is so obvious . . .

I would even believe that you painted yourself into a corner in your
marriage, striking attitudes you do not and can not in your heart of
hearts believe, burning the wrong bridges for all the wrong reasons.
Just imagine what it would be like trying to make a life with someone
who has set himself up as being always right about everything? One
would have to either begin to resist such destruction of their own personality or turn into a submerged "owned" creature. No person of any
pride or spirit could long endure such an artificial role.

Here is what happened. I got your letter back in August and I wrote
an innocuous reply. You know. I gave you all the strokes, and I handled
my teacup with excruciating care. And then I read it over and said
to myself, what the hell. Am I his friend, or am I an acquaintance?

As his friend I will try to jolt him back into enough self-awareness
so that he can see what he has been doing to himself and his friends.

And thus I spend the coin of friendship. In hopes. Maybe you will
find this letter too tough to take, and scratch me off your list. I would
feel a great sense of loss at that. Even so, I cannot honorably avoid
taking the risk. You are the guy who, years ago, used to joke about
the Star Syndrome. I think you can extricate yourself, and become
once again aware of this aspect of life and reality, as well as the others.
Who knows? You might not even get divorced. Mutual confession of
error would be a start.

Yr friend

John

MacDonald to Rowan

[*Note scrawled on a machine copy of a Sydney J. Harris syndicated
column carried in the Sarasota Herald Tribune a few days earlier*]

Nov. 23, 1974

Have *really* missed hearing from you, Dan. Leaving for Florida on
Tuesday. Sister finally died. Have no address for you.

John

[*Excerpt from Harris column titled "The Only Good Debates Are Between Friends"*]

It is one of the paradoxes of human relationships that in order to have a good and productive argument with a man, you first have to be a friend of his.

Strangers can only be ineffectually polite or abrasively rude: It requires friends to quarrel to a conclusion or at least a compact. When strangers have an argument about politics or religion or art, they are busier defending their personality than their point of view. Two friends can come to grips with the subject honestly and deeply.

That is why so many social altercations are fruitless and shallow. Each adversary is secretly striving to prove his supremacy to the other; logic and reason are only incidental weapons, and truth is subdued to plausibility.

A debate, like a love affair, must be intensely honest to be satisfactory. The debaters, like the lovers, must not lie to each other; but more important, they must not lie to themselves. Two friends who know each other well are under no necessity to pretend they are nobler or wiser or more dispassionate than they really are.

Friends have the privilege of piercing beneath the "good" reason and exposing the real reason for the opponent's convictions and opinions and prejudices masking as "fact."

MacDonald to Rowan

[*Written after Rowan called the MacDonalds and began the conversation by saying, "Hello? This is Scrooge."*]

Christmas Day 1981

Hey, Dan

So very good to hear your voice today. Thanks, Sept '74 to Dec '81 is seven years, three months. A fine New Year to you and yours.

As ever,

John D.

A NOTE ON THE TYPE

The text of this book was set in a digitized version of the type face called Primer, designed by Rudolph Ruzicka, who was earlier responsible for the design of Fairfield and Fairfield Medium, Linotype faces whose virtues have for some time now been accorded wide recognition.

The complete range of sizes of Primer was first made available in 1954, although the pilot size of 12-point was ready as early as 1951. The design of the face makes a general reference to Linotype Century—long a serviceable type, totally lacking in manner or frills of any kind—but brilliantly corrects its characterless quality.

Composed by PennSet, Inc.,
Bloomsburg, Pennsylvania

Printed and bound by The Haddon Craftsmen,
Scranton, Pennsylvania

Typography and binding design by
Dorothy Schmiderer